Regulating Vertical Agreements

International Competition Law Series

VOLUME 87

Editor

In its series editor, Alastair Sutton, Kluwer is fortunate to engage and benefit from the experience and expertise of one of the world's outstanding authorities on European Union and international economic law.

Introduction

In their efforts to regulate competition in an increasingly complex business environment, competition authorities face a daunting task. The European Commission and Courts, as well as national courts and legislatures, policymakers, and regulators, are constantly proposing, enacting, reviewing, and enforcing new legal measures, often addressing novel situations. Every industry and service is affected.

Contents/Subjects

With many titles currently available and new ones appearing regularly, the series' coverage includes detailed analyses of relevant legislation and case law in major global trading jurisdictions, defences used in cases involving the digital network economy, state aid cases, enforcement methodologies and a great deal more.

Objective & Readership

The purpose of Kluwer's International Competition Law Series is to follow the ever-changing contours of this dynamic area of the law, keeping the practice in sharp focus so that practising lawyers (including in-house counsel) and academics can be assured of the most up-to-date guidance and sources, in the widest possible range of applications.

The titles published in this series are listed at the end of this volume.

Regulating Vertical Agreements

A Comparative Law and Economics Review of the EU and Brazil

Maria Fernanda Caporale Madi

Wolters Kluwer

Published by:
Kluwer Law International B.V.
PO Box 316
2400 AH Alphen aan den Rijn
The Netherlands
E-mail: international-sales@wolterskluwer.com
Website: lrus.wolterskluwer.com

Sold and distributed by:
Wolters Kluwer Legal & Regulatory U.S.
7201 McKinney Circle
Frederick, MD 21704
United States of America
Email: customer.service@wolterskluwer.com

ISBN 978-94-035-2650-8

e-Book: ISBN 978-94-035-2651-5
web-PDF: ISBN 978-94-035-2652-2

Para meus pais, Alejandra e Helio

Table of Contents

Foreword

This book is the commercial edition of the PhD dissertation successfully defended by Maria Fernanda Caporale Madi at the Erasmus University Rotterdam, the Netherlands, on 29 June 2020. The book by Dr Caporale Madi is on an important and timely topic: she conducts a Comparative Competition Law and Economics analysis of the Brazilian and European Union (EU) competition rules relating to vertical distribution agreements. The start point for her research is the change in Brazilian competition law (Resolution No. 17/2016) from an *ex ante* notification system towards an *ex post* assessment of vertical restrictions. The author convincingly shows that copying the EU approach towards vertical restraints has not been optimal, since a switch from *ex ante* notification to *ex post* assessment crucially depends on the skills and available information of the competition authorities, the information of private actors and the overall institutional framework. These factors vary considerably between the EU and Brazil. Her analysis also reveals the persisting weaknesses of the European Block Exemption Regulation, particularly relating to the increasing importance of online retailing.

The central research question of this book is the following: in the case of vertical distribution agreements, what are the advantages and disadvantages of a switch from an *ex ante* notification system to an *ex post* monitoring system? The benefits to be obtained from such a law change are illustrated with the effects of the EU experience: beneficial effects of decentralization, lower enforcement costs and improved transparency. Particularly in the legal literature, the last benefit is emphasized since it generates a high degree of legal certainty. Dr Caporale Madi questions whether such benefits have also materialized in Brazil. The author investigates different types of costs: information costs, incentive costs and administrative costs. The enforcement costs of vertical restraints are analysed with the help of a cost curve indicating the optimal point to switch from *ex ante* notification towards an *ex post* assessment. This part of the book offers its most original contribution: it deepens the existing analysis of vertical restraints in the academic literature and allows better-informed policy conclusions.

The candidate's methodology nicely fits in the tradition of Comparative Law and Economics. Different legal rules are analysed within a framework elaborated with tools from economics science. Besides its explanatory power, which enables a better understanding of the institutional and legal differences between the EU and Brazil, it also informs the political discussion and permits nuanced conclusions for the current policy debate. The growth of online sales, which has been accelerated by the COVID-19 pandemic, invites to a renewed discussion of the traditional free-riding justification for resale price maintenance. The classic argument holds that fixed minimum resale prices may protect small specialized stores from ruinous price competition by large retail chains by protecting the level of services offered by the former shops. However, in the internet context, free-riding is no longer necessarily a negative externality. One may not exclude that consumers shop for information online and then buy the product that best fits their preference in a specialized store. This raises the question to what extent the latter effect outbalances the negative impact of reduced service by brick-and-mortar stores. The new uncertainties caused by the digital economy are elaborated in the fourth chapter of this book. Particular attention goes to selective distribution systems and most-favoured nation clauses in vertical distribution agreements.

In sum, this book substantially enriches the literature on vertical restraints, and it is highly relevant for scholars and competition law practitioners not only in Brazil but also in the EU.

Prof. em Dr Roger Van den Bergh
Rotterdam Institute of Law and Economics
Erasmus University Rotterdam, the Netherlands

List of Abbreviations

ACM	Autoriteit Consument & Markt (Dutch Competition Authority)
AFCA	Austrian Federal Competition Authority
ANAC	Agência Nacional de Aviação Civil (Brazilian Civil Aviation Agency)
ANATEL	Agência Nacional de Telecomunicações (Brazilian Telecom Agency)
ANEEL	Agência Nacional de Energia Elétrica (Brazilian Energy Agency)
ANP	Agência Nacional do Petróleo, Gás Natural e Biocombustíveis (Brazilian Agency for Petrol and Gas)
ANTT	Agência Nacional de Transportes Terrestres (Brazilian Transport Agency)
CADE	Conselho Administrativo de Defesa Econômica (Brazilian Competition Authority)
CEE	Central and Eastern Europe
CF	Constituição Federal do Brasil (Brazilian Federal Constitution)
CMA	Competition and Markets Authority (Current British Competition Authority)
DG Comp	Directorate-General (for Competition)
e.g.	Exempli Gratia (for example)
ECJ	European Court of Justice
ECN	European Competition Network
EEA	European Economic Area
EEC	European Economic Community
EU	European Union
FCA	French Competition Authority
FCO	German Federal Cartel Office (in German, Bundeskartellam)

FOHB	Brazil Forum of Hotel Operators (Fórum de Operadores Hoteleiros do Brasil)
GDP	Gross Domestic Product
HRS	Hotel Reservation Service
i.e.	Id est (that is)
IHG	InterContinental Hotels Group
MFN	Most Favoured Nation (clause)
NCA	National Competition Authority
OECD	Organisation for Economic Co-operation and Development
OFT	Office of Fair Trading (Former British Competition Authority)
OTA	Online Travel Agency
RPM	Resale Price-Fixing
SBDC	Sistema Brasileiro de Defesa da Concorrência
SBDP	Sociedade Brasileira de Direito Público
SDE	Secretaria de Direito Econômico (Brazilian Secretariat of Economic Law)
SEAE	Secretariat for Economic Monitoring
TFEU	Treaty on the Functioning of the European Union
UK	United Kingdom
US	United States of America
VBER	Vertical Block Exemption Regulation

List of Figures

List of Tables

Acknowledgements

This book is a result of my doctoral research that was defended in June 2020 at the Erasmus University Rotterdam, the Netherlands.

I am grateful to Erasmus University Rotterdam, University of Bologna, Italy, and University of Hamburg, Germany, for ensuring the necessary infrastructure for conducting this research.

I would also like to express my deepest gratitude to my supervisors Professor Roger van den Bergh (Erasmus School of Law) and Professor Niels Philipsen (Erasmus School of Law/University of Maastricht, the Netherlands), for all the knowledge, enthusiasm, inspirational and motivational supervisions.

I would like to extend my acknowledgements to the honourable members of my PhD defence Committee Professors Paula Forgioni (University of São Paulo, Brazil), Thomas Eger (University of Hamburg), Jacques Steenbergen (Katholieke Universiteit Leuven, Belgium), Caroline Cauffman (University of Maastricht), Jarig van Sinderen (Erasmus School of Economics) and Sharon Oded (Erasmus School of Law) for their careful reading of my manuscript and for the insightful remarks that certainly improved the latest version of this book.

CHAPTER 1

Introduction

This book discusses antitrust policies applicable to vertical agreements. It focuses on a comparative analysis of the current vertical agreement's legal framework in Brazil and the European Union (EU). By comparing the challenges of antitrust enforcement in two jurisdictions, this study opens up new perspectives to analyse the evolution of the rules and the institutional set-up of antitrust authorities concerning the complex assessment of vertical agreements.

1.1 SETTING THE SCENE: MOTIVATIONS AND CONCERNS

1.1.1 The Complex Assessment of Vertical Agreements

Vertical agreements represent a broad variety of supply and distribution contracts involving diverse market players, such as suppliers of diverse inputs, manufacturers, distributors and retailers.[1] These agreements are signed among businesspeople on a daily basis, and therefore antitrust experts around the world are often asked to advise on whether those agreements have any negative impact on competition or whether they infringe antitrust law. The study of vertical agreements is always a complex subject and constitutes a lively dispute for antitrust enforcement. An explanation for this complexity is the fact that these commercial contracts have different motivations and they can enhance mixed impacts on markets, depending on the context in which they are implemented.

Vertical agreements are considered 'good' or 'procompetitive' when the contractual terms do not restrict competition and when the effects in the market increase consumer welfare. Vertical agreements are considered 'bad' or 'anticompetitive' when they provoke negative outcomes, such as collusive practices, that consequently reduce social welfare. There are other types of vertical agreements that do not necessarily fit

1. S. Colino, *Vertical Agreements and Competition Law: A Comparative Study of the EU and US Regimes*, Portland, Hart Publishing, 2010, p. 1.

into these two extreme categories, i.e., there are agreements that can reduce consumer welfare while also enhancing efficiency gains that outweigh the welfare losses. For this reason, the examination of the competitive effects of vertical agreements should be conducted taking into consideration the market conditions that firms face in each situation. These puzzling characteristics of vertical agreements justify the presence of conflicting positions when it comes to their regulation. This regulatory dilemma is one of the motivations for this book.

In terms of the scope of antitrust field, it is intriguing to study how the legal rules and the decision-making process of antitrust enforcers have developed over the years. In the United States of America (hereinafter called the 'US'), for example, certain vertical agreements (for instance, those with resale price maintenance (RPM) clauses) were for several decades considered as illegal practices. In the 1970s, the scenario has slowly changed, since economic-oriented arguments were then recognized by US Courts that started analysing such agreements under the rule of reason. Important decisions to be mentioned are the *Sylvania*[2] case about non-price restraints, the *Khan*[3] case decision regarding maximum RPM and, more recently, the *Leegin*[4] case that is considered the most significant about minimum RPM. The shift in the American antitrust case law can be justified by the spread of the Chicago school of thought that is counted among the important contributions of Robert Bork and Richard Posner.[5]

Although there is some consensus on both sides of the Atlantic regarding the possible existence of efficient outcomes as a result of vertical contractual relations, new discussions have been raised. The rise of new technologies, the spread of the internet, the expansion of e-commerce, new applications of algorithms, big data and artificial intelligence have brought innovative queries to academics and policymakers. It is uncertain whether the novel forms of vertical relations give rise to new forms of anticompetitive behaviour. Different examples of vertical restraints in the context of digitalization, such as the hub-and-spoke conspiracy involving price algorithms, put into question the legality of these contractual forms and, moreover, the enforcement challenges (the lack of legal tools) that arise from them. The discussion of the antitrust enforcement of these contractual innovations is an additional motivation for this book.

Because of the complex assessment of vertical agreements, their legal framework must be analysed within the institutional set-up of each jurisdiction. The interpretation of the competition rules applicable to vertical agreements must be built beyond their technical aspects and it should also include the competitive market features and the characteristics of the institutional environment. In addition to the evaluation of the methodology of public policies related to vertical agreements, concern relies on the

2. *Continental TV Inc v. GTE Sylvania Inc* (1976) 433 US 36; *GTW Sylvania Inc v. Continental TC Inc* (1976) 537 US 980.
3. *State Oil Co v. Khan* (1997) 522 US 3.
4. *Leegin Creative Leather Prods v. PSKS Inc* (2007) 127 US 2705.
5. *See*, for example, R. Bork, 'The Rule of Reason and the Per Se Concept: Price-Fixing and Market Division', *Yale Law Review*, Vol. 75, No. 5, 1965, pp. 775-847; R. Bork, *The Antitrust Paradox: A Policy at War with Itself*, New York, Basic Books, 1978; R. Posner, 'The Rule of Reason and the Economic Approach: Reflections on the Sylvania Decision', *University of Chicago Law Review*, Vol. 45, No. 1, 1977, pp. 1-20.

historical evolution of the law-and decision-making in Brazil and in the EU because of the relevance of comparative studies in law and economics.

At the core of this book, it is assumed that the primary goal of competition policies should be the promotion of economic welfare. As explained by Richard Posner, the economic welfare concept involves the understanding of the term 'economic efficiency':

> Firms should be assumed to be rational profit maximisers, so that the issues in evaluating antitrust significance of a particular business practice should be whether it is a means by which a rational profit maximiser can increase its profits at the expense of efficiency, and that the design of antitrust rules should take into account the costs and benefits of individualized assessment if challenged practices relative to the costs and benefits of rule-of-thumb prohibitions.[6]

1.1.2 The Recent Changes in the Brazilian Legal Framework

The motivation to choose Brazil as a case study is not only due to personal background. The current challenges encountered by the Brazilian Antitrust Authority (in Portuguese, 'Conselho Administrativo de Defesa Econômica' and hereinafter called 'CADE') regarding the enforcement of vertical agreements can be compared to those observed in other jurisdictions that face similar economic and institutional realities. This comparison is relevant in order to learn and share lessons for the future. Indeed, several countries around the globe have experienced deep economic and social transformations in the past decade that include the implementation of legislative and institutional frameworks for enforcing antitrust laws. Brazil is one example of an emerging economy that has put efforts in implementing a competition policy. In the past decade, CADE has updated its legal framework, has undoubtedly structured a more efficient merger control system and strengthened its leniency programme and fight against cartels, and, as a result, it 'has consolidated its position among the main antitrust jurisdictions around the world'.[7]

A lot has been said and/or written about CADE's achievements, and the impact of its decision in the Brazilian economy and the evolution of national competition policy. However, the existing studies often rely on the legal aspects of the decision- and lawmaking process. Less attention has been given to CADE's historical institutional design and the challenges related to it.

When it comes to regulating vertical agreements, CADE has changed its policy twice in the past decade. In 2014, the authority defined clear parameters of notification of vertical agreements based on the firm's turnover and market shares within the *ex ante* merger control review. In 2017, CADE brought an end to the *ex ante* notification of vertical agreements, favouring the *ex post* control of vertical restraints. Nowadays, if a company is in doubt about the legality of a certain agreement, it cannot anymore notify the authority and wait for the 'green sign'. The company has instead to

6. R. Posner, *Antitrust Law*, 2nd ed., Chicago, The University of Chicago Press, 2001, at ix (Preface).
7. OECD, *Peer Review of Competition Law and Policy: Brazil*, 2019, p. 15.

self-assess the potential anticompetitive effects of the commercial practice (mostly with the help of their legal advisors) and it has to bear the costs of legal uncertainty and/or potential future litigations.

In this book, it is to be wondered whether the sole *ex post* control of vertical agreements is capable of both guaranteeing legal certainty to business people and giving them enough incentive to stop engaging in 'bad' agreements and to start engaging in procompetitive ones. Brazil faces challenges when it comes to antitrust enforcement of vertical agreements, since the relevant parties are not always instructed to self-assess their business practices. Moreover, the authority has limited personnel and budget for the enforcement of restrictive practices outside the scope of cartels. Indeed, CADE has for years been considered as 'one of the most under-staffed competition enforcement authorities', having nowadays around five people to handle all the antitrust cases that are not cartels or mergers.[8]

Brazil is a continental country, the 9th largest world economy (in terms of nominal gross domestic product (GDP)),[9] with thousands of business transactions being signed on a daily basis. An efficient monitoring of most of the industries and business transactions in this country of continental scope seems to be a difficult task. According to Paula Forgioni, because of this continental dimension, vertical restraints imposed by companies with economic power are capable of truly causing short- and long-term 'disasters' in Brazil.[10] There are regions in Brazil in which the closing of distribution channels, including the suppressing of traditional commerce, 'may foster unemployment, reduce the economic activity and undermine development'.[11] According to the author, competition policies must consider the reality of the country and the magnitude of its territory to ensure that the benefits of this policy actually reach most of the population.

The adequate regulation of vertical agreements gains importance in this context. It should be able to stimulate producers to improve access to their retailers and to provide them with the most diversified products. It should also encourage retailers to distribute their products with fair prices and quality to the largest number of consumers in the country, not only in the big metropolitan areas but also in the most remote countryside locations. Taking into account the challenges to regulation, what attracts the attention is whether the policy options of the antitrust agency in recent years have taken into consideration the Brazilian economic reality and social needs.

Another crucial point that motivated the study of antitrust policies in Brazil is the fact that in the past years, the country has faced a scenario of political turbulence that weakened the institutional set-up and fostered a deep economic and political crisis in the country. In this scenario, the public interest was put into question in several fields of law- and decision-making. The antitrust study has been one of these spheres. According to Article 6 of the Brazilian Competition Law, CADE's Administrative

8. OECD, 2019, *supra* note 7, p. 21.
9. According to the World Bank, in 2019, Brazil had a GDP equivalent to USD 1.9 trillion.
10. P. A. Forgioni, *Os fundamentos do antitruste*, 9th ed., São Paulo, Editora Revista dos Tribunais, 2016.
11. Forgioni, 2016, *supra* note 10, p. 18.

Tribunal, composed of the president of the authority and the Commissioners, are appointed by the President of the Brazilian Republic, following the Federal Senate approval. Their names are therefore subject to the influence of political pressure groups.

1.1.3 The Experience from the EU and Its Upcoming Challenges

The EU has always been, together with the US, the most influential antitrust regime in the world. The study of the evolution of competition policies oriented to vertical agreements in the EU is one of the drivers of interest in comparative law and economics.

Historically, Council Regulation 17/1962 created an enforcement system of vertical agreements based on an *ex ante* authorization regime that was applied for almost forty years without significant changes. By that time, the European Commission had the monopoly in the assessment of the economic effects of vertical agreements and therefore in granting exemptions. Forty years later, EU Regulation 1/2003 installed the *ex post* control of vertical contracts putting an end to the centralized notification system among Member States. Nowadays, all European Members States apply Regulation 1/2003 in parallel to their national competition law. In the EU, this change from an *ex ante* to an *ex post* control of vertical agreements happened after decades of having a notification system of agreements, and the reform was complemented by the Vertical Block Exemption Regulation (VBER) and further guidelines to help business people and law enforcers in self-assessing the potential anticompetitive effects of such contracts.

However, the new reality of a more globalized, technology-driven, and digitalized competitive environment has challenged the European Commission's approach to date. The following years will be dynamic in the discussion of online and offline vertical agreements, since more enforcement action is expected regarding sales restrictions and digital conducts. Moreover, the VBER is now under review,[12] and the Geo-Blocking Regulation 302/2018 is also applicable. The clear expansion of e-commerce in Europe, from 30% of the population in 2007 to 55% in 2016, is calling the attention of the European Commission.[13] In 2017, as part of the 'Digital Single Market Strategy',[14] the authority published the 'E-commerce Sector Inquiry', taking a look at the market tendencies, and the indication of market barriers to the growth of e-commerce.[15]

12. The current Vertical Block Exemption Regulation (Commission Regulation 330/2010) will expire in 2022.
13. More data available at: https://ec.europa.eu/commission/priorities/digital-single-market_en (25/7/2019).
14. The 'Digital Single Market' is a strategy plan created by the European Commission to outline policy actions in order to foster innovation and to stimulate a fair competition in the digital economy among the EU Member States. More information about the plan is available at: https://ec.europa.eu/commission/priorities/digital-single-market_en (25/7/2019).
15. European Commission, *Final Report on the E-commerce Sector Inquiry*, 2017.

This study devotes attention to relevant information regarding the dynamics of vertical agreements. First, the majority of manufacturers reacted to e-commerce and have started selling their products directly to consumers, therefore, competing directly with their own independent distributors. Second, the number of selective distribution contracts has risen considerably over the past decade, as manufacturers want more control of their distribution networks (in terms of both price and quality) within the scope of e-commerce. Finally, and most importantly, the development of online commerce encouraged the adoption of several other vertical restraints in the EU. Among them are highlighted the reinforcement of price restrictions, exclusionary practices in respect to online distributors, platform bans, and so on. These restrictions are often justified by the fact that producers are afraid of losing control of their distribution channels in this new digital reality.

Figure 1.1 identifies the most common commercial restrictions in vertical agreements that were identified by the Commission.

Figure 1.1 Proportion of Retailers with Contractual Restrictions, per Type of Restrictions

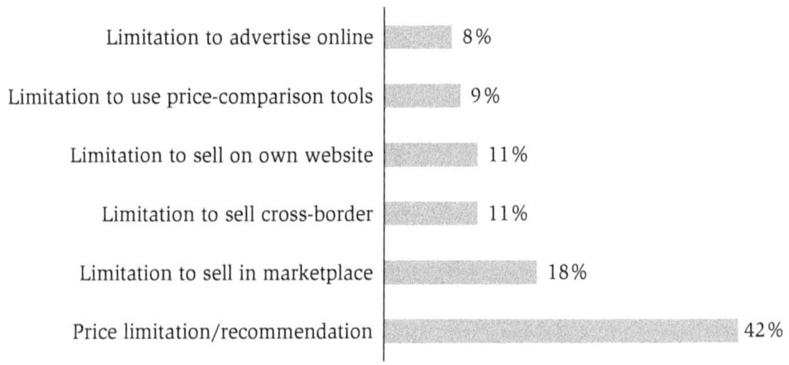

Source: European Commission, *Final Report on the E-commerce Sector Inquiry*, 2017, p. 9.

The recent attempts in discussing the competitive outcomes of digital economies in Europe certainly broaden the views on the new forms of market power that can offer useful insights to other countries.

Apart from the challenges of regulating vertical agreements in the digital markets, the EU also faces challenges when it comes to the different levels of enforcement across the National Competition Authorities (NCAs). About that, the main question at stake is whether, in the legal process related to vertical agreements, all Member States may be able both to acquire a similar level of knowledge and to guarantee adequate institutional set-ups for the enforcement of restrictive commercial practices.

Reinforcing interest in comparative law and economics, the European experience when it comes to regulating vertical agreements, opens new perspectives about normative discussions. Indeed, several arguments motivate the comparative study of Brazil and the EU. The first argument is that Brazil has historically followed the EU civil law legal traditions.[16] Second, when it comes to competition policy, both jurisdictions have an administrative model, and their legal systems passed through a change in policies oriented to vertical agreements: from an *ex ante* notification of agreements to an *ex post* control of anticompetitive practices, although with some crucial differences. The European antitrust regime has inspired the Brazilian antitrust law. In truth, the analysis of Article 101 of the Treaty on the Functioning of the European Union (TFEU) and Article 88 of Law No. 12.529/2011 in Brazil – the legal texts on anticompetitive agreements – shows that the inspiration of the European system was largely literal.[17] Third, the political and institutional reality in Brazil can be directly compared to some less developed EU countries, e.g., Central and Eastern European (CEE) countries. This means that the challenges encountered by these jurisdictions, mainly related to a late development of market economies and late implementation of competition law – and the way they are overcoming them – can also be considered comparable to those encountered in the Brazilian reality.

1.2 THE AIM OF THE BOOK

The main objective of this book is to open a discussion about the different policy options for an efficient antitrust enforcement applicable to vertical agreements, considering the different institutional realities. In this attempt, this study intends to explore the evolution of the legal framework and the institutional set-up in Brazil and in the EU with the aim of evaluating lessons to be learned from these jurisdictions, considering their promises and drawbacks. This book challenges the reader to answer the following question:

> How should an antitrust policy be designed to efficiently deter anticompetitive vertical agreements and encourage pro-competitive ones?

In order to guide the reader, the book proposes other groups of sub-questions.

The first group addresses economic-oriented questions: *Under which conditions should vertical agreements be considered efficiency enhancing? How can vertical agreements lead to anticompetitive outcomes?*

The second group refers to legal-oriented questions, such as: *What are the possible legal treatments for vertical agreements? What are the promises and drawbacks of the legal treatment chosen by Brazil and by the EU? To what extent has the evolution of the Brazilian and European regulation been conditioned by the interests of private relevant actors?*

The third and most important group of sub-questions is related to the law and economics analysis. The following questions will guide us to the normative analysis:

---

16. The law in Brazil law was mainly influenced by Roman law and the law of contemporary European countries, such as Portugal, France, Italy and Germany. G. Angelozzi, *História do Direito no Brasil*, Rio de Janeiro, Freitas Bastos Editora, 2009.
17. *See*, for instance, work of Verissimo, in which he does the literal analysis of the text of the Brazilian and European competition provisions. M. P. Verissimo, 'A "regra da razão" e o controle de condutas anticompetitivas pelo CADE', *in* C. Campilongo & R. Pfeiffer (eds), *Evolução do antitruste no Brasil*, São Paulo, Editora Singular, 2018, p. 910.

Does a change in antitrust policies from ex ante *to* ex post *control of vertical agreements always enhance the efficiency of the enforcement of competition law? What are the direct and indirect enforcement costs in a notification system of vertical agreements and in an* ex post *monitoring system? Which elements affect those different costs?*

To answer the proposed questions, this book applies a comparative law and economics methodology. It relies on comparative legal methods to provide an overview of the evolution and recent developments of antitrust policies applicable to vertical agreements in Brazil and in the EU. The studies of these different jurisdictions open new perspectives of interpretation and transformation of public policies. Through a process of learning, new practices should be studied to enhance economic efficiency and social welfare in the markets. The book also counts on the analysis of institutional factors of these jurisdictions that have affected the optimal enforcement of legal rules. In more detail, the research primarily connects the analysis of antitrust law in different jurisdictions to the economic theory of vertical agreements, in order to justify the need for an economic-oriented normative analysis.

1.3 OVERVIEW OF THE CHAPTERS

This book is organized into six chapters.

After *Chapter 1*, which introduces the goals, motivations and the aims of the book, *Chapter 2* is centred on the economic analysis of vertical agreements. It summarizes the debate about the effects of these commercial contracts in terms of economic efficiency and potential anticompetitive outcomes. This chapter provides a literature review that discusses the complex assessment of vertical agreements and the difficulties in designing optimal antitrust policies. Considering different approaches to the economic analysis of vertical agreements, it highlights the main efficiency arguments, such as solving double markup problem, preventing free-riding, and lowering transaction costs of the firms that are in the vertical structure. In addition, those efficiency arguments are analysed more particularly in cases where vertical restraints are implemented in online markets.

Taking into account the anticompetitive effects of vertical agreements, Chapter 2 presents a selected literature review which explains that vertical agreements may help maintaining horizontal cartels, exacerbating market imperfections and increasing the market power of incumbent firms. The anticompetitive effects of the increase of collusion practices, the reduction of intra- and inter-brand competition, and market foreclosure are understood as related processes. To enrich the discussion, some considerations about the anticompetitive outcomes in the context of online markets are presented.

Chapter 3 discusses the regulation of vertical agreements and the enforcement activities in Brazil mainly from 1994 until 2019. The chapter gives a brief historical perspective of the Brazilian Competition Law, including the discussion regarding the goals of the competition policy in the country. It explores the evolution of policies applicable to vertical agreements, including the recent changes in legislation after 2016. Moreover, it focuses on the jurisprudence of vertical cases and on the institutional design that allows the *ex post* enforcement of vertical agreements. The chapter discusses the new legal framework in Brazil by analysing the lawmaking process (i.e., the public consultation) that caused the end of the *ex ante* control of vertical agreements.

Chapter 4 presents the evolution of policies oriented to vertical agreements in the EU in the period starting from 1957 - when the internal market was established - until the late 2010s, as well as its current challenges. After briefly describing the origins of antitrust policy in the EU, the Council Regulation 17/1962, and the first sector exemptions for vertical agreements, the chapter outlines the modernization of the competition policies in Europe under Regulation 1/2003 (also called 2004 Reform). Historically, Regulation 1/2003 replaced the centralized *ex ante* notification system of vertical agreements to a decentralized *ex post* control of these business practices. Chapter 4 finally identifies the pillars that made the 2004 Reform possible and the challenges that jeopardize the optimal enforcement among the different Member States.

Chapter 5 develops a normative analysis of antitrust policies applicable to vertical agreements. For this analysis we consider the antitrust enforcement cost framework and a comparative analysis of the Brazilian and the EU experiences. The chapter looks at three main types of costs faced by the antitrust agency when enforcing vertical agreements. First, it focuses on the information costs that are involved in the assessment of vertical agreements, that is to say, the costs of gathering relevant information for an antitrust assessment and the costs of assessing the complex effects of vertical agreement. Second, the chapter describes the incentive costs which are related to the legal uncertainty of parties in a given framework. These costs are measured by analysing the level of fines of different jurisdictions, the probability of error, the role of private enforcement, and the general trust in institutions. Third, the administrative costs of enforcement practices are considered. Following the cost analysis, the chapter presents a normative discussion of efficient policies of vertical agreement taking into consideration different scenarios of enforcement costs. Chapter 5 also offers policy recommendations for Brazil and the EU.

Finally, *Chapter 6* summarizes the conclusions of the book and prospects for further research.

CHAPTER 2
Economic Analysis of Vertical Agreements

The study of vertical agreements is always a complex subject and constitutes a lively dispute for antitrust enforcement. An explanation for this complexity is the fact that these commercial contracts have different motivations and they can enhance mixed impacts on markets, depending on the context in which they are implemented. On the one hand, these commercial practices can bring economic efficiencies to markets, increasing the total welfare. On the other hand, they can generate negative outcomes, be harmful to consumers and producers, reducing the total welfare of the specific market. This 'regulatory dilemma' is also reinforced in the context of digital economies, e-commerce transactions, and marketplace platforms. This study explores the economic analysis of vertical agreements and guides the reader to this enduring debate on policymaking.

2.1 INTRODUCTION: THE REGULATORY DILEMMA OF VERTICAL AGREEMENTS

This chapter is centred on the economic analysis of vertical agreements. The aim is to summarize the debate regarding the effects of these commercial contracts, focusing on the efficiency theories and on the potential anticompetitive outcomes. The expression 'vertical agreements' can be described as a commercial agreement between firms at distinct stages of the supply chain.[1] Vertical agreements basically represent a broad variety of supply and distribution contracts involving diverse market players, such as suppliers of diverse inputs, manufacturers, distributors and retailers. Vertical agreements gain importance in a context in which technological advances are dynamic and are changing all the time. This is the case because they allow companies to form commercial alliances in order to strengthen themselves and to be able to compete in diverse markets. Added to the technological question, turbulence in the global

1. S. Colino, *Vertical Agreements and Competition Law: A Comparative Study of the EU and US Regimes*, Portland, Hart Publishing, 2010, p. 1.

economic scenario and uncertainties in the financial markets also give greater prominence to the issue. Vertical agreements are signed among businesspeople on a daily basis, and therefore antitrust experts around the world are often asked to advise on whether those agreements have any negative impact on competition or whether they infringe antitrust law.

Herbert Hovenkamp highlights important conceptual differences between vertical and horizontal agreements for antitrust law enforcers:

> The conceptual differences between a horizontal agreement and a vertical agreement are significant. For example, competitors meeting together to discuss market prices may provoke considerable suspicion. But a supplier and a dealer are necessarily parties to a buyer-seller agreement, and they presumably discuss prices all the time. As a result, in vertical cases the evidentiary focus tends to be the *content* of the agreement, while horizontal cases tend to focus on the *fact* of agreement.[2]

Indeed, vertical agreements can contain specific clauses that restrict competition on upstream and/or on downstream levels. Those restrictions are hereinafter called 'vertical restraints', and they can be categorized as: price and non-price restraints.

The first ones are restrictions on the downstream markets (i.e., on distributors, retailers, and buyers) as to the price at which they may resell their products and/or services. Resale price-fixing (also referred in the literature as resale price maintenance or just RPM) is an example of it, since the retailer is obliged to not sell its products below a certain price threshold, fixed by the producer. The second type of vertical restraints, the non-price restraints, corresponds to all the other categories of restrictions that are not related to price. As examples of non-price restraints we have *geo-blocking clauses* (also known in the literature as exclusive territory clauses) in which distributors are prohibited from selling in certain geographic regions; *exclusive distribution and supply clauses*, when the producer imposes a restriction on the distributor in order to be the only one contracting with it; *selective distribution*, when the producers require distributors to meet certain criteria before entering into the network and *franchising*, in which a license is granted to trade under a brand, provided that the licensor's standards for the business are maintained.[3]

In the scope of contract law, the term 'freedom of contracts' refers to a main legal principle. It means that parties should be free to decide upon the terms of any agreements.[4] It also means that parties are presumed to be equal when they decide upon the contractual terms. This important expression captures the volunteer aspect of the contract, and therefore, parties in the contract are 'protected against coercion and fraud'.[5] The principle of *freedom of contracts* is also applied to commercial contracts, such as vertical agreements. When companies opt to sign vertical agreements, it is expected that parties (e.g., producer and distributor) benefit from this transaction. Parties believe that the agreement itself would make them better off.

---

2. H. Hovenkamp, *Principles of Antitrust*, St. Paul, West Academic Publishing, 2017, p. 435.
3. L. A. Sulivan, *Antitrust*, Minnesota, West Publishing, 1976, p. 400.
4. *See* P. Atiyah, *The Rise and Fall of Freedom of Contract*, Oxford, Oxford University Press, 1979.
5. H. Collins, *The Law of Contract*, 2nd ed., London, Butterworths, 1993, p. 17.

However, this principle is not absolute.[6] As we will discuss along this chapter, parties may have different bargaining positions and might want to use these agreements to intensify their market power, increase market imperfections, or to maintain an anticompetitive behaviour, exclude rivals from the markets, and/or deter entry. All these possible effects decrease the overall welfare in the specific market.

In the scope of Competition Law, according to Patrick Rey and Francisco Caballero-Sanz, who prepared an important policy-evaluation document about vertical restraints for the European Commission in 1996, there are different explanations for the existence of vertical agreements.[7] The first one refers to the need to fix market failures and guarantee vertical coordination in the manufacturer-retailer relationship. The authors claim that, because producers may have market power, distributors do not always keep all the benefits of their sales efforts, which is what drives them to maintain their sales effort at a sub-optimal social level. As an answer to these market imperfections between producers and retailers, vertical agreements are introduced so as to prevent the negative outcomes of that externality. The second explanation draws attention to the use of vertical agreements as a way to restrict competition. This is the case because these contracts can be used by firms as instruments to maintain collusive behaviour and to increase their market power to the detriment of rivals, new entrants and consumers.[8]

The study of vertical agreements was always a complex subject, constituting a lively discussion for antitrust enforcement. These commercial alliances among firms have different motivations and may cause different effects on markets, according to the context where they are used. On the one hand, they carry important economic efficiencies, and, on the other hand, they may generate anticompetitive concerns. As described by Sandra Colino, 'these puzzling characteristics justify conflicting positions when it comes to their regulation'.[9] Other authors also have highlighted the complex issue when it comes to regulating vertical agreements. For Posner, the nature of vertical restrictions challenges the development of an ideal antitrust policy, in his words, it is hard 'to enforce antitrust against practices that we are not prepared to treat (as we are in the case of price-fixing) as entirely lacking in possible redeeming economic virtues'.[10] This difficulty characterizes the regulatory dilemma that motivates this book.

This chapter provides a literature review that discusses the complex assessment of vertical agreements and the difficulties to design optimal antitrust policies. Some related questions are highlighted: Under which conditions should vertical agreements be considered efficiency enhancing? How can vertical agreements lead to anticompetitive outcomes?

---

6. *See* discussion in P. Logelain, *Competition Law: Self-Assessment of Contracts – Interaction of EU Competition Law with Contract Law and Tort Law*, Bruxelles, Larcier, 2011, p. 18.
7. P. Rey & F. Caballero-Sanz, 'The Policy Implication of the Economic Analysis of Vertical Restraints', *European Commission Economic Paper*, No. 119, 1996, p. 5.
8. Rey & Caballero-Sanz, *supra* note 7, pp. 5-6.
9. Colino, 2010, *supra* note 1, p. 1.
10. R. Posner, 'Vertical Restraints and Antitrust Policy', *University of Chicago Law Review*, Vol. 72, 2005, p. 241.

To answer these questions, the chapter is organized as follows. Section 2.2 presents the main economic efficiency theories of vertical agreements. Among these theories, we highlight the double markup theory, the free-riding theory, and the transaction cost theory. Section 2.3 analyses the potential anticompetitive outcomes of these commercial structures. This section generally discusses the collusion theory, the reduction of intra- and inter-brand competition and the theories of market foreclosure and barriers to entry. Sequentially, section 2.4 discusses the double-side effects of vertical agreements illustrated by selective vertical restraints: retail price-fixing; geo-blocking and selective distribution. Section 2.5 briefly introduces a political economy discussion which shows that welfare-oriented arguments might not always be the motivation of policymakers. Finally, the chapter ends with some conclusive remarks about the enduring debate on policymaking.

2.2 THE ECONOMIC EFFICIENCIES OF VERTICAL AGREEMENTS

The purpose of this section is to present an overview of some relevant topics about vertical agreements that have been highlighted in economic theories. Economic efficiency, in the case of vertical agreements, can be mostly defined as allocative efficiency, the situation in which the total welfare of the market is guaranteed (optimal prices and greater levels of output in the market). Briefly speaking, in some situations where prices are persistently held above marginal cost and the output is reduced, vertical agreements can be used to guarantee that the market outcomes will go back to the efficient level.[11]

It is worth pointing out that every vertical structure faces a diverse range of decisions on its daily activities that goes from retail and wholesale prices, to locations for the distribution, quality demands for their distributors, sales efforts, and so on. Some decisions are only controlled by producers, while others are controlled by the distributors. In some cases, the decision over some variables affects the payoffs of each party involved, as well as the welfare outcomes.[12] In other words, because the choices of one company (e.g., the producer) can directly influence the profit of other companies (e.g., the distributors), the outcome of the firm's decision-making may generate inefficiencies in markets, if not correctly assessed.[13] Vertical restraints can be used as a way of repairing the externalities related to the coordination problem among the agents in the same vertical structure.

Considering different approaches to the economic analysis of vertical agreements, three main efficiency arguments are highlighted. First, vertical restraints can solve the double markup problem. Second, vertical restraints can prevent free-riding in both upstream and downstream markets. Third, vertical restraints can lower the transaction costs of the firms that are in the vertical structure. Lastly, we also point out

11. M. Motta, *Competition Policy: Theory and Practice*, Cambridge, Cambridge University Press, 2004, p. 303.
12. Colino, 2010, *supra* note 1, p. 11.
13. Colino, 2010, *supra* note 1, p. 12.

the context of those efficiency arguments when vertical restraints are imposed in online markets.

2.2.1 Solving the Double Markup Problem

Over the years, economists have developed models to explain the outcomes of monopolies (higher prices, lower outputs), and also of successive monopolies (double marginalization). Double marginalization was first analysed by Spengler in the 1950s and corresponded to circumstances in which manufacturers and retailers have some market power.[14] When this situation is observed, one company usually does not consider the effect of the price on the profit of the other company when setting its own price. Therefore, they set an additional markup to their costs that results in excessive prices to final consumers.

In the light of increasing retail prices, for example, the distributor raises the profit margin to decrease the volume of sales, but while doing so, the distributor does not take into account that the reduction of the volume of sales has negative effects on the volume of profits of the producer. Such a principal-agent problem[15] leads to a final price that is higher than the level that maximizes both the producer's and distributor's total profits.

If it is not possible for the firms to integrate vertically, different types of restraints can remove the market power of the retailers, putting an end to this negative externality.[16] RPM appears to be a simple solution to the problem, since the producer can simply impose the resale price on the retailer, instead of waiting until the retailers define the price that maximizes their profits. It is worth emphasizing that since the double markup generates excessively high prices, any vertical restrictions used solely to eliminate this problem lead in fact to lower prices, benefitting both companies and consumers. In these cases, vertical restraints guarantee lower prices, more outputs, therefore increasing total surplus and guaranteeing efficient outcomes in the markets.

2.2.2 Preventing Free-Riding

The first important consideration to note is that distributors typically offer a variety of services to consumers that directly affect the demand for the selling good.[17] Among

14. J. Spengler, 'Vertical Integration and Antitrust Policy', *Journal of Political Economy*, Vol. 58, No. 4, 1950, pp. 347-352.
15. Briefly speaking, in Law & Economics, the term 'principal-agent problem' addresses the difficulties that can arise in conditions of asymmetric and incomplete information. For instance, situations in which a Company A (principal) takes a certain decision regarding its business practice based on their own interest, not necessarily considering the interest of the other contract party (agent). J. Stiglitz, 'Principal and Agent', *The New Palgrave: A Dictionary of Economics*, Vol. 3, 1987, pp. 966-971.
16. S. Bishop & M. Walker, *Economics of E.C. Competition Law: Concepts, Application and Measurement*, 3rd ed., London, Sweet and Maxwell, 2010, p. 198.
17. From microeconomic theory, the demand curve of a product shows what happens to the quantity demanded of a good when its price varies, 'holding constant all the other variables that influence buyers'. If any of the other variables apart from price and quantity changes, the

these services, the most relevant are: information and guidance on presales to prospective clients, the size of showrooms, number of qualified sellers in the store, aftersales services, etc. In general terms, the fewer the services that are provided by the retailers, the smaller is the demand for their products.

There are diverse circumstances in which the behaviour of the retailer is unexpected and disadvantageous to the producer, for example, when retailers provide a sub-optimal level of services, which directly affect the number of sales. If retailers do not have the right incentives to appropriate the benefits of such services, they will not be motivated to invest in them, which will directly affect the producer's profit.[18] This is again another principle-agent problem that can somehow be fixed with vertical restraints.

In the 1960s, Lester Telser was a pioneer scholar in discussing that vertical agreements can be used to increase total level of sales in the market and therefore increase total welfare.[19] The author discusses that manufacturers can use contractual restrictions to prevent free-riding and to induce retailers to invest in services. As suggested by Telser, some retailers might have good reasons for not investing in presale treatments, since they do not bear the investment costs and therefore they can charge lower prices to consumers.[20] The consumers, in this sense, can get the information of presales services regarding a specific product from one retailer (i.e., the consumer would first visit the shop which offers additional services to take all the relevant information), and afterwards purchase the same product in another shop that has lower prices and does not invest in services.

This situation illustrates the free-riding problem: some retailers 'free-ride' on the investments made by other retailers. The expected outcome is that no retailer will have an incentive to invest in the presale services, unless the producers give them incentives to do so. In this context, price restrictions show up as an option. RPM guarantees a minimum gross markup for the retailers. They are therefore forced to find other forms of competitive strategies, such as the offer of special sales services, rather than relying only on price competition. One important point raised by Telser is that the nature of the product matters when applying this free-riding discussion. Branded products and new products that are unfamiliar to the mass of consumers are good 'candidates' for RPM.[21]

To sum up, Telser clarified that vertical price-fixing could benefit producers in the case where restraint is the only way to promote the sales services of distributors. Over the decades, his analysis was extended and complemented by several other scholars

demand curve shifts. Pre-sale services can be one factor that shifts the demand curve upwards, i.e., lead to a situation where the demand for such a product increases. *See* G. Mankiw, *Principles of Microeconomics*, 8th ed., Boston, Cengage Learning, 2018, p. 71.

18. Motta, 2004, *supra* note 11, p. 314.
19. L. Telser, 'Why Should Manufacturers Want Fair Trade', *The Journal of Law & Economics*, Vol. 3, October 1960, pp. 86-105.
20. Telser, 1960, *supra* note 19, p. 91.
21. Telser, 1960, *supra* note 19, p. 95.

such as Robert Bork[22] and Richard Posner[23] who also discussed on non-price restrictions.

In the late 1960s, Bork wrote the first article directly addressing the economic analysis of vertical restraints, mainly indicating the efficiency argument.[24] According to the author, the vertical restraints will lead to an efficient outcome only if both the producer of the goods and the consumer have their interests aligned. In other words, a producer imposes restraints only when these restraints are profitable, meaning, only if these restraints are able to expand the sales of the goods. And this expansion in sales will depend on consumer preferences. If consumers understand that it is worth paying more for goods that have the additional value of supplementary services, they will buy more of these specific goods. According to Bork, even though these vertical restraints are anticompetitive in their nature, the effects might be procompetitive, since the output has increased. In our example, consumers buy more goods with an increased level of services.

Following the authors' line of argumentation, every commercial restriction imposed by producers is procompetitive, and therefore, efficiency enhancing. Actually, Bork and Posner claim that, even when a firm has monopoly power, vertical restraints, such as RPM, can be procompetitive. According to the authors, it is crucial to conduct the rule of reason[25] analysis in such cases, which involves the balancing of potential economic efficiency and potential anticompetitive effects. Moreover, they present the argument that the increase of consumer welfare is not only due to lower prices and an increase in quality of products or services but also due to the increase in consumer satisfaction. This is why the increase in pre- or post-sales services can increase overall consumer satisfaction, which will lead to greater outputs.

The spread of the Chicago school of thought, which includes the contributions of Telser, Bork and Posner, started to influence US judges in the 1970s. Throughout many decades, vertical restraints in the US were considered illegal. This scenario started changing with the well-known *Sylvania*[26] case that was a crucial decision in the topic of vertical restraints, since it accepted the economic efficiency arguments and rule of reason approach. As the court in *Sylvania* noted, restrictions are necessary because, in their absence, any dealer who offers presale services would be inviting competing

22. *See*, for example, R. Bork, *The Antitrust Paradox: A Policy at War with Itself*, New York, Basic Books, 1978.
23. *See*, for example, R. Posner, 'The Rule of Reason and the Economic Approach: Reflections on the Sylvania Decision', *University of Chicago Law Review*, Vol. 45, No. 1, 1977, p. 4.
24. R. Bork, 'The Rule of Reason and the Per Se Concept: Price-Fixing and Market Division', *Yale Law Review*, Vol. 75, No. 5, 1965, pp. 775-847.
25. In practical terms, the term 'rule of reason' can be defined as the *legal approach* taken by law enforcers (antitrust agencies and courts) that considers the assessment both pro- and anticompetitive effect of a business practices in their decision-making process. It means that it is the opposite legal approach taken in cases of per se illegal practices. The rule of reason is the main approach taken by US courts. *See* discussion of R. Van den Bergh, *Comparative Competition Law and Economics*, Cheltenham, Edward Elgar, 2017, pp. 230-234. *See also* OECD, *Glossary of Industrial Organisation Economics and Competition Law*, p. 77.
26. *Continental TV Inc v. GTE Sylvania Inc* (1977) 433 US 36.

dealers to provide no (or fewer) services and thereby under-price them. This 'free-riding danger' would deter dealers from offering presale services, at least at the optimum amount.[27] As decided by American courts:

> Service and repair are vital for many products, such as automobiles and major household appliances. The availability and quality of such services affect a manufacturer's goodwill and the competitiveness of his product. Because of market imperfections such as the so-called 'free rider' effect, these services might not be provided by retailers in a purely competitive situation, despite the fact that each retailer's benefit would be greater if all provided the services than if none did.[28]

Following this analysis, William Comanor raises the critical question of whether customers are served better by reduced prices and fewer services or greater prices and more services.[29] The author argues that the assessment of whether a particular restraint increases or decreases the efficiency in a certain market largely depends on the relative preferences of different groups of consumers, i.e., it depends on how knowledgeable (or ignorant) they are in respect of a specific product. He argues that there are some consumers who do not perceive the value of additional services, meaning that they would prefer to pay less for the same product. Because of that, the economic efficiency argument elaborated by Bork would only make sense if the number of consumers who indeed value these services and are willing to pay more for the goods is greater than the number of consumers who are not willing to pay for these additional services.

In Comanor's words, 'the profitability of imposing a vertical restraint depends on the demand-stimulating effects of the additional information for marginal consumers'.[30] It means that vertical restraints, such as RPM, benefit 'ignorant' marginal consumers but harm 'knowledgeable' infra-marginal consumers who do not give the same value to the extra information. An interesting example discussed by Comanor is the case of new products. Whenever a new product is launched, more consumers are 'ignorant' when it comes to the use of such products, as well as their characteristics, meaning that more consumers are willing to pay more to get the sales services. This is different from a product that has been launched for years, and the market, in general, has enough information about the product, and the producer has less to add to it. Consequently, retail price-fixing is more likely to increase efficiency contrary to the case of an incumbent firm.[31] In a more qualitative analysis, Howard Marvel reaches similar conclusions.[32]

In the context of the free-riding theory, it is worth highlighting three additional efficiencies of vertical restraints. First, preventing free-riding among producers should

27. Posner, 1977, *supra* note 23, p. 10.
28. *Continental TV Inc v. GTE Sylvania Inc* (1977) 433 US 36, decision 23, June 1977, p. 2561.
29. W. Comanor, 'Vertical Price-Fixing, Vertical Market Restrictions, and the New Antitrust Policy', *Harvard Law Review*, Vol. 98, No. 5, 1985, p. 1001.
30. W. Comanor & J. Kirkwood, 'Resale Price Maintenance and Antitrust Policy', *Contemporary Economic Policy*, Vol. 3, 1985, p. 14.
31. Comanor & Kirkwood, 1985, *supra* note 30, p. 15.
32. H. Marvel, 'How Fair Is Fair Trade?', *Contemporary Economic Policy*, Vol. 3, 1985, pp. 23-35.

also be considered as an efficiency gain.[33] In this case, a producer may want to increase the effective distribution by making specific investments in the distribution channel (by training staff, investing in the shops, and so on).[34] However, rival producers could free-ride by using the same outlets without contributing to the investments, or using the same trained staff. In this situation, the first retailer may lose its incentives to investment in a better distribution system and therefore consumers are worse-off, since it affects the number of products available for them. This free-riding problem could be fixed by exclusive deals or geo-blocking clauses.

Second, there is a quality certification theory. Some retailers provide customers with a certification service that also involves some costs (rent of place in a good neighbourhood, hiring smart assistants, nice decoration) and therefore, other shops can benefit from these investments. This argument was developed by Marvel and Stephen McCafferty[35] who justify restraints such as RPM and selective distribution to solve the free-riding problem. Considering the latter case, usually related to luxury goods, only a specific type of shop (being in a nice shopping street, having dedicated personnel, having particular amenities, and so on) is entitled to sell the product. It is worth noting that not enabling a producer to safeguard the reputation of its goods is detrimental to the producer itself and also to the buyers who value the luxurious features of the goods.[36]

Third, the hold-up theory is relevant for this discussion. Distributors sometimes must make specific investments in their retail shops which may decrease their value, when the relationship is ended. The use of long-term contracts is often the way to guarantee and support these specific investments and avoid any type of opportunistic behaviour from the distributors.[37] Franchising contracts is the classic example of long-term commitments, but they are not the only ones. Exclusive arrangements, such as exclusive distribution or even selective distribution systems can guarantee an optimal level of investments and therefore effective level of sales. This specific efficiency is also discussed in the scope of the transaction cost theory and therefore, it gives us a link to the next subsection of this chapter.

2.2.3 Reducing Transaction Costs

The third economic efficiency argument of vertical agreements is the reduction of transaction costs. Ronald Coase first created the Transaction Cost Theory in his 1937 contribution 'The Nature of the Firm', and this publication formed the basis of the New Institutional Economics.[38] The main point of this theory is that transaction costs affect the ways in which markets are organized, that is to say, the interaction among

33. Before, the analysis was more focused on the free-riding among distributors.
34. G. Niels, H. Jenkins & J. Kavanagh, *Economics for Competition Lawyers*, 2nd ed., Oxford, Oxford University Press, 2016, p. 247.
35. H. Marvel & S. McCafferty, 'Resale Price Maintenance and Quality Certification', *RAND Journal of Economics*, Vol. 15, No. 3, 1984, pp. 346-359.
36. Motta, 2004, *supra* note 11, p. 334.
37. Rey & Caballero-Sanz, 1996, *supra* note 7, p. 16.
38. R. Coase, 'The Nature of the Firm', *Economica*, Vol. 4, November 1937, pp. 386-405.

companies. Examples of transaction costs include contract negotiation costs, research costs, contract implementation and enforcement costs, among others. One of the ideas behind Coase's theory is that, on the one hand, the higher the transaction costs perceived by companies, for example, in their contractual negotiations with other companies, the greater the incentives to maintain various activities within the company. On the other hand, if these transaction costs are lower, organizations will have incentives to sign various contracts with other companies.

In the 1970s, Oliver Williamson further developed the transaction cost theory in the scope of price theory.[39] The author explains that the size of transaction costs directly influences the choice in favour of certain governance structures (for instance, whether to centralize or not the governance of a firm through integration).[40] The work of Williamson has direct implications for antitrust discussions about vertical restraints and vertical integrations since he acknowledges that transaction costs should be considered in the analysis of antitrust cases.[41] As this idea will be better developed, in order to reduce transaction costs, companies will engage in vertical alliances to a greater or lesser degree.

In his book *Markets and Hierarchies*, Williamson recognizes that the self-interest of agents (opportunism) and the bounded rationality are important factors of the transaction cost theory to be taken into consideration. They allow the firms to choose among different governance structures.[42] Williamson refers to these features as the two human factors which might be a major source of risk and limitations on governance transactions. He indicates that the governance structure should be built in such a way as to minimize the bounded rationality of firms and consumers, and at the same time protect transactions against opportunism. In other words, the integrity of a distribution system should be protected against free-riders, and the quality of products should not be debased. If any of these features are observed in specific markets, vertical market restrictions may be necessary.[43]

According to Williamson, in a first extreme case, market solutions provide an efficient outcome. A market is an institution in which a significant number of products are changed regularly, and where the rules and structures of these negotiations and transactions are standardized. In markets, the observed behaviour pattern is based on individual interests, and social interaction without restrictions. The market offers choices, flexibility and opportunities. Markets are poor learning mechanisms and the transfer of technological know-how and information is freely available. Markets can be understood as situations where producers and distributors are free to contract, and no commercial restriction is imposed on any of them.[44]

39. Van den Bergh, 2017, *supra* note 25, p. 62.
40. *See*, for instance, O. Williamson, *Markets and Hierarchies: Analysis and Antitrust Implications*, New York, Free Press, 1975.
41. *See*, for instance, O. Williamson, 'Assessing Vertical Market Restrictions: Antitrust Ramifications of the Transaction Cost Approach', *University of Pennsylvania Law Review*, Vol. 127, No. 4, 1979, pp. 953-993.
42. Williamson, 1975, *supra* note 40, pp. 21-22.
43. Williamson, 1979, *supra* note 41, p. 958.
44. *See* discussion of Chapter 2 *in* Williamson, 1975, *supra* note 40.

In the second extreme case, hierarchies are needed to achieve efficiency. A hierarchy is a network of relational contracts between individuals to efficiently organize the process of production. Hierarchies permit better specialization and decision-making, better controlling and coordination among agents (in his words 'lower communication expenses'), less uncertainty related to unexpected costs or small-number of exchangers.[45] Finally, according to Williamson, hierarchies narrow the information gap that exists between autonomous agents,[46] since the transactions and the flow of resources that were previously conducted in the market are then internalized. Employees operate under the system of administrative procedures and play roles shaped by senior supervisors in the context of an authority system. Whereas the tasks are usually very specialized, internal activities are highly interdependent. Hierarchies are constituted by vertically integrated firms, with their own routines, expectations and detailed knowledge.

In 1985, Williamson included in his analysis a more profound attention to asset specificity. According to the author, the decision of firms in respect of their governance structures is mostly dependent on the degree of asset specificity.[47] In more detail, if the degree of asset specificity is low, firms depend less on these assets in order to keep their economic activity, and, when necessary, tend to sign short-term agreements with other companies. The degree of asset specificity does not bring excessive transaction costs to companies, and therefore market-based transactions are preferred. In these circumstances, the market itself, supported by contract law, should be able to provide effective protection mechanisms to the transacting parties. On the contrary, when the degree of asset specificity is large, companies are more dependent on this asset, and usually require large investments to have it. Therefore, the idea of engaging in long-term contracts with another company with more expertise becomes attractive to the firm. It becomes more effective to keep the assets within the company, for instance, via vertical integration.

An important contribution of Williamson that has direct relevance for this book is the recognition of hybrid structures of governance.[48] In between a pure market setting and a hierarchy, the author defines the hybrid forms of relationship derived from collaboration between agents. As stated previously, an increase in the degree of asset specificity most often creates a bilateral dependence between buyers and sellers, which promotes the formation of long-term contractual arrangements among parties. Therefore, the hybrid form is a 'specialized governance structure to address a bilateral dependence without promoting integration'.[49] The usual explanation for bilateral dependency invokes the existence of specific assets that create some 'lock-in' among

45. Williamson, 1975, *supra* note 40, pp. 49-54.
46. Williamson, 1975, *supra* note 40, pp. 49-54.
47. O. Williamson, *The Economic Institutions of Capitalism*, New York, Free Press, 1985.
48. O. Williamson, 'Comparative Economic Organization: The Analysis of Discrete Structural Alternatives', *Administrative Science Quarterly*, Vol. 36, No. 2, 1991, pp. 269-296.
49. Williamson, 1991, *supra* note 48.

agents and simultaneously generate appropriate quasi-rents.[50] The lock-in effect, therefore, provides an explanation regarding the long-term characteristics of vertical agreements. Practical examples of hybrid forms are franchising agreements, long-term supply and distribution contracts with exclusive clauses.

Regarding coordination, hybrid forms generally require planning and management decisions, both within and between firms (otherwise the market would be sufficient). They develop specific features (contractual restrictions) to maintain long-term relationships between the parts of the arrangement, while ensuring efficient coordination and acceptable interests to generate income.[51] As discussed in the previous subsection, vertical restraints can indeed guarantee better coordination between producers and distributors, generating market efficiencies.

The mutual dependence, observed in hybrid forms of governance, is an important feature that explains the rationale of certain vertical agreements, and can be developed, for instance, because of the existence of asset specificity. In this respect, Williamson defines asset specificity as the 'degree to which an asset can be redeployed to alternative uses and by alternative users without sacrifice of productive value'.[52] He classifies asset specificity into six kinds and concludes that especially in its first five forms (described below), asset specificity creates bilateral dependency, which justifies the existence of certain contractual designs:

> (1) *site specificity*, as where successive stations are located in a cheek-by-jowl relation to each other so as to economize on inventory and transportation expenses;
> (2) *physical asset specificity*, such as specialized dies that are required to produce a component;
> (3) *human-asset specificity* that arises in learning by doing;
> (4) *brand name capital*;
> (5) *dedicated assets*, which are discrete investments in general purpose plant that are made at the behest of a particular customer; and
> (6) *temporal specificity*, which is akin to technological non-separability and can be thought of as a type of site specificity in which timely responsiveness by on-site human assets is vital.[53] (Emphasis added)

Asset specificity can take a variety of forms, and in general, a condition of bilateral dependency (or the creation/need of vertical restraints) builds up as asset specificity develops. An important challenge for firms that engage in hybrid forms (or vertical agreement with commercial restraint) is to commit with their contractual obligations that naturally create mutual dependence, and at the same time, remaining

50. The lock-in effect was discussed in B. Klein, R. Crawford & A. Alchian, 'Vertical Integration, Appropriable Rents, and the Competitive Contracting Process', *The Journal of Law & Economics*, Vol. 21, No. 2, 1978, pp. 297-326.
51. C. Menard, 'On Clusters, Hybrids, and Other Strange Forms: The Case of the French Poultry Industry', *Journal of Institutional and Theoretical Economics*, Vol. 152, No. 1, 1996, pp. 154-183.
52. Williamson, 1991, *supra* note 48, p. 281.
53. Williamson, 1991, *supra* note 48, p. 281.

independent when it comes to the firm's decision-making process and protection of property rights.[54]

A quick look at the model developed by Williamson in 1991 shows that markets (M), hierarchies (H) and hybrid forms (X) are functions of asset specificity and governance costs.[55] When there is no asset specificity of any kind, then markets are preferred to hierarchies. In this case, the costs related to the internal bureaucracy of an organization are bigger than the costs of market structures, since the latter is superior in adaptation respects.[56] Expanding the analysis and considering also the hybrid forms of governance: $M(0) < X(0) < H(0)$. When we look at the marginal value of those functions, we can state that $M' > X' > H' > 0$, and this is because the variation in governance costs in relation to asset specificity is lower in hierarchies than in hybrid forms and therefore higher in hybrid forms than in market structures.

In sum, in the view of the transaction cost theory, vertical agreements are developed when specific investments are needed, and at the same time, companies do not want to lose the advantages of making autonomous decisions. The dependency created by asset specificity within a vertical arrangement, especially in long-term relationships, explains contractual risks. Also, vertical agreements bring uncertainty to both parties. Uncertainties may explain the potential coordination problems discussed in the previous sections. The combination of the risk of opportunism and the risk of coordination clarifies the existence of various forms of governance, including the decision of parties to have long-term contract-based solutions. Hence, risks must be balanced in such a way that the form of governance chosen by parties (markets, hybrids or hierarchies) is efficient and advantageous for the markets.

2.2.4 Other Efficiency Arguments: Considerations Regarding Online Markets

The topic of vertical restraints has been catching specific attention of antitrust authorities around the world when related to cases involving digital markets. A literature review on e-commerce highlights some features that may affect the traditional efficiency analysis of vertical restraints.[57] First, in online markets, the search costs of consumers are relatively low, which means that they can more easily compare prices among competitors.[58] Second, e-commerce has expanded the geographic scope

54. C. Menard, 'The Economics of Hybrid Organizations', *Journal of Institutional and Theoretical Economics*, Vol. 160, No. 3, 2004, p. 355.
55. Williamson, 1991, *supra* note 48, pp. 283-286.
56. Actually, according to Williamson, 'adaptation' is a key concept in the study of economic organizations, since it can be understood as the ability of a form of governance to handle disturbances which continually arise between agents that tend to transact over time. O. Williamson, *The Mechanisms of Governance*, New York, Oxford University Press, 1996, pp. 101-102.
57. *See* E. Lieber & C. Syverson, 'Online Vs. Offline Competition', *in* M. Peitz & J. Waldfogel (eds), *The Oxford Handbook of the Digital Economy*, Oxford, Oxford University Press, 2012.
58. *See*, for instance, the study of Brown and Goolsbee about insurance markets. J. R. Brown & A. Goolsbee, 'Does the Internet Make Markets More Competitive? Evidence from the Life Insurance Industry', *Journal of Political Economy*, Vol. 110, No. 3, 2002, pp. 481-507.

of business transactions, encouraging competition among producers and retailers that do not exist in the offline market.[59] Third, the effect on distribution costs and the relationship of producers-distributors-consumers have changed considerably. Several producers started selling directly to consumers, sometimes with the help of price-comparison platforms. Some retailers are motivated to enter the markets because, in online shops, distribution costs (and stocks) are minimized in a way that retailers can offer a better variety of goods to consumers.[60] Lastly, e-commerce has an impact upon consumer and producer information asymmetries. Buying online may create greater information asymmetry between producers, distributors and consumers, because consumers cannot try the goods out before purchasing them, making it harder for both producers and distributors to create a good reputation.[61]

Taking this background into account, there are some considerations to be made regarding the efficiencies of vertical restraints in online markets. A first point to note is that the internet may increase the scope of the free-riding argument.[62] Because price competition becomes more evident in digital markets, distributors might have no incentive to invest in pre- and post-sales services. Therefore, the magnitude of the free-riding effect may become bigger and retailers have even more reasons to focus their marketing strategies on guaranteeing lower prices to consumers. In this context, RPM, selective distribution systems, among other vertical restraints, can also encourage online retailers to keep an optimal level of services. In a similar way, vertical restraints may also overcome the hold-up problem of online platforms, guaranteeing the return of their specific investments. Online platforms must bear high costs of software and design development, and exclusive arrangements can also counterbalance this negative externality.

Cristina Cafarra and Kai-Uwe Kühn, in a study prepared for the OECD, analyse the problem of asymmetric information and incomplete contracting in multisided platforms.[63] They argue that producers cannot sign complete contracts with their retailer stipulating an optimal level of 'sales effort/services' because the producer has asymmetric information on the amount and effectiveness of the retailer's 'sales effort' on its online platforms. According to the authors, the design of complete contracts becomes even more difficult within the scope of multisided platforms (such as price-comparison websites). This is because demand for goods is more elastic in

59. It is worth noting, however, that some scholars show that internet users tend to buy online from sellers that are in the same geographic areas, i.e., they do not fully explore this limitless reach of the internet. *See*, for instance, A. Hortaçsu, F. Martínez-Jerez & J. Douglas, 'The Geography of Trade in Online Transactions: Evidence from eBay and Mercadolibre', *American Economic Journal: Microeconomics*, Vol. 1, No. 1, 2009, pp. 53-74.
60. According to Brynjolfsson, Hu, and Smith, there was an increase in consumer welfare by seven to ten times due to the expansion of online book retailers. Their research shows that, on average, an online book retailer, such as Amazon, trends to offer fifty-seven times more book titles than a traditional large bookstore. *See* E. Brynjolfsson, Y. Hu & M. Smith, 'Consumer Surplus in the Digital Economy: Estimating the Value of Increased Product Variety at Online Booksellers', *Management Science*, Vol. 49, No. 11, 2003, pp. 1580-1596.
61. OECD, *Vertical Restraints for Online Sales*, 2013, p. 20.
62. Van den Bergh, 2017, *supra* note 25, p. 252.
63. OECD, *The Competition Analysis of Vertical Restraints in Multi-Sided Markets – Note by Cafarra and Kuhn*, 2017, pp. 4-5.

platforms and the 'service level' offered by the platform cannot usually be priced. Selective distribution can be a form of tackling the problem of incomplete contracting.

It is worth noting that the free-riding argument in the context of e-commerce can also be challenged. Lao, for instance, argues that consumers may free-ride in the opposite direction, i.e., consumers first compare the prices of certain goods online, and then go to the physical outlets to buy the goods.[64] In this way, online retailers are harmed, but offline retailers may benefit from this positive externality. Because of these controversial effects that are raised with digitalization, the author brings attention to the possible limitations of traditional efficiencies arguments in this new scenario.

2.3 ANTICOMPETITIVE EFFECTS OF VERTICAL RESTRAINTS

Market functioning is researched by the industrial organization field. Its focus is not only on analysing how companies exercise market power in imperfectly competitive markets but also on their interactions, welfare results and rationale for public measures. Vertical agreements can also be explained and explored considering theories of harm which put the emphasis on how companies can enhance their competitive performance by obtaining better market positions. Porter, for example, argues that 'the relative position which firms occupy within their industry's structure determines the generic strategies which are the most viable and profitable for them'.[65] Vertical agreements can modify the general dynamics of a certain market, offering an advantage to the parties who are cooperating in strengthening their market positions. In fact, these contracts may allow companies to increase their market power, or in the worst case, to abuse that power.

This section aims at presenting the anticompetitive effects of vertical agreements. A selected literature review shows that vertical agreements may help in maintaining horizontal cartels, exacerbating market imperfections, and increasing the market power of incumbent firms. This section is organized in order to highlight the anticompetitive outcomes of the increase of collusion practices, the reduction of intra- and inter-brand competition, and the foreclosure of markets. In the same way as in the previous section, and to enrich the discussion, some considerations about the anticompetitive outcomes in the context of online markets will be added.

2.3.1 Increasing Collusion in Markets

From microeconomic theory, we know that a cartel (just like a monopoly) chooses a price that maximizes profits, and this price is higher than the prices in competitive markets. Unlike a monopoly, a cartel faces special difficulties related to the actual conflicting interests of its members. Insights from game theory explain the logic behind

64. M. Lao, 'Resale Price Mantenance: The Internet Phenomenon and "Free Rider" Issues', *Antitrust Bulletin*, Vol. 55, No. 2, 2010, pp. 473-512.
65. M. E. Porter, *Competitive Strategy: Techniques for Analyzing Industries and Competitors*, New York, Free Press, 1980.

the cartel instability.[66] Within a cartel, each member is interested in the others cooperating with the agreed terms. At the same time, each cartel member has his/her own incentives to break the agreement. For example, if all companies cooperate and charge the same (monopoly) price for a given product, they all make higher profits than the ones in a competitive market. In the same example, if a firm decides to break the terms of the collusive agreement, and charge less for the same product, the same firm will naturally capture a large number of consumers who would like to pay less for the same product. Then, the 'cheating' firm increases its sales, reducing the profits of other cartel members. In this context, the cartel needs clear and easy-to-monitor rules to prevent members from escaping the deal. RPM is a way of facilitating coordination between companies, as retail prices become easy to detect and it prevents the cheating behaviour.[67]

Indeed, firms can use vertical agreements to sustain cartels both in upstream (producers) as well as in downstream markets (retailers).[68] With regard to upstream markets, retail price-fixing increases transparency and price observability,[69] and it makes collusion more likely by eliminating the retail price variation. In the late 1990s, Frank Mathewson and Ralph Winter explored this argument:

> With a competitive retail market and stable retail cost conditions, manufacturers could assume agreed-upon retail prices by fixing their wholesale prices appropriately. In reality, however, variation over time in the costs of retailing would lead to fluctuating retail prices. If wholesale prices are not easily observed by each cartel member, cartel stability would suffer because members would have difficulty distinguishing changes in retail prices that were caused by cost changes from cheating on the cartel. [Resale price-fixing] can enhance cartel stability by eliminating the retail price variation. The facilitating power of [Resale price-fixing] is in the increased cartel stability.[70]

Bruno Jullien and Patrick Rey also formalized the same argument, stressing that RPM contributes to the detection of price deviations in tacit collusion, since it makes it easier for producers to follow the same price. This is because fixed retail prices are noticeably less responsive to demand shocks.[71]

In the downstream market, vertical restraints, such as retail price-fixing, can lead to a decrease in competition because retailers cannot anymore compete in price. In the absence of RPM, final prices to consumers are more exposed to diverse shocks in retail markets, making it more difficult for producers to distinguish changes in retail prices that are caused by different retail conditions from cheating on cartels.[72] Collusion in downstream markets is usually enforced by boycotting any producers who refuse to

66. *See*, for instance, discussion of Chapters 12 and 13 of R. Pindyck & D. Rubinfeld, *Microeconomics*, 7th ed., Essex, Pearson/Prentice Hall, 2009.
67. Telser, 1960, *supra* note 19, p. 96.
68. Telser, 1960, *supra* note 19; Posner, 1977, *supra* note 23.
69. Motta, 2004, *supra* note 11, p. 359.
70. F. Mathewson & R. Winter, 'The Law and Economics of Resale Price Maintenance', *Review of Industrial Organization*, Vol. 13, No. 1/2, 1998, pp. 57-84.
71. B. Jullien & P. Rey, 'Resale Price Maintenance and Collusion', *The RAND Journal of Economics*, Vol. 38, No. 4, 2007, pp. 983-1001.
72. Motta, 2004, *supra* note 11, p. 359.

impose RPM. Also non-price restraints may sustain the equilibrium of collusive practices among distributors since they 'limit the scope for deviations from the collusive path'.[73]

2.3.2 Reducing Intra- and/or Inter-brand Competition

Briefly speaking, intra-brand competition is characterized by competition among retailers who sell products from different producers (i.e., the competition among the same brands that are sold in different shops), and inter-brand competition is defined by the competition among different branded products sold by each retailer.[74] Let us think about an example related to the beer manufacturers: Heineken and Budweiser sell their products in different supermarket chains, for instance, Walmart and Carrefour. In this case, intra-brand competition is characterized by the competition among retail shops, so it refers to the competition between Walmart and Carrefour. The inter-brand competition is defined among brands, so it is related to the competition among Heineken and Budweiser inside each retail shop. It goes without saying that the dynamic of the intra- and inter-brand competition depends on several variables, such as market power in the upstream and downstream levels, economies of scale, entry barriers, rivalry, buying power. However, vertical agreements can also alter the dynamics of these markets in different ways. When vertical restraints diminish intra-brand and inter-brand competition, they also reduce total welfare in a given market, and therefore they are likely to be anticompetitive.

Exclusive distribution, selective distribution, exclusive territory restrictions, and RPM are examples of restriction in vertical agreements that decrease the level of intra-brand competition. If a producer grants exclusive distribution to a single retailer, no other retailer will then be able to sell this specific product, and therefore intra-brand competition becomes non-existent. The important question to be raised is how these vertical restraints may affect the strategic interaction and the behaviour between producers, retailers and their rivals. In other words, what happens if this reduction in intra-brand competition also leads to a decrease in inter-brand competition? The answer to this question will depend on how imperfect is the market in the production (upstream) level, since the reduction of inter-brand competition exacerbates existing market imperfections.[75]

If the market is concentrated in the upstream level (in our example, the markets for beers), contractual restrictions such as exclusive distribution lead to a reduction of intra-brand and consequently a reduction of inter-brand competition, since the options for consumers become very limited in most of the retail shops. However, if the upstream market is not concentrated (in our example, if there are many beer producers in certain geographic area), then the reduction of competition among retailers does not necessarily weaken inter-brand competition, since consumers, in this situation, still face several options of substitute goods in different retail shops.

73. OECD, 2013, *supra* note 61, p. 14.
74. Motta, 2004, *supra* note 11, pp. 306 and 347.
75. Rey & Caballero-Sanz, 1996, *supra* note 7, pp. 17-18.

Exclusive territory restrictions can also reduce intra-brand competition in a certain marketplace (i.e., only one specific retailer is able to sell in a certain geographic market) and this scenario creates incentives for rival producers to undercut each other, reducing therefore the inter-brand competition in different geographic areas.[76]

To sum up, the effects of vertical restraints on intra- and inter-brand competition are hard to clearly assess, because each type of restraint can lead to different consequences in terms of encouraging or restricting competition. Indeed, in specific cases, these effects can be dubious and very hard to weigh. The US Supreme Court in the *Sylvania* case illustrated this concern:

> Vertical restrictions reduce intra-brand competition by limiting the number of sellers of a particular product competing for the business of a given group of buyers [...]. Vertical restrictions promote inter-brand competition by allowing the manufacturer to achieve certain efficiencies in the distribution of his products. These 'redeeming virtues' are implicit in every decision sustaining vertical restrictions under the rule of reason. Economists have identified a number of ways in which manufacturers can use such restrictions to compete more effectively against other manufacturers. For example, new manufacturers and manufacturers entering new markets can use the restrictions in order to induce competent and aggressive retailers to make the kind of investment of capital and labour that is often required in the distribution of products unknown to the consumers.[77]

2.3.3 Market Foreclosure and Higher Barriers to Entry

Vertical agreements can be used in an attempt to foreclose markets. This argument calls the attention of competition agencies around the world, especially in highly concentrated markets. Certain types of vertical restraints, such as exclusive distribution, exclusive supply and geo-blocking, might allow firms to enjoy a dominant position and deter the entry of competitors in the market, by making it harder or more costly for the entrant to acquire the necessary inputs.[78]

Entry conditions may be affected at every level of the supply chain. In the upstream level, market foreclosure may be the result of exclusive arrangements that force potential new producers to set-up their own distribution systems. Some vertical restraints may discourage potential producers because these agreements would impose restricted access to retailers who would therefore have difficulty reaching prospective customers. Similarly, such restrictions can be implemented to exclude competitors from market by limiting the opportunities for distribution. If the distributors are generally subjected to large economies of scope or scale in a specific market, exclusive arrangements would also increase the costs of entry of potential competitors. Moreover, the practice of exclusive dealing may encourage potential rivals to distribute their products less efficiently and with higher costs.[79]

76. Rey & Caballero-Sanz, 1996, *supra* note 7, p. 16.
77. *Continental TV Inc v. GTE Sylvania Inc* (1976) 433 US 36, pp. 54-55.
78. Motta, 2004, *supra* note 11, p. 362.
79. Rey & Caballero-Sanz, 1996, *supra* note 7, p. 19.

The risk of an entry barrier is also observed at the downstream level. This is the case because entering the distribution market can also be difficult and expensive. For instance, retailers might face a hard time in finding as good retail locations as its incumbent competitors. Again, holding the finest distributors or places in exclusive long-term agreements would raise the cost of distribution for potential entrants and could therefore ban potential competitors from entering the market. This challenge is more frequent where economies of scale are already considered natural entry barriers to a certain market.

More generally, these examples are part of the so-called raising rivals' cost strategy, developed by Thomas Krattenmaker and Steven Salop in the late 1980s.[80] Considering the upstream and/or downstream market, such practices can be used against rivals to reduce their presence in the market or to decrease their market share significantly. They can also delay or prevent competitors from entering the market. The authors explain that retailers are not necessarily harmed by exclusive agreements. Even though they face limited lines of products to supply to their consumers, they may also be compensated by the producers, in case these firms decide to share the extra profits of deterring an entrant.[81] According to Krattenmaker and Salop: 'By embedding a collusive agreement in a vertical contract that raises input prices by restraining sales to rivals, the firm reduces coordination costs, making it more efficient at preventing cheating and distributing the gains from collusion. Thus, these strategies involve creating additional horizontal market power through the mechanism of vertical contracts.'[82]

Moreover, long-term exclusive dealing provisions or exclusive territory provisions proposed by producers generate a restrictive situation with distributors who even protect these brands against competing products. In these situations, producers and distributors are less willing to engage in a price war. It goes without saying that all these anticompetitive effects have socially negative outcomes.[83]

2.3.4 Other Anticompetitive Effects: Considerations Regarding Online Markets

Following on from the discussion brought by section 2.2.4, the features of online markets may extend and/or reinforce the above-mentioned anticompetitive effects of vertical restraints. Because online markets reduce search costs for consumers and increase price transparency among retailers, it can be expected that these markets also facilitate tacit collusion among competitors.[84] Vertical restraints may reinforce the magnitude of these effects. In the event of an explicit collusion scheme created by RPM mechanisms, they become even easier to monitor via the internet.

80. T. Krattenmaker & S. Salop, 'Anticompetitive Exclusion: Raising Rivals' Costs to Achieve Power over Price', *The Yale Law Journal*, Vol. 96, No. 2, 1986, pp. 209-293.
81. Rey & Caballero-Sanz, 1996, *supra* note 7, pp. 18-19.
82. Krattenmaker & Salop, 1986, *supra* note 80, p. 224.
83. Rey & Caballero-Sanz, 1996, *supra* note 7, p. 21.
84. *See* analysis of Brown & Goolsbee, 2002, *supra* note 58, pp. 481-507.

Furthermore, to create a successful online retailer shop, it is necessary to build a strong reputation and network, which requires huge investments. Network effects increase barriers to entry in digital markets.[85] It can be the case that a producer signs exclusive clauses with a specific online retail shop (established firm), and because of that, the producer cannot set better prices than the ones agreed with the established platform, not even with new entrants. These exclusive clauses among sellers and online retail platforms directly discourage new platforms and e-shops from entering the market, since they know that they cannot compete in price in these specific goods. Most-favoured nation clauses are examples of that. In the next section, there is a brief introduction to this vertical restraint.

Within the digital market scope, another frequent vertical restraint is the so-called platform bans. These bans are related to restrictions imposed on online distributors regarding sales conditions in their online shops. Platform bans can be understood as a special form of selective distribution system, and they have very peculiar and controversial characteristics. As we have seen in the previous sections, a producer may want to place restrictions on its distribution network to make sure that the product has its image protected, especially in the case of luxury goods. However, these restrictions do not always match the online shop businesses, where consumers have no physical contact with the product, and much information, linked to the characteristics of the goods, is lost. In other words, some features of the internet and online shops directly conflict with the purpose and rationality of certain types of vertical agreements, mainly selective distribution systems. That was the conclusion reached by Paolo Buccirossi, who emphasizes that 'e-commerce tends to increase price competition and poses some problems of asymmetry of information that may exacerbate the difficulties that selective distribution is meant to overcome'.[86] The internet may therefore be an unsuitable marketplace for certain products, and this fact underlines the preference of certain producers to prevent internet sales altogether.

Finally, new forms of hub-and-spoke conspiracies also arise in this context. Let us take as an example the market for pricing services. In the upstream market there is the creator/developer of the pricing-algorithm (e.g., *Bloomberg Commerce*) and in the downstream market there are several industries that use this pricing-algorithm either to determine their market prices or to respond to market fluctuations.[87] A sole vertical agreement that supplies price algorithm services to a specific industry is not necessarily anticompetitive. The problem comes when several of the same vertical agreements are signed among competitors in the same industry. Since rival firms end up using the same price suggestions, and therefore aligning their prices, the competition in this

85. G. Werden, 'Network Effects and Conditions of Entry: Lessons from the Microsoft Case', *Antitrust Law Journal*, Vol. 69, No. 1, 2011, pp. 87-111.
86. P. Buccirossi, 'Vertical Restraints on E-commerce and Selective Distribution', *Journal of Competition Law and Economics*, Vol. 11, No. 3, 2015, pp. 747-773.
87. *See*, for example, A. Ezrachi & M. Stucke, *Virtual Competition: The Promise and Perils of the Algorithm-Driven Economy*, Cambridge, Harvard University Press, 2016.

market is harmed. This situation is also referred to in the literature as hub-and-spoke cartels that are originated by vertical agreements in the digital markets.[88]

2.4 THE DOUBLE-SIDED ASPECT OF SELECTED VERTICAL RESTRAINTS: AN OVERVIEW OF ECONOMIC EFFICIENCIES AND ANTICOMPETITIVE EFFECTS

This section draws attention to selected vertical restraints considering both economic efficiencies and anticompetitive effects in our analysis. The nature of vertical restraints can be relatively complex, since restrictive clauses can affect different levels of the supply chain in diverse forms. Also, their effects in marketplaces are subjected to the behaviour of several players. To reflect upon these issues, the following subsections aim at taking a closer look to specific restraints, considering the theories discussed in the previous sections. The cases of RPM, geo-blocking restrictions and selective distributions schemes will be considered in order to highlight the complexity of the market dynamics that need to be considered in an economic analysis of vertical agreements.

2.4.1 Resale Price-Fixing (Resale Price Maintenance or RPM)

Resale price-fixing is a restriction under which the producers determine the final price charged to consumers by distributors. There are several variants to this restriction, including price ceilings, price floors, and recommended prices. The contributions of Telser and other Chicago scholars have shed light on the procompetitive effects of RPM.[89]

First, RPM can be very useful to combat double markup problems. As we have seen in previous sections, a producer that wants to protect its sales and avoid the reduction of quantity sold by retailers can control the profit of the distributors by fixing retail prices. Second, this price restraint can help producers and distributors to avoid free-riders of both levels of the supply chain. Third, still related to the second point, RPM, by preventing free-riding, is likely to improve presales and postsales services. Considering that the demand for goods is affected by the number of services provided, it means that this restriction, in the end, can increase demand in specific markets and therefore increase total welfare. Fourth, RPM protects the image of certain branded (luxury) goods and quality standards, which would otherwise be less valued by consumers. Lastly, in the short-run scenario, RPM can have a positive impact on inter- and intra-brand competition. This happens because other producers might be attracted to enter the market if certain profitability is guaranteed. Also, it might raise the interest of other distributors that would hesitate to join a certain distribution network in other circumstances.

88. For a more extensive discussion on hub-and-spoke conspiracy within the digital markets, *see*: B. Klein, 'The Apple E-books Case: When Is a Vertical Contract a Hub in a Hub-and-Spoke Conspiracy?', *Journal of Competition Law & Economics*, Vol. 13, No. 3, 2017, pp. 423-474.
89. *See* discussion in section 2.2.

However, in the absence of a free-riding problem, this specific vertical restraint does not truly enhance consumer and total welfare. As discussed before, if consumers are knowledgeable in respect of a specific product, the producer may take the risk of providing more information than is necessary, and therefore, charging higher prices. It means that vertical restraints, such as RPM, benefit 'ignorant' marginal consumers but harm 'knowledgeable' infra-marginal consumers who have to pay more for the goods.

Moreover, several other risks might be associated with price restrictions. They can facilitate collusion (explicit or tacit) between producers by enhancing price transparency. In the case of explicit collusion, RPM helps the maintenance of a cartel, making it harder for rivals to 'cheat'. In the case of tacit collusion, however, producers can observe very easily the prices of competitors, which may directly affect the way they define their own prices. RPM can also facilitate collusion between distributors, i.e., in the downstream market. This may happen because this vertical restraint eliminates price competition (intra-brand competition) among retailers, who lose part of their freedom in setting their own prices. It means that price restraints can soften competition between producers and distributors, thus increasing market imperfections. In less competitive markets, not only are prices higher and quantities offered lower, but at the distribution level, dynamism and innovation are also compromised. Finally, RPM can foreclose markets and deter entry in relation to the long-term, although this effect is clearer with non-price restrictions.

Table 2.1 aims at summarizing the potential multiple outcomes both regarding economic efficiencies and anticompetitive effects. It is worth noting that the table does not give an answer to whether RPM is pro- or anticompetitive, since each possible effect has different sizes and the competition assessment is influenced by market conditions, and mainly, by the goals of competition law in the given jurisdiction.

Table 2.1 The Possible Double-Sided Effects of Resale Price-Fixing

Resale Price-Fixing	
Economic Efficiency	**Anticompetitive Effects**
Fights double markup	Encourages tacit collusion
Prevents free-riding	Reduces intra-brand competition
	Reduces inter-brand competition

Source: Compiled by the author.

It is worth noting that when it comes to online markets, new forms of price-restrictions have been popping up. For instance, most favoured nation clauses (or MFN clauses) are vertical restraints between suppliers and distributors that generally consist of an offer by the supplier of a price or rate to a client no higher than the lowest offered to other clients. For instance, in the online hotel booking sector, an MFN clause obliges hotels to always give to the platform the best price for online hotel bookings, among other most favoured conditions.[90] Competition authorities are mainly concerned that

90. *See* discussion of MFN clauses in Chapter 4.

such restrictions constitute a form of RPM that could limit price competition, and raise entry barriers among online travel agents (OTAs), preventing their expansion.

2.4.2 Geo-Blocking

The territory designated to a certain distributor can be limited by geo-blocking provisions. When producers grant exclusive territory to certain distributors, the last ones are the only ones to serve customers in that geographic area. On the one hand, geo-blocking provisions can be efficiency enhancing. Most of the objective justifications are related to the free-riding theory. Geo-blocking clauses prevent free-riding on the production side. In case a producer makes specific investments on a certain distribution network (for instance, training of staff), they would not want other competitors (producers) to free-ride on these investments. Regarding the downstream level, geo-blocking clauses may be adopted to better coordinate retail services, since it aims at eliminating or at least reducing the scope of such externality. Even if free-riders are inexistent, a producer may target the allocation of exclusive territory clauses so that retail services are better monitored, especially the ones that attract marginal consumers.[91] This is because this vertical restraint also assists in overcoming the hold-up problem of specific investments, and therefore reduces transaction costs related to economies of scale in logistics.[92]

On the other hand, these provisions can provoke a negative impact on the competitive environment. First, geo-blocking restrictions may facilitate collusion in the short-run. Producers might agree on dividing territories to guarantee better profits in those locations. Client division is one type of cartel that is constantly on the radar of antitrust agencies and they can be reinforced by exclusive territory restrictions. Second, and most importantly, geo-blocking clauses can foreclose markets and deter entry by raising a rival's cost, mainly if parties have some degree of market power. It means that those smaller producers that do not belong to a specific distribution network might not be able to reach their consumers. Similarly, smaller distributors might not have access to producers, and intra-brand competition is therefore harmed.

It is worth noting that the magnitude of negative effects of territorial restrictions on intra-brand competition and market foreclosure depends on whether the producers give the distributors any freedom to set their own prices. In this case, the anticompetitive effects tend to be lower.[93] Table 2.2 presents a summary of the double-sided analysis.

91. Telser, 1960, *supra* note 19.
92. A more descriptive analysis is carried out in subsection 2.2.3.
93. Rey & Caballero-Sanz, 1996, *supra* note 7, p. 25.

Table 2.2 The Possible Double-Sided Effects of Geo-Blocking Clauses[94]

Geo-Blocking	
Economic Efficiency	**Anticompetitive Effects**
Prevents free-riding in the production side	Facilitates collusion
Prevents free-riding in case retail services are necessary	Forecloses markets
Reduces transaction costs	Deters entry

Source: Compiled by the author.

2.4.3 Selective Distribution

Selective distribution is a practice characterized by the engagement of a supplier with a restricted number of distributors. The EU VBER defines that it is 'a distribution system where the supplier undertakes to sell the contract goods or services, either directly or indirectly, only to distributors selected on the basis of specified criteria'.[95] It means that within the selective distribution system, distributors must fulfil a number of specific features to be eligible to commercialize the manufactured products or services. The producers may request, for example, that the retail shop should be situated in a popular shopping street, or that it should have highly trained staff, or even a particular furnishing style. As discussed in the previous sections, suppliers may engage in these restrictive agreements to preserve the image of their brands, in particular for luxury goods.[96] Selective distribution systems may prevent free-riding problems in the downstream markets and, because of it, these vertical restrictions may help distributors to promote specific investments. Selective distribution may also increase economic efficiencies in cases of products that require presale services or branded products. In these cases, even if intra-brand competition is reduced by the contractual restraint, the inter-brand competition remains strong.

This vertical restraint is however considered anticompetitive when producers use this vertical restriction to reduce significantly the number of outlets that sell their products. Considering a scenario where inter-brand competition is also weak, the selective distribution scheme will allow prices to rise above competition level.[97] These distribution systems can also restrict intra-brand competition and, as a result of this,

94. Like Table 2.1, Table 2.2 does not give an answer to whether geo-blocking is pro- or anticompetitive, since each possible effect has different sizes and the competition assessment is influenced by market conditions, and mainly, by the goals of competition law in the given jurisdiction. As we will *see* in Chapter 4, the market integration goal of European Competition Policy outweighs the potential anticompetitive effects of geo-blocking clauses.
95. Article 1 of EU Regulation 330/2010.
96. *See* discussion of section 2.2.
97. *See*, for instance, the paper of Rey and Stiglitz that demonstrates that within an exclusive distribution system (and to a certain extent selective distribution systems), a producer is less aggressive in setting their prices, which also influences the competitors to set higher prices as well. P. Rey & J. Stiglitz, 'The Role of Exclusive Territories in Producer's Competition', *The RAND Journal of Economics*, Vol. 26, 1995, pp. 431-451.

customers will cope with fewer alternatives available for certain brands/products. Besides, these selective systems can both generate entry barriers in some markets and promote market foreclosure. Finally, if producers and retailers have market power, the risk of double-marginalization may enhance higher prices for consumers.

Recently, several cases of selective distribution in online platforms and online marketplaces have come to light around the world. The most prevalent limitation that producers impose on retailers aims to restrict the scope of their online products in selective distribution networks. There are some features of online sale restrictions, such as increased competition in prices and information asymmetry issues that 'may conflict with the objectives of a selective distribution organization'.[98] The internet may therefore not be a suitable marketplace for some products, and this, in theory, can help explaining why a producer might want to totally avoid internet sales.[99] The outcome of these cases has been dubious, since national authorities have been deciding differently upon this topic.[100] Table 2.3 highlights the main outcomes in terms of efficiency and anticompetitive effects that may be assessed in selective distribution cases.

Table 2.3 The Possible Double-Sided Effects of Selective Distribution[101]

Selective Distribution	
Economic Efficiency	**Anticompetitive Effects**
Prevents free-riding	Reduces intra-brand competition
Ensures pre- and post-sale services	Raises search costs for consumers
Protects brands	Forecloses markets
Protects specific investments	Deters entry
	Encourages double markup

Source: Compiled by the author.

2.5 THE POLITICAL ECONOMY OF COMPETITION POLICIES

This chapter is mostly focused on the economic analysis of vertical agreements, and on the need to think about policies of vertical agreements that guarantee an optimal level of welfare in society. This specific section, however, briefly introduces the discussion that welfare-oriented arguments – such as the ones presented in sections 2.2 and 2.3 – might not always be the motivation of policymakers. Competition policies (and in this case, policies applicable to vertical agreements) can also be inspired by private interests such as the interest of the competition authorities, the interest of industries and their lobby groups, of legal representatives, among others. Given the complexity of

98. OECD, 2013, *supra* note 61, pp. 25-26.
99. Buccirossi, 2015, *supra* note 86, pp. 747-773.
100. *See* in Chapter 4 the examples of the European Union.
101. This table does not give an answer to whether selective distribution systems are pro- or anticompetitive, since each possible effect of these practices has different sizes, and the competition assessment is influenced by market conditions, and mainly, by the goals of competition law in the giving jurisdiction.

the assessment of vertical agreements, the political economy discussion gains importance.

Generally speaking, regulation is motivated and explained by public interest argumentation, meaning that the law and decision makers should operate to be able to ensure the promotion of economic efficiency. In theory, externalities, information asymmetry, market power and public goods are the market failures that give grounds for regulation. Even knowing that public interest grounds might vary among different societies, they are usually intended to tackle those conventional forms of market failures in those given contexts.[102] When studying competition law, monopolies are the classic examples of market failures, as they might lead to an abuse of market power. The previous sections also showed that price and non-price restrictions that result from vertical agreements can also lead to collusion, reduction of competition and market foreclosures. Usually, competition policies are the main instruments for dealing with those issues.[103]

However, in certain contexts, the law- and decision-making processes do not follow what is optimal for society, or they do not achieve the public interest goals. One explanation for that has been brought by public choice theory.[104] The primary concept of the public choice theory is that an individual's preferences are reflected in the lawmaking process and therefore affect the social welfare. George Stigler,[105] Sam Peltzman,[106] Richard Posner[107] and Gary Becker[108] all pointed out, for instance, the fact that various interest groups compete when it comes to achieving political favours. A basic assumption of this private interest approach to regulation is that there is a demand and supply for regulation.[109] With regard to the demand for regulation, interest groups (such as businesses, government authorities, industry associations, legal representatives) attempt to influence the law- or decision-making process in order to pursue benefits for themselves.[110] In other words, from a public choice point of view, the evolution of legislation also responds to the demands of private interests.[111] In this way, legislation can almost never be 'allocative efficient' in the Pareto sense, since it

102. A. Ogus, *Regulation: Legal Form and Economic Theory*, Oxford, Hart Publisher, 2004, p. 71.
103. *See*, for example, F. M. Scherer, *Industrial Market Structure and Economic Performance*, 2nd ed., Chicago, Rand McNally, 1980.
104. The proposition that private interest drive policy outcomes was articulated in its modern form by Stigler in G. Stigler, 'The Theory of Economic Regulation', *The Bell Journal of Economics and Management Science*, Vol. 2, No. 1, 1971, pp. 3-21.
105. *See*, for instance, Stigler, 1971, *supra* note 104.
106. *See*, for instance, S. Peltzman, 'Toward a More General Theory of Regulation', *Journal of Law and Economics*, Vol. 19, No. 2, 1976, pp. 211-240.
107. *See*, for instance, R. Posner, 'Theories of Economic Regulation', *The Bell Journal of Economics and Management Science*, Vol. 5, No. 2, 1974, pp. 335-358; R. Posner, 'The Social Costs of Monopoly and Regulation', *Journal of Political Economy*, Vol. 83, No. 4, 1975, pp. 807-827.
108. *See*, for instance, G. Becker, 'A Theory of Competition among Pressure Groups for Political Influence', *Quarterly Journal of Economics*, Vol. 98, No. 3, 1983, pp. 371-400.
109. Stigler, 1971, *supra* note 104.
110. G. Shen & N. Philipsen, 'Regulation of the Inter-Provincial Establishment of Companies: Applying the Private Interest Approach to China', *in* N. Philipsen, S. Weishaar & G, Xu (eds), *Market Integration: The EU Experience and Implications for Regulatory Reform in China*, London, Springer, 2016, p. 194.
111. Ogus, 2004, *supra* note 102, p. 63.

will invariably impose losses on some individuals. William Schughart summarizes the theory by saying:

> The model of public choice insists that the same rational, self-interest-seeking movements that animate human action in ordinary markets be applied to decision making in the public sector as well. The assumption that all individuals, in or out of government, pursue their own self-interests is the fundamental tenet of public choice. Just as consumers want to maximize their utility and firms want to maximize their profits, public policy makers want to maximize their own welfare.[112]

Taking this perspective, public choice theorists argued that special-interest groups have a powerful influence not only over politicians but over the whole lawmaking process. This is the case because there are several different approaches in which those groups affect policymaking. In the antitrust field, no different from economic regulation in general, the agencies, the judges and the antitrust bureaucrats[113] are also assumed to operate in the public interest.

Critical scholars of antitrust policy argue that the failures in implementing these policies are due to several reasons, for instance: the errors in the application of the law, the lack of knowledge of agencies, of courts and of lawyers in correctly applying the relevant economic theories, and/or the constant replacement of existing policies.[114] However, historical records of unsuccessful legislations and bad antitrust decisions in different countries prove that the private interest of certain groups also has an influence on the levels of optimal enforcement. That is to say, while antitrust can be a way of promoting public interest goals, it can also be used to benefit some groups to the detriment of others. Armando Rodriguez and Ashok Menon when enumerating the limits of competition policies argue that the fundamental competition problem is the ability of domestic interest groups to easily influence government in their policymaking process.[115] The authors focus their analysis on developing countries and highlight that the governmental institution in those countries seems to be exceptionally vulnerable to pressure from interests groups compared to developed ones.[116]

Robert Tollison was a pioneer scholar in discussing public choice theory to understand why competition law is often unsuccessful in achieving its goals oriented to consumer protection and protection against abuse of market power.[117] After Tollison's contribution, a whole new research agenda was created. An extensive literature, which included several empirical studies, started suggesting that antitrust enforcement was

112. W. F. Schughart II, 'Public-Choice Theory and Antitrust Policy', *in* F. Mc Chesney & W. F. Schughart II (eds), *The Causes and Consequences of Antitrust: The Public Choice Perspective*, Chicago, The University of Chicago Press, 1995, p. 9.
113. Expression used by Tollison in R. Tollison, 'Public Choice and Antitrust', *Cato Journal*, Vol. 4, Winter, 1985, p. 905.
114. F. Mc Chesney & W. F. Schughart II, *The Causes and Consequences of Antitrust: The Public Choice Perspective*, Chicago, The University of Chicago Press, 1995, p. 2.
115. A. Rodriguez & A. Menon, *The Limits of Competition Policy: The Shortcomings of Antitrust in Developing and Reforming Countries*, Biggleswade, Kluwer Law International, 2010, p. 136.
116. Rodriguez & Menon, 2010, *supra* note 115.
117. Tollison, 1985, *supra* note 113.

often working in favour of private interest groups and against consumers, by interfering with the allocation of resources within society. For example, William Long, Richard Schramm and Tollison[118] provided empirical evidence that the goals of competition law, such as consumer welfare, are not always observed in the allocation of antitrust cases.

This political economy approach opens up a debate about the limitation of the welfare-oriented arguments as main drivers of antitrust regulation. It also appears to be important since it allows us to develop an alternative look at the Brazilian and European experiences when regulating vertical agreements. Regarding the Brazilian case, Chapter 3 discusses the extent to which the self-interest of the relevant stakeholders explains the recent changes in regulation oriented to vertical agreements. Taking into account the European case, Chapter 4 introduces some ideas about the public choice perspective to the analysis of the policy options on vertical agreements adopted by the EU in the early 2000s.

2.6 THE COMPLEXITY OF VERTICAL AGREEMENTS AND THE ENDURING DEBATE ON POLICYMAKING

This chapter argues that vertical agreements have different effects in the marketplace. They can often increase economic efficiency and total welfare in certain markets, and in other cases generate anticompetitive outcomes, harm consumers and create welfare loses. Because vertical agreements are complex in their nature, this creates difficulties for policymakers to assess the overall effects in the markets. A vertical restraint can constitute a solution to a market failure, and at the same time encourage anticompetitive behaviour. Moreover, different forms of vertical restraints have diverse outcomes in the markets, and therefore require case-by-case assessments. For example, RPM and geo-blocking restrictions may combat free-riding, which is a procompetitive effect. RPM and geo-blocking clauses may also facilitate collusion and foreclose markets, which are anticompetitive effects. However, RPM may also combat double marginalization problems, while territorial protection may increase those problems.

Balancing pro- and anticompetitive effects of vertical agreements also has limitations. First, incomplete information of parties harms the antitrust analysis. Second, the interrelations between producers and distributors, during a time period and the resulting outcomes, are not always the same (not even fully predictable). Indeed, the effects of these interrelations are sometimes contradictory. Moreover, the economic analysis of vertical agreements is largely dependent on the assessment of the features of specific markets (such as market concentrations, rivalry, entry conditions, buying power) that add complexity to the overall analysis.

On behalf of the regulatory dilemma of vertical agreements, the enforcement of such practices turns out to be one of the most animated disputes in competition law nowadays. The exemplary literature review of the advantages and disadvantages of

118. W. Long, R. Schramm & R. Tollison, 'The Economic Determinants of Antitrust Activity', *in* F. Mc Chesney & W. F. Schughart II (eds), *The Causes and Consequences of Antitrust: The Public Choice Perspective*, Chicago, The University of Chicago Press, 1995, p. 95.

vertical agreements proves that there are many reasons to justify contradictory types of regulation. As shown in the next chapters, some jurisdictions changed their policies over the years from prohibition of certain types of vertical agreements to a rule of reason approach, from notification system of agreements to legal exception regimes, or even from *ex ante* notification systems to an *ex post* control of such contracts. The chapter introduces the argument that contradictory regulations might be justified by private interest of different agents, rather than by welfare-oriented arguments.

The chapter also briefly shows that what can be called the ‘regulatory dilemma’ may be reinforced in the context of digital economies, e-commerce transactions, and marketplace platforms. This is the case because new forms of contractual arrangements, with innovative features, are now being spread and bring into question their legality when it comes to competition policy. The assessment of the competition implications of vertical restraints in digital markets seems inherently more complex on behalf of multiple interactions, network externalities and vertical relationships between the marketplace platforms and consumers. This scenario potentially implies more difficult antitrust analysis with multiple foreclosure effects.

This chapter provides an opportunity to rethink and explore some foundations of competition law and its purposes. One can conclude, first, that the effects of vertical restraints are limited and less problematic when compared to the effects of horizontal restraints, so the policy options of the first restrictions should be carefully assessed. The complexity of vertical agreements also requires the conceptualization by the competition authorities of what is harmful to society, in order to guarantee that restrictions to competition do not take place. And whether a country will choose a lighter or stricter approach towards vertical agreements will depend on the goals of competition policy in the jurisdiction, i.e., what policymakers believe competition policy should aim at protecting. As shown in the upcoming chapters, the understanding of sociopolitical and economic circumstances is a crucial feature to allow an optimal normative discussion.

Considering this background, the following chapters intend to discuss different applications of competition policies oriented to vertical agreements. As this book enhances a comparison between the competition policies in Brazil (Chapter 3) and in the EU (Chapter 4), the upcoming chapters will analyse the evolution of those competition policies and the attempts of the authorities to handle vertical restraints. One of the main policy features to be considered refers to the enforcement costs of the chosen policies because of the complexity of these commercial structures. Since the welfare outcomes of vertical restraints (in both online and offline markets) are not clear, a case-by-case analysis appears to be a good policy option. However, case-by-case analysis raises significant enforcement costs. A critical evaluation of these enforcement costs will be presented in Chapter 5.

CHAPTER 3
Antitrust Enforcement of Vertical Agreements in Brazil

Recent changes in the Brazilian competition regulation put an end to the *ex ante* notification of vertical agreements, favouring the *ex post* control of vertical restraints. In order to understand the motivations of the Brazilian Competition Authority (CADE) when it comes to this policy choice, several legal and institutional aspects shall be considered: the historical perspective of the Competition Law in Brazil, the goals of competition policy in the country; the evolution of case law applicable to vertical agreements, and the self-interest of parties in the lawmaking process. For this reason, this study aims to discuss the evolution of vertical agreements regulation and enforcement activities in Brazil, considering their strengths and weaknesses.

3.1 INTRODUCTION: THE CHOICE OF BRAZIL AS A CASE STUDY

The previous chapter discussed that vertical agreements face a regulatory dilemma and the enforcement of such practices turns out to be one of the most animated disputes in competition law. The exemplary literature review of the advantages and disadvantages of vertical agreements on competition proved that there are a lot of reasons to justify contradictory types of regulation. Following this discussion, this chapter aims to discuss vertical agreements regulation and enforcement activities in Brazil. The selection of Brazil as a case study is not only because of the author's background. The current challenges encountered by the Brazilian authority in the enforcement of vertical agreements can be compared to the ones observed in other jurisdictions that face similar economic and institutional realities in order to learn and share lessons for the future.

Briefly speaking, the recent change in Brazilian competition regulation put an end to the *ex ante* notification of vertical agreements, favouring the *ex post* control of vertical restraints. Nowadays, if a company is in doubt about the legality of a certain agreement, it cannot anymore notify the authority and wait for the 'green sign'. The company has instead to self-assess the potential anticompetitive effect of the commercial practice (mostly with the help of their legal advisors) and still has to bear the costs of legal uncertainty and/or potential future litigations.

In comparative terms, one cannot forget that this prioritization to an *ex post* monitoring of commercial agreements also happened in the EU in the 2000s. However, two important differences should be highlighted here. First, in the EU, the change from an *ex ante* control of agreements to an *ex post* monitoring system happened after forty years of implementation of a notification system of agreements. This learning period allowed firms, agencies and courts to create knowledge regarding what kind of agreements were anticompetitive or not. Second, the *ex post* control policy was introduced together with a revised VBER and guidelines for the self-assessment of parties. This second issue is particularly important as these legal instruments helped to reduce uncertainty among business people.[1]

This chapter explores that in Brazil, the end of the *ex ante* notification system happened in a different format and context. The country had only a few years of a regulation that clearly defined the notification system of vertical agreements before changing the rules to the *ex post* control of these commercial contracts. There was not enough time and/or opportunity to create a consolidated antitrust jurisprudence regarding the legality of vertical agreements in the country as only a few of these cases were actually notified to CADE. Moreover, CADE has not yet published any detailed guidelines to help business people to self-assess the potential anticompetitive effects of their vertical agreements, or to help the agency staff to conduct an adequate effect-based analysis in its investigations.

Several factors might explain this change in legislation, from an inadequate legal transplant to budget reasons regarding the high administrative costs of analysing all notified contracts, the technical failure of lawmakers, or even the self-interest of the interacting groups of agents (antitrust authorities, lawyers, business people and their lobby groups). For these reasons, the following question emerges in this chapter: *Is the new legal framework that favours* ex post *control of vertical agreements aligned with the goal of competition law in Brazil and its institutional design? To what extent does the analysis of the interests of private relevant actors help explaining the recent changes in the Brazilian regulations?*

To answer these questions, the chapter is organized into six sections, including this introduction and the concluding remarks. Section 3.2 illustrates a brief historical perspective of the Competition Law in Brazil as well as the goals of competition policy in the country. Section 3.3 explores the evolution of policies applicable to vertical agreements, including the recent changes in legislation. Section 3.4 focuses on the jurisprudence of vertical cases in Brazil and on the institutional design of law enforcers that allows the *ex post* enforcement of these agreements. This section explores CADE's limited case law regarding RPM and geo-blocking practices. Lastly, section 3.5 discusses the context of the new legal framework in Brazil by looking at the self-interest of parties in the lawmaking process. The section describes the public consultation that

1. Chapter 4 presents an extensive analysis of the European experience.

resulted in Resolution No. 17/2016 which terminated the *ex ante* control of vertical agreements in Brazil. Finally, there is a summary of the findings and an outline of the prospects for the following chapters.

3.2 HISTORY AND FRAMEWORK OF THE BRAZILIAN COMPETITION LAW AND POLICY

3.2.1 The Origins of Competition Policy in Brazil: From 1934 to 2011

In Brazil, the first time the protection of economic freedom was elevated to constitutional status was in the 1934 Federal Constitution that enhanced the organization of the 'Economic Order' in accordance with the principles of justice and human dignity.[2] Three years later, the 1937 Constitution emphasized the relevance of economic and industrial development and gave to the state the possibility of implementing direct and indirect interventions in the economy when necessary to guarantee the public interest. Both the 1934 and the 1937 Brazilian Constitutions defended the promotion of the 'popular economy' and consumer protection.

As explained by Paula Forgioni:

> The evolution of the [antitrust] discipline, in Brazil, did not happen as in countries with a certain antitrust tradition: *antitrust was not born, in Brazil, as a link between economic liberalism and (maintenance of) economic freedom. It was born as a repression against the abuse of economic power, having the interest of the population and the consumer protected by the Constitution.*[3]

In the period between 1934 and 1988 - year when the current Brazilian Federal Constitution (CF) entered into force - several norms started to give attention to competition issues. In 1938, the publication of Decree No. 869/1938 defined crimes against the 'popular economy'. This decree delineated provisions designed to sanction businesses for anticompetitive behaviour, such as: acquiring a dominant position in the market, engaging in predatory pricing, price-fixing, and entering into agreements to exclusively deal. While aiming to protect the 'popular economy' and consumer welfare, the 1938 Decree can be regarded as the first compendium of antitrust rules in Brazil.[4]

Years later, in 1945, a new regulation, Decree No. 7.666 entered into force. This decree, also known as 'Lei Malaia', defined actions contrary to the moral and economic order. It established competition offences, such as the formation of trusts, monopolies, and the concentration of power (via incorporation, merger, association or grouping of

2. Some authors discuss the origins of competition and economic freedom in Brazil long before the twentieth century, since the colonial period. *See*, for instance, R. Simonsen, *História Econômica do Brasil*, São Paulo, Companhia Editora Nacional, 1957. However, this section will briefly introduce the historical period from 1934, when the economic freedom was elevated to constitutional status in the country.
3. Free translation, P. A. Forgioni, *Os fundamentos do antitruste*, 9th ed., São Paulo, Editora Revista dos Tribunais, 2016, p. 102.
4. V. Bagnoli, *Direito Econômico e Concorrencial*, 7th ed., São Paulo, Revista dos Tribunais, 2017, p. 317.

companies). 'Lei Malaia' is considered to be the regulation which established the need for mandatory controls over market concentration and it established administrative proceedings and institutions to be used for reviews of anticompetitive practices.[5] Due to the novel administrative characteristic of anticompetitive practices, 'Lei Malaia' mandated the creation of an administrative agency to handle cases, the Administrative Commission for Economic Defence (in Portuguese, 'Comissão Administrativa de Defesa Econômica'), precursor to the current competition agency in Brazil. Resistance to 'Lei Malaia' quickly emerged from various sectors of the economy and this decree was repealed after only three months in force.

Some years later, in 1962, the first Competition Law (Law No. 4.137/1962) was enacted in Brazil. Law No. 4.137/1962 regulated abuses of market power and created CADE as the governmental body responsible for enforcement of the law. CADE's powers included the power to open administrative proceedings, the power to investigate anticompetitive practices, and the power to determine penalties and fines for violations. This legal mandate was inspired by the Constitution of 1946, which had foreseen (for the first time) the principles of protection against abuse of economic power in Brazil. The terms of the 1946 Constitution and Law No. 4.137/1962 resulted in an antitrust policy in Brazil which was no longer solely focused on the principle of protection of the 'popular economy', but also included protections against abuses of market power.[6] However, Law No. 4.137/1962 was not successfully implemented. The failure of Law No. 4.137/1962 was due to political and economic forces which controlled the priorities of the Brazilian government at the time. As observed by Roberto Pfeiffer:

> Law No. 4.137/1962 was known for its low effectiveness, in particular because: 1) there were other public policies to encourage business concentration (especially under the National Development Plans); 2) the high inflation that disrupted economic activity; 3) the instruments of price control implemented by the Federal governments that ended up encouraging uniform and concerted practices between companies.[7]

It was only in 1988, in a scenario of democratization, that the 1988 Brazilian Federal Constitution (or simply 'CF/1988') entered into force promoting several institutional changes and supporting the creation of a law to defend the constitutional principles of free competition. The Constitution of 1988 stated a change to market-oriented policies, which was followed by a sequence of economic reforms, such as the privatization of state-owned companies, price liberalization and deregulation.[8] In this context, several independent regulatory agencies were created, such as the regulatory agency for the telecommunication sector (ANATEL), the agency for the electricity sector (ANEEL), for petroleum and natural gas (ANP), for transportation (ANTT) and

5. *See* Forgioni, 2016, *supra* note 3, p. 107.
6. I. Vaz, *Direito Econômico da Concorrência*, Rio de Janeiro, Editora Forense, 1993, p. 250.
7. Free translation, R. A. C. Pfeiffer, *Defesa da concorrência e bem-estar do consumidor*, PhD thesis filed at University of São Paulo, São Paulo, 2010, p. 120.
8. OECD, *Peer Review of Competition Law and Policy: Brazil*, 2019, p. 17.

for the air transport sector (ANAC).[9] The democratic Constitution was published in a new political and economic context where there was a strong policy orientation towards economic liberalization and price stabilization.

In this historical context, Law No. 8.884 of 11 June 1994 was the Brazilian law that successfully systematized the antitrust discipline in the country and improved the legislative treatment to the topic. This law turned CADE as a self-contained independent federal body linked to the administrative structure of the Ministry of Justice.[10] This law also established the attributions of the Brazilian Secretariat of Economic Law ('SDE' is its Portuguese acronym) - a body from the Ministry of Justice, and the Secretariat for Economic Monitoring ('SEAE' is its Portuguese acronym). These three bodies together composed the Brazilian Competition Defence System (in Portuguese 'Sistema Brasileiro de Defesa da Concorrência' or SBDC). Under this structure, CADE oversaw the administrative proceedings related to anticompetitive conduct and the mergers subject to its review system. The proceedings were instructed by SDE and SEAE. These two bodies were responsible for issuing technical but non-binding opinions to CADE.[11]

Having this structure, Law No. 8.884/1994 foresaw two main regulatory activities against abuse of economic power: the repressive and the preventive control. The *ex post* repressive control of anticompetitive conduct, including cartels and anticompetitive agreements was based on Article 20 of Law No. 8.884/1994. The *ex post* repressive control aimed at investigating the illegality of concrete commercial practices.[12] The *ex ante* preventive intended to take care of market concentration of commercial structures and certain types of cooperation among firms.[13] It was based on Article 54 of Law No. 8.884/1994, and was mostly related to the notification system of mergers that were capable of harming competition in the Brazilian markets.[14] Among many other reforms, this law consolidated a mandatory merger control system, established policies oriented to fight against cartels (as for instance, the introduction of a leniency procedure or even the growing interaction with the federal prosecutors), and initiated

9. It is worth noting that the privatization process did not affect all sectors in the Brazilian economy. The Brazilian government remained in control of the oil and gas sector, through Petrobras, in the electricity generation sector and, also, in the banking sector (e.g., via Banco do Brasil).
10. Even knowing that CADE was only treated as an independent agency in 1994, Law No. 4137/1962 was the one that originally created the agency. However, by that time, CADE could not successfully implement its policies, and one of the reasons was the military coup of 1964: 'The antitrust statute had been passed in 1962, but its implementation was left to the upcoming authoritarian regime. The statute proved to be largely ineffective.' For more detailed information about the dictatorial period and its impact on competition policy, *see* F. Todorov & M. Torres Filho, 'History of Competition Policy in Brazil: 1930-2010', *The Antitrust Bulletin*, Vol. 57, No. 2, 2012, pp. 207-257.
11. Information available at CADE's official website: http://en.cade.gov.br/topics/about-us/our-history (7/12/2017).
12. C. Salomão Filho, *Direito Concorrencial: As Condutas*, 1st ed., São Paulo, Editora Malheiros, 2007, p. 14.
13. C. Salomão Filho, *Direito Concorrencial: As Estruturas*, 3rd ed., São Paulo, Editora Malheiros, 2007, p. 265.
14. F. Abreu & J. Honda, 'Associative Agreements under the Brazilian Antitrust Law', *in* C. Zarzur, L. Katona & M. Villela (eds), *Overview of Competition Law in Brazil*, São Paulo, Editora Singular, 2015, p. 138.

the control of unilateral behaviour, besides the promotion of competition advocacy, in order to increase the competition culture in the country.

In 2011, the Brazilian antitrust policy passed through an important institutional reform. Law No. 12.529/2011 – known as the new Brazilian Competition Law – altered important proceedings, such as the merger review system, and the structure of the antitrust agencies. As described above, before Law No. 12.529/2011 entered into force, the SBDC was composed of three agencies, CADE being the main one. With the advent of the new law, CADE took over the role of the other two agencies (SDE and SEAE), being unified as a solely investigatory and decision-making body dealing with antitrust matters. Nowadays, CADE's structure is composed of (i) an Administrative Tribunal that comprises a President and six Commissioners; (ii) a Directorate-General for Competition (DG Comp), the investigative body in matters related to anticompetitive practices; and (iii) an economics department.

It is worth noting that both Law No. 8.884/1994 and the current Law No. 12.529/2011 guaranteed a legal foundation that were essential for the growth, and consolidation of competition policy in Brazil. CADE has certainly gained greater efficiency in the merger review system and has also shown a notable development in its leniency program. Additionally, in the last few years, the Brazilian authority has published several guidelines to society, and it is now recognized as a leading competition authority in Latin America and in the world.

3.2.2 The Current Goals of Competition Law in Brazil

In a democratic country such as Brazil, all power relations, including economic power, must be exercised in accordance with fundamental rights and other constitutional principles.[15] Each legal system has a set of principles and goals – directly linked to its historical, economic and social contexts – that underlines its regulatory and decision-making process. Those goals are essential for the better understanding of the local competition law- and decision-making process.

Over the decades, several schools of thought in the field of competition theory and competition law have tried to define and explain the goals of a competition policy. For instance, among those schools of thought are the Ordoliberal School, the Harvard School, and the Chicago School. Some scholars have discussed the different consequences of consumer welfare and total welfare as goals of competition policies. Others brought the different concepts of efficiency (allocative, productive and dynamic) as policymaking orientation. In addition to the strict economic aims, different competition policy goals have already been attributed to different legal systems, such as market integration (as in the EU), income redistribution, protection of small businesses, price control, control of corruption and fairness.[16] Although many jurisdictions have formally assigned certain goals to their competition policies, in practice, those goals are

15. A. Frazão, *Direito da Concorrência: pressupostos e perspectivas*, São Paulo, Editora Saraiva, 2017, p. 46.
16. *See* for instance the discussion in Chapter 3 in R. Van den Bergh, *Comparative Competition Law and Economics*, Cheltenham, Edward Elgar Publishing, 2017.

not observed in the regulatory or decision-making process; or even there are cases in which the goals of certain jurisdictions contradict one another.

In Brazil, the discussion related to the foundations and principles of the economic order, and therefore on the competition policy goals, is directly linked to the analysis of constitutional principles, and it has been extensively debated in the national antitrust literature. First, it is worth noting that every national legislation (including competition law) should bring with it the general principle that permeates all the CF/1988: the principle of human dignity and social justice, reinforced by Articles 1 and 3 of the *Carta Magna*.[17]

When considering the specific principles applied to the economic order, which includes competition policy, the 1988 Constitution highlights, among others, the free enterprise (Articles 1 and 170 CF/1988), the principle of free competition (Article 170, IV, CF/1988) and the principle of consumer protection (Article 170, V, CF/1988). Historically, as indicated in the previous section, the principles of economic order were directly linked to the protection of popular economy. Nowadays, the Constitution established that the law should prevent the abuse of economic power that aim at the domination of markets, elimination of competition and arbitrarily increasing profits (Article 173 § 4, CF/1988).[18]

With regards to the principle of free enterprise, Eros Grau explains how in Brazil this principle has 'dual-characteristics'. In addition to the attributes related to economic freedom (freedom of commerce and industry; freedom of economic initiative), the principle of free enterprise also reinforces the 'social value of work' as one of the fundamental elements of the Federative Republic of Brazil (Article 1, IV, CF/1988). Moreover, Grau highlights how the principle of the 'social value of the free enterprise' is always combined with the dignity of human work.[19]

As to the principle of free competition, Grau explains that it derives from the principle of free enterprise. According to the author, the principle of free competition has as its premise market efficiency, and therefore a fair playing field among market

17. Brazilian Federal Constitution, 1988: 'Art 1 The Federative Republic of Brazil, formed by the indissoluble union of States and Municipalities, as well as the Federal District, is a Democratic State of Law founded upon: I. sovereignty; II. citizenship; III. human dignity; *IV. social values of work and free initiative*; V. political pluralism. [...] The fundamental objectives of the Federative Republic of Brazil are: I. to build a free, just and unified society; II. to guarantee national development; III. to eradicate poverty and substandard living conditions and to reduce social and regional inequalities; IV. To promote the well-being of all, without prejudice as to origin, race, sex, color, age and any other forms of discrimination.' (Emphasis added).
18. Brazilian Federal Constitution, 1988: 'Art 170 The economic order, founded on the appreciation of *the value of human labor and free enterprise*, is intended to assure everyone a dignified existence, according to the dictates of social justice, observing the following principles: I. national sovereignty; II. private property; III. social function of property; *IV. free competition; V. consumer protection*; [...]Art 173 With the exception of the cases provided for in this Constitution, direct exploitation of an economic activity by the State shall only be permitted when necessary for the imperatives of national security or a relevant collective interest, as defined by law.[...] §4°. *The law shall repress abuse of economic power seeking to dominate markets, to eliminate competition and to increase profits arbitrarily.*' (Emphasis added).
19. E. R. Grau, *A Ordem Econômica na Constituição de 1988*, 15th ed., São Paulo, Malheiros Editores, 2012, p. 203.

competitors. It also has the 'legal equality' as a main framework.[20] The principle of free competition in Brazil also assumes the repression of the abuse of economic power, precisely to prevent market dominance.

The current Brazilian Competition Law (Law No. 12.529/2011) acknowledges the principle of free competition in its Article 1:

> Art. 1. This Law structures the Brazilian System for Protection of Competition – SBDC and sets forth preventive measures and sanctions for violations against the economic order, guided by the constitutional principles of *free competition, freedom of initiative, social role of property, consumer protection and prevention of the abuse of economic power.*[21] (Emphasis added)

Indeed, having as a background the constitutional principles of economic order in Brazil, one can say that the evolution of the law- and decision-making regarding antitrust rules in Brazil should have observed wider goals than efficiency and the free market.[22] In like manner, the Brazilian Supreme Court, as part of a decision upon an Action for Declaration of Unconstitutionality,[23] indicated that the principle of free competition should be considered in a broad perspective than the one adopted by classic economic liberalism. In a broader perspective, free competition encompasses the 'social values of free enterprise' that also refer to consumer protection and reduction of social inequalities.[24]

According to Forgioni, the goal of the competition law in Brazil is to preserve, under the constitutional principles, an environment in which companies have effective incentives to compete, innovate and satisfy the demands of consumers; and to protect competition and prevent markets from being harmed by agents with a high degree of economic power.[25] In complement to that, the author also describes that competition law is an instrument for the achievement of social justice and human dignity.[26]

César Mattos, in his analysis of the goals of Brazilian Competition Law, highlighted the clear prevalence of consumer welfare: 'Despite the fact that Law 12.529/2011 and the old Law 8.884/1194 tried to approach economic efficiency goals in its text, the tone is clearly favouring consumer welfare.'[27] This view is reinforced by the fact that, in practice, no case (mergers or anticompetitive conduct) has been decided on the sole basis of economic efficiency.

Despite the obvious semantic connections between the wording of the Constitution and the wording of the current Brazilian Competition Law, the law- and decision-making processes in Brazil have not always been fully connected to the goals of the

20. Grau, 2012, *supra* note 19, p. 206.
21. For the whole content of the Brazilian Competition Law, please access: http://www.cade.gov.br/assuntos/internacional/legislacao/law-no-12529-2011-english-version-from-18-05-2012.pdf/view (25/1/2018).
22. *See* Forgioni, 2016, *supra* note 3, p. 193.
23. Case Reference: ADIn 319/4/DF. Relator Ministro Moreira Alves [03-03-1993].
24. *See* Forgioni, 2016, *supra* note 3, p. 193.
25. Forgioni, 2016, *supra* note 3, p. 194.
26. Forgioni, 2016, *supra* note 3, p. 192.
27. C. Mattos, 'Um pouco da História da Lei 12.529/11', *in* C. Campilongo & R. Pfeiffer (eds), *Evolução do antitruste no Brasil*, São Paulo, Editora Singular, 2018, p. 45.

country. In 2009, Luis Fernando Schuartz was one of the first authors to explicitly argue that antitrust decisions in Brazil are not always based on constitutional principles, including references to Article 1 of the National Competition Law. This phenomenon was named by the author as the 'deconstitutionalization' of the Brazilian competition rules,[28] as he argues that the implementation of competition policies in Brazil does not have as its main goal the national constitutional principles but rather the Chicago School's assumptions.

Schuartz describes that by the time Law No. 8.884/1994 entered into force, the antitrust discussions were not yet developed in the country. For these reasons, the decisions, that were mostly transplanted from the most advanced American jurisprudence and sophisticated academic discussions, filled a theoretical and practical gap without significant resistance. While in the US, the antitrust cases evolved with fissures and tensions – partially resulting from complex law and economics discussions – in Brazil, the undisputed normative framework was created for immediate use without taking into consideration the main goals and constitutional principles of the country.[29]

Indeed, even taking into consideration the constitutional principles, it is still unclear what are prevalent goals that, in practice, lead the law- and decision-making process of Brazilian competition policies. Consequently, when the goals of a law are not fully clear or respected in a country, it creates a window of opportunity for relevant actors to behave in favour of their private interests, rather than in favour of the public interest.

3.3 THE EVOLUTION OF BRAZILIAN COMPETITION LAW ORIENTED TO VERTICAL AGREEMENTS

This section offers an analytical description of the current state of the art of the Brazilian competition policy related to vertical agreements and is divided into two subsections. The first subsection (3.3.1) analyses the policies under the old Brazilian Competition Law from 1994 until 2011, and the second subsection (3.3.2) analyses the most recent policies in the context of the new Competition Law from 2011 until 2018.[30]

28. L. F. Schuartz, 'A desconstitucionalização do direito de defesa da concorrência', *Revista do IBRAC*, Vol. 16, No. 1, 2009, p. 327.
29. Schuartz, 2009, *supra* note 28, p. 334.
30. It is worth noting that commercial agreements have primarily to observe the rules of contract law (private law). In Brazil, the Brazilian Civil Code is the main legal instrument that sets the principles and rules for commercial contracts. However, the focus of this book is on the effects of these contracts in the markets and economic welfare, and therefore the antitrust legal framework is highlighted. The study of vertical agreements under contract law in Brazil can be found at: P. A. Forgioni, *Contratos Empresariais: Teoria Geral e Aplicação*, 4ª ed., São Paulo, Revista dos Tribunais, 2019; P. A. Forgioni, *Contratos de distribuição*, São Paulo, Editora Revista dos Tribunais, 2005.

3.3.1 Vertical Agreements under Law No. 8.884/1994: An Unclear Legal Framework

According to Law No. 8.884/1994, there was no explicit rule oriented to vertical agreements. Because certain vertical agreements can reduce consumer welfare,[31] these practices were interpreted as anticompetitive conduct prosecuted under Articles 20 and 21 of Law No. 8.884/1994. In addition to that, given the broad scope of the old merger system, vertical agreements were also somehow interpreted as within the notification threshold.

In more detail, the scope of all anticompetitive practices, including the different types of vertical restraints, was analysed under the *ex post* control of Articles 20 and 21. Actually, these articles covered all types of antitrust conduct other than mergers that could '(i) limit, restrain or in any way injure open competition or free enterprise; (ii) control a relevant market of a certain product or service; (iii) increase profits on a discretionary basis; and (iv) abuse of market power'.[32] While Article 20 had more generic language, Article 21[33] brought an exemplary list of practices, which included provisions of RPM and exclusive territory provisions. In contrast with other jurisdictions, the Brazilian Competition Law has never differentiated the provisions regarding anticompetitive agreements from the provisions of unilateral conduct. Indeed, they were all analysed under the same articles.[34]

Actually, in 1999, CADE published Resolution No. 20/1999 to settle a framework for analysing anticompetitive conduct in Brazil, including vertical agreements. For instance, Annex I of Resolution No. 20/1999 introduced, for the first time, the idea of an effects-based analysis in the assessment of vertical restraints:

31. *See* economic analysis of vertical agreements in Chapter 2.
32. Article 20 Law No. 8884/94: 'Notwithstanding malicious intent, any act in any way intended or otherwise able to produce the effects listed below, even if any such effects are not achieved, shall be deemed a violation of the economic order: I – to limit, restrain or in any way injure open competition or free enterprise; II – to control a relevant market of a certain product or service; III – to increase profits on a discretionary basis; and IV – to abuse one's market control. Paragraph 1. Achievement of market control as a result of competitive efficiency does not entail an occurrence of the illicit act provided for in item II above. Paragraph 2. Market control occurs when a company or group of companies controls a substantial share of a relevant market as supplier, agent, purchaser or financier of a product, service or related technology. Paragraph 3. The dominant position mentioned in the preceding paragraph is presumed when a company or group of companies controls twenty percent (20%) of the relevant market; this percentage is subject to change by CADE for specific sectors of the economy.'
33. Some items of Article 21 Law No. 8884/94 could be applied to vertical restraints, such as 'Article 21. The acts spelled out below, among others, will be deemed a violation of the economic order, to the extent applicable under article 20 and items thereof: [...]II – to obtain or otherwise procure the adoption of uniform or concerted business practices among competitors; III – to apportion markets for finished or semi-finished products or services, or for supply sources of raw materials or intermediary products; IV – to limit or restrain market access by new companies; [...]VI – to bar access of competitors to input, raw material, equipment or technology sources, as well as to their distribution channels.'
34. In Europe, for example, Article 101 TFEU deals with anticompetitive agreements while Article 102 deals with abuses of dominant position. More details about the European experience can be found in Chapter 4.

> As in the case of horizontal restrictions, vertical restrictive practices presume, in general, the existence of market power in the relevant market of origin, as well as an effect on a substantial share of the market that is the target of such practices, typifying a risk of harming the competition. Although these restrictions are, in principle, limitations to free competition, they may also bring benefits ('economic efficiencies'), which must be weighed against the potential anti-competitive consequences, in accordance with the rule of reason.[35]

Following this general guideline, CADE had, in theory, to follow a three-step approach towards vertical restraints consistent with: (i) verifying the existence of a dominant position of the parties involved in the investigation; (ii) proving the anticompetitive effects of the vertical restraint, in particular the market foreclosure conditions; and (iii) balancing these potential anticompetitive effects with the potential economic efficiencies of the transaction. The terms of the resolution were not objective enough in order to guarantee that business people and the authority could prepare a good assessment of the investigated restraints. Although Resolution No. 20/1999 introduced to the national competition policy an important tool for the analysis of vertical restraints, it left significant room for CADE to create more accurate criteria via its jurisprudence.[36]

In parallel with the enforcement of Articles 20 and 21, some companies opted to submit their vertical agreements (such as supply and distribution agreements) to the merger control system of Article 54 of Law No. 8.884/1994. This happened because, under Law No. 8.884/1994, transactions subject to mandatory filing explicitly included not only 'acts aiming at economic concentration' (Article 54, paragraph 3) but also 'any act, under any form, that has the potential to limit or restrain competition or result in market domination' (Article 54, *caput*). During the years of implementation of Law No. 8.884/1994, the lack of objective criteria/thresholds regarding the notification of vertical agreements, and the vague boundaries of such broad notion of Article 54, encouraged CADE to publish important administrative decisions on the matter for further clarification.

Indeed, CADE's precedents under Law No. 8.884/1994 tried to create some objective criteria for the notification (or not) of commercial agreements.[37] Following the jurisprudence, there were a few parameters that defined which agreements were not subjected to the notification system, based on market share, the existence of an exclusivity clause, the duration of the agreement, and so on. In more detail, the agreements that were not subjected to the *ex ante* merger control were the ones where (i) the volume of sales represented less than 20% of a specific relevant market; (ii) the duration lasted less than five years; (iii) they did not carry any type of exclusivity

35. Resolution No. 20/1999, Annex I, Item B.
36. This criticism was also brought by D. Geradin & C. M. Pereira Neto, *Restrições verticais adotadas por empresas dominantes: uma análise do Direito Concorrencial no Brasil e na União Europeia*, Edição Bilingue, São Paulo, Editora Revista dos Tribunais, 2013, p. 153.
37. *See*, for example, CADE's decision on the cases: Case No. 08012.005367/2010-72 involving *Monsanto do Brasil Ltda* and *Dow Agrosciences Industrial Ltda* and Case No. 08012.004571/2010-76 involving *Basf S.A* and *Syngenta Crop Protection.*

clause; and (iv) they did not affect the independence of asset-related decision-making.[38] Those parameters, however, did not cover several business practices and they remained mostly unknown to the business community.[39]

This background reveals that the legal framework established by Law No. 8.884/1994 was not necessarily favouring the enforcement of anticompetitive vertical agreements in the country. Even though one can conclude that both *ex ante* notification of agreements and *ex post* control of vertical restraints were somehow covered by the national legislation, the enforcement of such practices was far from being optimal. This can be explained because: (i) there were no clear parameters for the notifications of agreements and the antitrust jurisprudence regarding the need of notification did not cover many vertical agreements that could potentially have anticompetitive effects; and (ii) the level of *ex post* enforcement was still very low and it relied on an instable pattern of jurisprudence. With regard to this last point, since this book emphasizes the importance of having consolidated antitrust jurisprudence to guarantee better legal certainty to parties, a section of this chapter will focus on the analysis of some relevant Brazilian case law.

3.3.2 Vertical Agreements under Law No. 12.529/2011: Favouring *Ex Post* Enforcement

As discussed in the previous section, the new Law No. 12.529/2011 did not introduce significant changes with regard to the substantive law. For instance, with regard to anticompetitive practices (including vertical agreements), the substantive provisions of the new Competition Law were not considerably modified when compared to the previous law. In practical terms, Article 36 of the new Competition Law comprises a merger of Articles 20 and 21 of Law No. 8.884/1994. This Article 36 establishes that a violation of competition law is observed when any act has the object, or is able, to produce anticompetitive effects in the Brazilian market, irrespective of its intention. Under this new institutional environment, CADE has not issued any regulation that sets out criteria for the economic assessment of the positive and negative effects of such conduct. The authority has based their decision-making process primarily on Resolution No. 20/1999, which is rather generic and outdated.

With regard to merger control, the new law introduces some procedural changes. Most importantly, it institutes a pre-merger regime[40] and redefines the very hypothesis

38. Abreu and Honda describe in more detail the former parameters of Law 8.884/1994. *See*, Abreu & Honda, 2015, *supra* note 14.
39. The Brazilian competition law and case law have very rarely imposed specific sector-oriented rules, as it was observed in the European Union (*see*, for instance, in Chapter 4 the discussion on the first block exemptions). I highlight, for instance, that certain vertical agreements in the car industry are regulated by Law No. 6,729 of 28 November 1979 (Law No. 6,729/79), also known as 'Lei Ferrari', which determines specific rules on territorial and customer restraints. *See* E. Grau & P. A. Forgioni, 'Restrição à concorrência, autorização legal e seus limites, Lei 8.884, de 1994, e Lei 6.279/1979 ("Lei Ferrari")', *Revista do IBRAC*, Vol. 6, 1999, pp. 5-27.
40. According to the former competition law, the notification of a transaction to CADE was not suspensory and could be made up to fifteen business days after the execution of the first binding document between the parties (i.e., a post-merger notification regime).

of transactions subject to mandatory filing. Law No. 12.529/2011 envisages, for instance, that associative agreements should be subjected to the merger control system.[41] As the enactment of the new Brazilian Competition Law did not make clear the terms of Article 54 of Law No. 8.884/1994 – i.e., what kind of agreements could be considered as associative – it immediately generated an immense debate regarding the meaning of the term 'associative agreements'. Indeed, this kind of contract did not represent a typical category of commercial agreements. Moreover, the term had never been used before in Brazilian legislation and it had not been considered a historical reference in antitrust practice.

For these reasons, the first attempt to clarify the notification requirements for horizontal and vertical agreements was Resolution No. 10/2014. Pursuant to Article 2 of Resolution No. 10/2014, horizontal and vertical agreements had to be filed under the pre-merger review system if they lasted for two years or more and the following additional conditions were met:

> (i) the agreement gives rise to a horizontal overlap between the contracting parties or their respective groups, and their combined market share is equal to or in excess of 20%; or (ii) the agreement gives rise to a vertical link between the contracting parties or their respective groups, and one of them has a market share of at least 30% in one of the markets affected by the agreement, provided that (a) the agreement contains a profit/loss sharing provision; or (b) the agreement contains exclusivity obligations.[42]

Whenever the contractual transaction fell within any of the above-mentioned cases, the contracting parties had to assess whether the turnover thresholds for mandatory filing set forth in the Brazilian antitrust law were also met.[43] In the case where such thresholds were met, the parties had to submit the agreement to CADE's pre-merger control before taking any measure to implement it. For example, a two-year exclusive distribution agreement with effects in Brazil was considered an associative contract whenever the manufacturer of the product to be distributed held a market share equal to or in excess of 30% in the market at issue. So, even though one can understand that notification of vertical agreements was covered in the national legislation since 1994, it was only twenty years later, in 2014 that an explicit provision entered into force.

41. Law No. 12.539/2011: 'Art. 90. For the purposes of Article 88 of this Law, a concentration act shall be carried out when: I – two (2) or more previously independent companies merge; II – one (1) or more companies acquire, directly or indirectly, by purchase or exchange of stocks, shares, bonds or securities convertible into stocks or assets, whether tangible or intangible, by contract or by any other means or way, the control or parts of one or more companies; III – one (1) or more companies incorporate one or more companies, or IV – two (2) or more companies enter into an *associative contract*, consortium or joint venture.' (Emphasis added).
42. Free translation from Article 2, CADE Resolution No. 10/2014.
43. According to the Brazilian Antitrust Law, an agreement is subject to CADE's pre-merger control if it has effects in Brazil. Second, if at least one of the groups involved in the transaction has gross revenues in Brazil of BRL 750 million or more (equivalent in May 2019 to around EUR 165 million) in the fiscal year immediately prior to the execution of the agreement; and if at least one other group involved in the transaction has gross revenues in Brazil of BRL 75 million or more (equivalent in May 2019 to around EUR 16 million) in that same fiscal year.

It should be noted that some of the wording of Resolution No. 10/2014 remained unclear to the business community, such as 'sharing of risks', 'sharing of profits and losses', 'inter-dependence relationship', and 'exclusivity relationship', also because no guideline was provided to parties to understand these concepts. Indeed, the first difficulty arising from the wording of Resolution No. 10/2014 was the lack of clarity about the essential elements of the definition of associative agreement, established in Article 2 ('horizontal or vertical cooperation or sharing of risk resulting in an interdependence relationship').

Moreover, because Resolution No. 10/2014 was too broad in scope, companies started not complying with the law. This fact meant that they preferred rather taking the risk of being caught by the authority than to bear the costs of undergoing the whole notification system. Indeed, the terms of Resolution No. 10/2014 led to high costs both to companies that were obliged to bear the non-negligible costs of communicating such agreements to CADE and to the authority itself, which had to assess these transactions.[44] Curiously, the number of associative agreements notified to CADE since Resolution No. 10/2014 entered into force was much smaller than expected. From January 2015 to November 2016 (when Resolution No. 10/2014 was revoked), only fifty associative agreements among horizontals and verticals were filed in the period (less than 5% of total merger transactions filed in the same period), out of which fifteen were considered non-mandatory notifications.[45] All other filed agreements were approved without restriction.

It is possible to speculate on the reasons for such a small number of agreements communicated to CADE. Maybe the rule itself was not totally comprehended by the companies – which is evidenced by the high percentage of cases where the agreement notified was not considered mandatory by the authority (30%). Notwithstanding that the reduced number is not realistic, mainly if we take into consideration the size of the Brazilian economy and the number of commercial transactions that are held in the country on a daily basis. It is unlikely that in almost two years there have been more mergers than, for example, supply and distribution agreements that contained exclusivity clauses. In other words, it would be erroneous to assume that there was significant compliance with the obligation to file vertical agreements under Resolution No. 10/2014.

In 2016, CADE decided to change the rules once again. The agency published Resolution No. 17/2016 that brought new conditions for the notification of commercial agreements, therefore revoking Resolution No. 10/2014. The new resolution established the basis for significant changes in the rules for mandatory filing of both vertical agreements and horizontal collaborations. The great innovation introduced by

44. An extensive cost analysis of different enforcement costs will be discussed in Chapter 5.
45. Under Resolution No. 10/2014, fifteen notified agreements were considered by CADE as non-mandatory notification, which reflects the vague/imprecise terms of the law (i.e., the parties thought they had to notify and in the end, CADE decided that those agreements were not in the scope of the notification system). Among the reasons for these decisions, CADE claimed: (i) the non-existence of a horizontal or vertical relation; (ii) the non-fulfilment of the market share thresholds; and/or (iii) the non-existence of exclusivity clauses or sharing of revenues and losses.

Resolution No. 17/2016 is that vertical agreements are no longer subjected to the *ex ante* notification system, meaning that they were excluded from the preventive provisions. The rule brought by the new Resolution is clear in the sense that only horizontal agreements, meaning, only agreements performed by firms that compete in the same relevant market, should be subjected to a merger review. Besides the conditions related to horizontal overlap, Article 2 of Resolution No. 17/2016, the agreement must cumulatively fulfil some other criteria for the antitrust filing: (i) the contract should have two years term or longer; (ii) parties should set up a common undertaking for the exploitation of a business activity;[46] and (iii) parties should share risks and results in the business activity under the agreement.

Actually, although Resolution No. 17/2016 tries to overcome the uncertainties from previous regulation, it still leaves some discussions open. It is worth remembering that, since 2014, Brazil has been passing through a deep political and economic crisis and, therefore, strategic alliances among competitors tend to occur more often as an important strategy of cost reduction and market expansion. Sectors such as food/beverage, chemical, pharmaceutical, among others, where players typically engage in various types of distribution and supply relationships and partnerships, have to carefully assess in order to check how these constant changes in regulation affect their business in Brazil.

The first case in which CADE applied the rules set forth in Resolution No. 17/2016 was Case No. 08700.008484/2016-25 (decided by CADE on 16 January 2017). The contract was between the pharmaceutical companies Medley Farmacêutica Ltda. ('Medley') and Aurobindo Pharma Limited ('Aurobindo'). Because they were direct competitors in the pharmaceutical market, they decided to notify their contract. However, the agreement referred to distribution, license and supply of three generic medical products (not covered by patent rights), i.e., it referred to a vertical agreement celebrated by direct competitors. In this case, CADE concluded that the agreement was not subject to mandatory review. In practice, the contract would result in an additional distributor for Aurobindo's products, without exclusivity. With this decision, CADE confirmed the understanding that typical vertical agreements are no longer subject to mandatory filing, even if between competitors, since they do not establish a common undertaking to perform an economic activity.

Lastly, it is worth noting that, in 2015, CADE issued Resolution No. 12/2015 about its Consultation Procedure. Within the scope of this Consultation Procedure, parties can directly contact CADE regarding the interpretation of legislation, or even regarding the legality of acts, contracts and commercial practices that have (or have not) been initiated by economic agents. Therefore, if parties have doubts regarding the legality of their vertical agreements, they can consult the authority. This procedure, however, appears to have been underused, looking at the available statistics. From 2015 to 2019, twenty-five consultations were judged by the authority, being only three

46. Resolution No. 17/2016 defines 'business activity' as the 'acquisition or offer of goods or services in the market, even if with no profit purposes, provided that such activity is exploited by for-profit corporations in the private sector'.

of them related to the legality of vertical clauses.[47] From these three cases, two of them (Case No. 08700.001930/2019-13 and Case No. 08700.009476/2014-34) were inconclusive because of the lack of information provided by the parties. In Case No. 08700.004594/2018-80, however, *Continental do Brasil Produtos Automotivos Ltda* asked CADE whether its resale price policy in the auto parts aftermarket was in accordance with the law. The Reporting Commissioner Paulo Burnier da Silveira concluded that the practice was legal since the company did not have market power in this market, and moreover, there was no discrimination between resellers affected by the minimum price policy.

When discussing vertical agreements in Brazil it is possible to conclude that the legal framework changed in 2016 in a way that turned out to prioritize the *ex post* enforcement of these practices. This book puts into question whether the legal framework that excluded vertical agreements from the notification system and, therefore, prioritized *ex post* enforcement of vertical restraints is an optimal policy. One way of answering this query is through the analysis of some of CADE case law that refers to *ex post* control. This discussion could be fruitful for predicting whether the precedents of the authority's behaviour are able to guarantee greater legal certainty to firms. The other way involves a discussion about whether the legal reform was duly justified considering the public interest and the goals of the Brazilian Competition Law. Both discussions are described in sections 3.4 and 3.5.

3.4 THE EX POST ENFORCEMENT IN BRAZIL: RELEVANT JURISPRUDENCE AND CURRENT CHALLENGES

Nowadays, the main rule applicable to anticompetitive vertical agreements is Article 36 of Law No. 12.529/2011, which corresponds to the *ex post* control of these practices. In Article 36(3), one can find a non-exhaustive list of business practices that may be deemed to be infringements of antitrust law if they have as their object, or effect, distorting competition. Law No. 12.529/2011, however, does not define vertical restraints. Over the years, CADE has investigated only a few cases related to vertical restraints, among them are RPM cases and exclusive agreements. Table 3.1 presents the data of (i) opened cases of vertical agreements and (ii) total decisions taken by CADE's Tribunal from 2013 until 2017.[48]

---

47. Data available at: http://cadenumeros.cade.gov.br/ (24/6/2019).
48. This is the most recent data available, in which vertical agreement cases are disaggregated from other anticompetitive practices.

Table 3.1 Enforcement of Vertical Agreements in Brazil, 2013-2017

Vertical Agreements	*2013*	*2014*	*2015*	*2016*	*2017*
Matters Opened	3	3	9	5	4
Total decisions	5	0	0	0	0

Source: CADE's General Superintendence and OECD, 2019. Compiled by the author.

From Table 3.1, one can conclude that from 2013 to 2017 CADE has decided very few cases involving vertical agreements. This can be explained by the fact that vertical restraints are not prioritized by the authority, and/or that most of the cases (if not the totality of them) are solved by settlement agreements.

Indeed, to resolve its investigations, CADE depends heavily on settlements.[49] Actually, in recent years, the authority has changed its settlement procedures with the aim of increasing cooperation among business people, and this has proven to be very effective. The increase in the number of settlements is impressive, from five agreements signed in 2012, when the new law entered into force, to seventy-five signed in 2017.[50] In 2018, the amount of fines that resulted from settlement decisions amounted to BRL 530 million (equivalent to around EUR 120 million). This number is ten times more than the value of fines that resulted from CADE's decision on administrative proceedings, that totalled BRL 50 million (equivalent to around EUR 12 million) in the same year.[51]

This substantial use of settlements by CADE has its drawbacks, mainly because it can give wrong incentives to parties. This is particularly the case when the discounts proposed by the settlements are substantial. Settlements can actually reduce legal certainty in the marketplace and slow the development of the jurisprudence in Brazil. With settlement agreements, no decisions are published by CADE and the cases are not reviewed by national courts. If, for instance, very few cases reach CADE's Tribunal in respect of vertical agreements, and the members of the Tribunal disagree among themselves, the clear view on the legality of verticals becomes a challenging issue.[52] As there are almost no recent cases in which CADE has conducted a full assessment of vertical restraints, this section will mostly rely on the older case law.

According to Paulo Furquim de Azevedo, and based on Resolution No. 20/1999, in order to investigate whether vertical restraints are anticompetitive, CADE's jurisprudence has usually followed three main criteria.[53] First, the analysis of market share and dominant position in both upstream and downstream markets. For instance, a franchising agreement of a medium-sized fast food chain that usually has several vertical restraints (such as geo-blocking clauses and RPM) cannot be considered an

49. The amount of settlement agreements signed by CADE in the last years was pointed out by OECD as an issue to be overcome by the authority in Brazil. OECD, 2019, *supra* note 8.
50. Most recent data, *see* OECD, 2019, *supra* note 8, pp. 104-108.
51. Data available at: http://cadenumeros.cade.gov.br/ (24/6/2019).
52. This concern was also raised by OECD, 2019, *supra* note 8, pp. 104-108.
53. P. F. Azevedo, 'Restrições verticais e Defesa da Concorrência: A experiência Brasileira', *Textos para Discussão FGV-EESP*, No. 264, 2010, pp. 9-11.

antitrust offence. The second criterion, according to Azevedo, is identifying the actual or potential negative outcomes in the market. For this second condition, CADE would observe whether the effect of the vertical restraint in market structure, rivalry between competitors and entry barriers is sustainable enough in order to foreclose markets. Once the potential anticompetitive effects of a particular vertical restraint are verified, CADE would go to the third and last step, which consists of verifying the relevant economic efficiencies. Azevedo shows (through case studies) that the three-step analysis is a pattern among CADE's decisions. However, the intention of conducting this approach does not say much about how the full assessment of vertical restraints is conducted, in terms of its complexity.

By the time the new Brazilian Competition Law entered into force in 2012, Damien Geradin and Caio Mario Pereira Neto conducted a study about vertical restraints in Brazil, looking mainly at CADE's decisions on exclusive dealing, conditional rebates, tying and bundling cases. The authors concluded that the effect-based approach conducted by CADE over the years relied on 'qualitative criteria and intuitive reasoning, rather than a rigorous and structured assessment, including quantitative elements, hence leading to inconsistency and uncertainty'.[54] The authors had a closer look at CADE's jurisprudence, showing significant discrepancies among the qualitative analysis of the authority:

> This variation generates inconsistency, especially when it comes to a definition of standards of proof in the context of the *rule of reason* analysis. Indeed, the relatively clear general framework for the effects-based analysis has not been capable of developing more detailed tests and standards to define when the net effects of a particular vertical restraint would be deemed negative to characterize conduct as illegal under the [Brazilian Competition Law]. In particular, Brazilian Competition Law System's initial analysis of effects has been relatively weak as it has not focused on demonstrating actual foreclosure effects or on developing a rigorous analysis of potential effects. Such assessments require a detailed, fact-based, analysis relying on objective economic criteria, such as, for instance, the 'equally efficient' competitor test in the case of rebates. However, the approach used by Brazilian authorities has not gone that far, sometimes limiting itself to observing hypothetical foreclosure to declare certain conduct anti-competitive.[55]

It should be highlighted that *ex post* enforcement in Brazil can also be accomplished by private actions. The Competition Law in Brazil foresees the possibility of damage claim actions against anticompetitive conduct, such as certain vertical restraints. Article 47 of the Brazilian Competition Law indicates that harmed parties 'may take legal action in defence of their individual interests or individual homogeneous interests, so that the practices constituting violations to the economic order cease, and compensation for the losses and damages suffered be received, regardless of the investigation or administrative procedure, which will not be suspended due to filing of court action'.

54. Geradin & Pereira Neto, 2013, *supra* note 36.
55. Geradin & Pereira Neto, 2013, *supra* note 36, p. 162.

However, there is no significant culture in Brazil when it comes to proposing damage claims.[56] In practice, filing private claims is not an easy task in Brazil, especially without having a corresponding CADE proceeding, since parties are required to demonstrate the harm of the alleged anticompetitive practice, as well as the duration of it. Just as in other jurisdictions, the need for complex economic analysis, evaluation of risk and the calculation of damages are natural barriers to these claims. In addition to these challenges, civil procedures can be very lengthy since parties should expect a minimum of five years for a final decision of the Superior Court of Justice.[57] Taking into account this scenario, the upcoming *ex post* enforcement analysis will focus exclusively on CADE's public enforcement and jurisprudence.

3.4.1 RPM: *SKF* Case

Traditionally, CADE adopted the rule of reason in RPM cases. Actually, for several years CADE seemed to prioritize the American approach regarding RPM.[58] The first and most relevant jurisprudence under Law No. 8.884/1994 was the *Kibon* case (or ice-cream price list case), adjudicated in 1997 by CADE.[59] In the *Kibon* case, the investigation started with a complaint by the Bakery Association of the State of São Paulo, which indicated that Kibon (ice-cream producer) set a price list for its resellers which directly affected their autonomy to define their prices in the markets. CADE dismissed the case and decided that the so-called price list referred only to the so-called 'recommended prices', since the ice-cream producer had not pressured at any time its resellers to follow the suggested prices. Not only that, CADE also pointed out that there were no sanctions to resellers that opted to offer prices below the suggested lists. Also, there were no threats from Kibon's side to stop supplying to such resellers. This position was confirmed by several other cases during the 1990s and the 2000s,[60] for

56. For more details, *see* submission of Brazil to OECD, *Relationship Between Public and Private Antitrust Enforcement: Brazil*, 2015.
57. Sociedade Brasileira de Direito Público (SBDP), *Revisão Judicial das Decisões do Conselho Administrativo de Defesa Econômica (CADE): Pesquisa empírica e aplicada sobre os casos julgados pelos Tribunais Regionais Federais (TRFs), Superior Tribunal de Justiça (STJ) e Supremo Tribunal Federal (STF)*, Belo Horizonte, Editora Fórum, 2010.
58. In the US, certain vertical agreements (for instance, with resale price-fixing clauses) were considered as per se illegal for several years. Since the 1970s, the US Courts have used the rule of reason to assess the cases involving vertical agreements. The highlight here is the famous *Sylvania* case (*Continental TV Inc v. GTE Sylvania Inc*, 1976, 433 US 36) about non-price vertical restraints. After the *Sylvania* case, the *Khan* case (*State Oil Co v. Khan*,1997, 522 US 3) judgment for maximum resale price maintenance and the *Leegin* case in 2007 (*Leegin Creative Leather Prods v. PSKS Inc*, 2007, 127 US 2705) accepted the efficiency arguments to allow minimum resale price maintenance.
59. *Kibon v. Bakery Association of the State of São Paulo*, Case No. 148/99.
60. *See* for example: *Kinder Ovo* Case No. 08000.0062701997-88; *Gomas de Mascar* Case No. 14/96; *Brahma* Case No. 08000.000146/96-55; *AmBev I* Case No. 08012.004363/2000-89; *Ambev 2* Case No. 08012.001626/2008-71; *CAA/DF* Case No. 08012.012420/99-6.

instance, in cases involving price lists set by car manufacturers,[61] and even in 2011 in cases involving vertical price-fixing for book publishers.[62]

Actually, until 2013, CADE had never condemned a company for RPM. Most of the above-mentioned cases were dismissed by lack of evidence of effective monitoring from the producers' side, i.e., a lack of monitoring mechanisms and punishment for the dealer that did not follow the fixed resale prices.[63] Other cases were dismissed because of the lack of market power of the economic agents. According to Amorim, the fact that CADE, until 2013, did not condemn any company on the basis of RPM and the existing jurisprudence supported agents to carry out the practice without apparent risks, ultimately encouraged this conduct in the country.[64]

However, this position was changed in January 2013 in the judgment of *SKF*.[65] In 2013, CADE published an infringement decision against SKF do Brasil Ltda, an auto parts manufacturer, subsidiary of the Swedish SKF group, for fixing minimum resale price for automotive bearings. In this decision, RPM was considered illegal since defendants were not able to prove efficiencies. Despite the duration of the practice and whether the distributors followed the fixed resale prices or not, the case was presumed to be illegal by the authority.

The *SKF* judgment was the first decision regarding RPM that was condemned by CADE. In detail, the investigated practice consisted of pre-definition of minimum markups in the resale of SKF products (automotive bearings) by its exclusive distributors in Brazil. SKF created a document called 'Preventive Measures' (in Portuguese 'Medidas Preventivas') in which they would fix resale prices. According to this document, SKF would punish the distributors that did not follow their resale price, for example, by cancelling the distribution contracts and/or any authorization to distribute SKF products. In practice, SKF did not terminate any contract but applied warnings to distributors that did not respect the fixed price.

During the investigation, SKF argued that (i) its commercial policy generated economic efficiencies to the market, and (ii) in practice the company did not set penalties for distributors who did not follow their fixed markups, meaning that distributors were free to set their own prices. The company also argued that the fixed markup was a request from the distributors themselves as a way of avoiding the free-riding problem as part of the 'price war' in the downstream market. The anticompetitive practice lasted seven months between 2000 and 2001.

In 2005, the SDE (the former investigation body) concluded the investigation in favour of SKF, arguing that there was not enough indication that SKF was dominant in the specific market or engaged in anticompetitive practice. When the case was

61. *See*, for example, *Volkswagen* Case No. 89/92; *FIAT* Case No. 08000.017766/95-33, judged in 1999.
62. Among others, *Ática* Case No. 08000.0018299/96-86.
63. M. M. Sampaio Ferraz, 'Fixação de preço de revenda no e-commerce: uma análise à luz da jurisprudência nacional e internacional', *Revista do IBRAC*, Vol. 23, No. 2, 2017, p. 453.
64. F. Amorim, *Fixação de preços de revenda no Sistema Brasileiro de Defesa da Concorrência: análise do direito sancionador antitruste à luz do princípio da segurança jurídica*, Master thesis filed at University of São Paulo, São Paulo, 2017.
65. *SKF v. Procon-SP*, Case No. 08012.001271/01-447.

forwarded to CADE, the Reporting Commissioner César Mattos, after years of further investigation, voted for dismissing the case, following the SDE's suggestion, since there was no indication of coordination in the upstream or downstream markets, and not enough evidence that SKF had market power.

Nevertheless, the Commissioner Vinícius Marques de Carvalho (who afterwards was appointed as president of CADE) requested a revision of the case and voted to condemn the company on the basis of the presence of a RPM policy combined with the threat of a punishment. According to him, that would be enough to create a 'coercion' regarding the commercial policy, even if the company, in fact, did not monitor the prices or apply specific penalties. Carvalho pointed out that the low market share of SKF as well as the efficiency defence presented by the defendant in the case files was not sufficient to characterize the legality of the practice. It is worth noting that the voting among CADE's Commissioners was not unanimous.[66] Four other Commissioners followed Carvalho's vote, while only one Commissioner voted for dismissal of the case following the Reporting Commissioner. CADE imposed on SKF a fine equivalent of BRL 2.7 million (equivalent to EUR 500 thousand).

SKF challenged CADE's decision in the judiciary, seeking its annulment. At the end of May 2015, the company obtained a favourable first instance decision from the Federal Court of Brasília. The decision shows that CADE had abruptly changed its position (by applying a different analysis to RPM), and therefore harmed the legal certainty of business people. The first instance decision, however, was based on formalistic arguments and did not analyse the scope of the practice and the effects in the market. In June 2015, CADE appealed to the Federal Regional Court, seeking to restore the terms of its 2013 decision, but the case is still under discussion.

The relevance of the *SKF* decision stems from the fact that CADE has gradually become more conservative in assessing the legality of vertical restraints. CADE's recent case law has returned the burden of proof to the companies, treating RPM as a sort of per se violation. Since this decision, companies that want to fix resale price must also be able to prove economic efficiency gains, i.e., prove that the positive effects generated by such restraint will be passed on to consumers.[67] The central point of the problem is this reversal of the burden of proof that directly alters the dynamics of the *ex post* enforcement of vertical restraints. On the one hand, if the burden of proof is on the side of the antitrust authority, it is more unlikely that the economic agent will be condemned by setting resale prices. On the other hand, if the burden of proof regarding the absence of adverse effects on competition rests with the company, it is very likely

66. In Brazil, every case of infringement of the economic order is voted by CADE's six Commissioners and President (Article 91, CADE's Internal Regulation). For every case, there is a Reporting Commissioner who is responsible to make a decision, and the other Commissioners can choose to follow it or not. If the votes are diverging (unusual to happen), CADE's President can nominate a Commissioner who will prepare a *casting decision*, which will go to a second vote among the Commissioners (Articles 92-100, CADE's Internal Regulation).
67. Amorim explains that this inversion in the burden of proof to the companies should not be confused with the rule per se, which considers an anticompetitive practice illegal by its very essence (as in the case of hardcore price-fixing cartels). The author concluded that resale price-fixing, despite the reversal in the burden of proof is still under the 'rule of reason', stipulated in Article 36 of Law 12.529/2011. Amorim, 2017, *supra* note 64, p. 95.

that it will be condemned by the authority, even though it can bring efficiencies to the markets.[68]

This means that the change in the burden of proof in cases of RPM may ultimately lead the authority to take sub-optimal decisions. Efficiency enhancing agreements may be condemned because proofing efficiencies is not an easy task. Still in the scope of the *SKF* case, CADE's Commissioner Olavo Chinaglia – one of the two Commissioners who voted in favour of dismissal of the case – stresses how difficult it can be for the firms to prove procompetitive outcomes:

> In this context, if the only way to decide upon the legality of the practice would be proving that economic efficiencies are greater than the damages, than the Defendant has almost no possibility of defence. In a case in which the documents are unable to conclude precisely that the investigated practice altered the functioning of the market and, consequently, are unable of proving any negative antitrust effect, the Defendant's necessity of proving economic efficiencies creates a very similar situation to what procedural theory has called as diabolical proof.[69]

According to Pedro Cristofaro, CADE did not present any constitutional or legal justification to adopt this reversal in the burden of proof for RPM.[70] The author explains that only a few exceptions in the whole Brazilian legal system accept the reversal in the burden of proof, and therefore the *SKF* decision could have failed to respect constitutional principles.[71]

After the *SKF* case, two other main cases involving RPM were judged by CADE. The first one, *Bematech,*[72] involving RPM in the market for a specific type of printer, resulted in settlement.

The second case involves RPM by *Raízen Combustíveis*, formerly Shell Brasil, a fuel distributor. In the *Raízen* case,[73] the company was accused of fixing resale prices (and markup margins) of fuels, imposing the standardization of accounting systems, prices and profit margins to distributors during the period of 1999 and 2003. Just as in the *SKF* case, CADE's Tribunal was again divided on how to assess those vertical restraints, and whether to consider the presumption of illegality. The Reporting Commissioner Alessandro Octaviani Luis voted for the condemnation of the company and presumed the vertical price-fixing to be illegal, since the company was incapable of proving the economic efficiencies of their business practice. In this sense, Octaviani Luis presented his arguments in a more formalistic approach and chose not to define any objective rule to be applied in RPM cases. The Commissioner Marcio de Oliveira Junior also voted for the condemnation of *Raízen* but based his arguments in the rule

68. It should be noted that the mere suggestion of resale price remains a lawful practice, when not accompanied by any price monitoring mechanism and/or retaliation of retailers that do not follow the price suggestions.
69. Free translation from Olavo Chinaglia's Vote on Case *SKF v. Procon-SP*, Case No. 08012.001271/2001-447, from 31 August 2011, case file p. 939.
70. P. Cristofaro, 'A categorização dos ilícitos concorrenciais e o direito concorrencial brasileiro', *in* C. Campilongo & R. Pfeiffer (eds), *Evolução do antitruste no Brasil*, São Paulo, Editora Singular, 2018.
71. Cristofaro, 2018, *supra* note 70.
72. *CADE v. Bematech S/A*, Case No. 08700.002692/2014-59.
73. *CADE v. Raízen Combustíveis S/A (former Shell Brasil Ltda)*, Case No. 08012.011042/2005-61.

of reason approach. His vote described a balance of the pro- and anticompetitive effects of the practice, taking into consideration the information that was available in the case files. In his words:

> There were no economic efficiencies generated by the practice: (i) it was not a mere suggestion of resale conditions to the distributor Shell, but instead the imposition of prices and operational conditions; (ii) the coercive mechanisms for the imposition of resale prices have eliminated the possible efficiencies of the practice; and (iii) the control over the services offered by distributors could have been made via other means rather than price-fixing, eg, via fuel quality inspections.[74]

Some recent literature challenged CADE's position with regard to RPM cases, while others recognize that the problems arise from a lack of cases being analysed by CADE. Priscila Brolio Gonçalves, for instance, explains that the lack of administrative precedents regarding RPM is partly related to government control exercised until the 1990s, and more recently, to the priority set by CADE in relation to horizontal conduct such as cartels.[75] The author stresses that the modest number of administrative decisions on this matter does not stem from the absence of such conduct in the Brazilian territory, or from the fact that the conduct does not harm competition and/or consumers.[76]

Nowadays, unfortunately, it is unclear the pattern of the jurisprudence regarding RPM, and there are divergent views in the Tribunal regarding the topic. This fact increases legal uncertainties and, and therefore, weakens the function of the Tribunal in guiding competition policy and enforcement. It is worth noting that in their decisions, none of the Commissioners mentioned the goals of competition law in Brazil as a way to clarify the choice for their line of argumentation. From the previous sections, it has been shown that among the goals of the competition policy in Brazil are economic efficiency and free-competition, i.e., the preservation of an environment in which companies have effective incentives to compete, innovate and satisfy the demands of consumers.

The use of presumption of illegality in RPM cases does not necessarily respect this goal, because RPM can bring economic efficiencies to markets, such as solving the double markup problem, preventing free-riding, or reducing transaction costs.[77] These economic efficiencies can help to create a level playing field among competitors that is intrinsically expressed in the constitutional principles, and therefore should be carefully assessed by the Brazilian authority in any analysis of vertical cases, even when they involve price restrictions.

74. *See* Vote of Commissioner Oliveira Junior on Case No. 08012.011042/2005-61, p. 135 (case file p. 1495).
75. P. A. Gonçalves, *Fixação e Sugestão de Preços de Revenda em Contrato de Distribuição*, 2nd ed., São Paulo, Editora Singular, 2016, p. 330.
76. Gonçalves, 2016, *supra* note 75, pp. 307-308.
77. *See* the economic analysis of resale price-fixing in Chapter 2.

3.4.2 Geo-Blocking: Iguatemi Cases

With regard to the jurisprudence of exclusive territory or geo-blocking agreements, CADE evaluated this problem in a few cases concerning leasing agreements in shopping malls. In the investigation and assessment of the authority, it was concluded that the negative outcomes of the restrictive agreements outweighed the potential benefits of it.

Iguatemi Shopping ('Iguatemi') was involved in two cases concerning the use of vertical restraints (exclusive territory), having been condemned in both. Iguatemi is a luxurious shopping mall located in the wealthy southern region of São Paulo. The first case (also called the *Iguatemi I* case[78]), judged in 2003, concerned leasing contracts[79] with exclusive territory clauses, in which Iguatemi prohibited the shop owners of luxury brands from opening other stores in malls that directly compete with Iguatemi. The second case (also called *Iguatemi II* case[80]), judged in 2007, involved another type of exclusive territory clause, defining that the same shop owners could not have other shops within a certain radius of its mall (hereinafter called 'radius clause'). In the next paragraphs, the focus is on the analysis of the second case.[81]

In *Iguatemi II*, SDE (the former investigatory body) concluded that the exclusive territory clause was lawful, and therefore recommended the dismissal of the case. SDE argued that these clauses are common in lease agreements in shopping malls and in franchising contracts because it brings economic efficiency to markets, such as elimination of the free-riding problem. CADE's Tribunal disagreed with SDE. The authority acknowledged the existence of efficiency gains from this vertical restraint but considered them to be insufficient and disproportionate to the restriction.

In detail, Iguatemi's lease agreements generally used a standard radius clause, which prevented shop owners from installing another facility within a radius of 2.5 kilometres away from its mall. Paulo Furquim Azevedo explains that, on the one hand, the radius clause restricts competition since it transfers to a single company (the shopping mall) the rights of other entrepreneurs to open a shop in a certain area.[82] Since the mix of stores is an important attribute of competition among shopping malls,[83] the radius clause limits the access of competing shopping malls to certain

78. *Participações Morro Vermelho Ltda. v. Condomínio Shopping Center Iguatemi e Shopping Centers Reunidos do Brasil Ltda*, Case No. 08012.009991/98-82.
79. Any store-brand that wants to have a shop in this Iguatemi mall has to sign a lease agreement with it.
80. *CADE v. Condomínio do Shopping Center Iguatemi/SP*, Case No. 08012.006636/97-43.
81. For the detail analysis of *Iguatemi I* case, *see*, for instance, P. F. Azevedo, 'Contratos de Exclusividade em Shopping Centers', *in* E. Pereira, E. Lagroteria & J. P. Lea (eds), *Concorrência e Regulação: Estudos e Pareceres Econômicos*, 1st ed., São Paulo, Editora Singular, 2004, pp. 163-186; R. Santacruz, 'Exclusividade e competição no mercado de shopping centers', *in* C. Mattos (org.) (ed.), *A revolução do antitruste no Brasil 2*, São Paulo, Editora Singular, 2008.
82. Azevedo, 2010, *supra* note 53, p. 27.
83. Commercial contracts with Shopping Malls are named in the literature as 'mix-tenant' contracts, since it is the mix of stores that guarantees enough incentives for shop owners to establish a store in these locations. For the analysis of such clauses in the Brazilian context, *see* R. Barcellos, *O Contrato de Shopping Center e os Contratos Atípicos Interempresariais*, São Paulo, Editora Atlas, 2009.

brands/shops and therefore weakens competition in the area under protection. In other words, intra-brand competition is harmed.[84] On the other hand, the radius clause discourages opportunistic behaviour of shop owners. In the absence of the radius clause, a shop owner could appropriate the collective benefits of the shopping mall (for instance, the number of consumers who visit that specific area) and set another shop just outside Iguatemi and profit from it without having to pay the high renting costs of the shopping mall and/or the royalties related to the volume of sales.[85]

In the first step of CADE's analysis, the authority suggested that Iguatemi is a mall with a clear dominant position in the marketplace because of its capacity to charge substantially higher prices for the leased space than similar malls in the city. Because of that, CADE had to assess as a second step whether there was the intention of Iguatemi to foreclose markets. In the case files there was strong evidence of other shopping malls being threatened not to enter into this luxurious shopping mall segment. In addition, there was also evidence of existing shopping malls (e.g., Eldorado Shopping mall) that failed to expand their activities to other segments because it was within the 2.5 kilometre radius.

Because of the market foreclosure evidence, CADE had (as a third step) to find a way to balance the pro- and anticompetitive effects of this vertical restraint. According to Azevedo,[86] the weighting in the *Iguatemi II* case could be done by means of radius dimension analysis. That is to say, if the radius was too small, the damage to competition would be proportionately smaller, and the benefits of keeping shop owners from installing a store next to the shopping mall would be proportionately larger than the damages in a way to conclude that the conduct was lawful. If the radius was too large, the damage to competition would increase as the protected area grew, while the benefits would remain the same since the gain in consumption deviation was fixed.

Considering that it was virtually impossible to accurately determine this borderline, in the present case, CADE concluded that the 2.5 kilometre radius was disproportional, and therefore the vertical agreement was illicit. This is because the area protected by the 'just 2.5 kilometres radius' actually corresponded to almost 20,000 kilometres square in the wealthiest area of São Paulo, which is the largest metropolis in South America.[87] This area would also cover almost the total of the consumers who would be willing to buy from those luxury shops. This area, according to CADE, is one of the world's most densely populated areas as well, and therefore, the efficiency arguments presented by Iguatemi were not enough to balance the anticompetitive effects of such practice.

Even though CADE did not assess too many cases involving geo-blocking clauses, the existing jurisprudence serves as important guidelines and respects the effect-based

84. M. Possas & J. Pondé, 'A análise de eficiência em práticas restritivas verticais: custos de transação e cláusulas de raio no mercado de shopping center', *in* C. Campilongo & R. Pfeiffer (eds), *Evolução do antitruste no Brasil*, São Paulo, Editora Singular, 2018, pp. 1012-1056.
85. In a lease agreement, shopping malls usually charge the shop owner a fixed component related to the renting of the place and a variable component related to the volume of sales (royalties).
86. Azevedo, 2010, *supra* note 53, p. 27.
87. *See* analysis of Azevedo, 2010, *supra* note 53.

analysis suggested by the Brazilian Law. Unlike the case of RPM, the few cases involving geo-blocking clauses are still analysed under the rule of reasoned approach. However, this does not mean that by signing geo-blocking agreements, firms are covered by legal certainty. And this can be explained by the fact that these decisions are rather outdated and not confirmed over the years as a way of creating a consolidated antitrust jurisprudence in the topic.

An important point that seems to be overlooked by CADE is the fact that the consideration of the geographical restraints should gain greater relevance in continental countries, such as Brazil. According to Forgioni, because of this continental dimension, vertical restraints imposed by companies with economic power are capable of truly causing short- and long-term 'disasters' in Brazil.[88] There are regions in Brazil where the closing of distribution channels, including the suppression of traditional commerce, 'may foster unemployment, reduce the economic activity and undermine development'.[89] According to the author, competition policies must consider the reality of the country and the magnitude of its territory to ensure that the benefits of these policies actually reach most of the population, not only in the big metropolitan areas but also in the most remote countryside locations. Therefore, one wonders whether the current enforcements efforts made by CADE in the past decades have taken into consideration this reality.

It is worth finally noting that with the ascension of digital economies and e-commerce, more cases discussing geo-blocking clauses could be in the radar of CADE. The growth of e-commerce may encourage producers to the adoption of marketplace restrictions, since they might be afraid of losing control of their distribution channels in this new digital reality. However, so far, no case of geo-blocking in the digital context has been assessed by the Brazilian authority.

3.4.3 Cases Involving Digital Businesses

CADE has not investigated many cases related to digital businesses.[90] Regarding vertical restraints, the authority has opened only one investigation of MFN clauses related to the market for online hotel booking. It is worth noting that the debate about MFN clauses is not recent, but it has already been under analysis by competition agencies in other countries.[91] MFN clauses that appear in vertical agreements between suppliers and distributors generally consist of an offer by the supplier of a price or rate to a client no higher than the lowest offered to other clients. For instance, in the online hotel booking sector, an MFN clause obligates the hotels to always give to the platform the best price for online hotel bookings, among other most favoured conditions.

88. Forgioni, 2016, *supra* note 3.
89. Forgioni, 2016, *supra* note 3, p. 18.
90. According to a report prepared by CADE in 2019, the authority has assessed over the years only few cases involving digital markets: five mergers, six cartels and five cases of unilateral conduct. For more information on the cases, *see* report 'BRICS in the digital economy: competition policy in practice', available at: http://www.cade.gov.br/acesso-a-informacao/publicacoes-institucionais/brics_report.pdf (1/10/2019).
91. *See*, for instance, Chapter 4 for the discussion about similar investigations in Europe.

In 2016, CADE started an investigation based on a representation filed by the Brazil Forum of Hotel Operators (*Fórum de Operadores Hoteleiros do Brasil or FOHB*).[92] In the representation, FOHB argued that the companies *Booking.com*, *Decolar.com* and *Expedia* were applying in their contracts hotel price parity clauses to ensure that they would have better prices/advantageous conditions to consumers when compared to competing platforms (including compared to the website of the hotels themselves). According to FOHB, these clauses infringed Brazilian Competition Law, particularly Article 36 of Law No. 12.529/2011. CADE, in practice, did not prepare an assessment of this case since the three companies decided to sign a settlement agreement with the authority before its final decision. The settlement specified that the use of price parity provisions in relation to offline sales channels and competing platforms should be terminated for the three firms.

It is worth noting that, in Brazil, digital businesses have grown significantly in the past years. For instance, e-commerce in Brazil presented an average growth of 13.2% in the past five years (2013-2018) and a turnover, in 2018, of more than BRL 50 billion (approx. EUR 12 billion), reaching a number of 58 million consumers.[93] It means that CADE, by signing the settlement agreements, once more missed the opportunity to start developing an antitrust jurisprudence in Brazil regarding digital business.

3.4.4 Challenges to *Ex Post* Enforcement

3.4.4.1 CADE's Institutional Design

From the previous sections, we can highlight that CADE faces the challenge of lack of more objective parameters in assessing vertical restraints. Indeed, the existing antitrust jurisprudence is not all clear, consistent, or vast enough to be able to conclude CADE's positions with regard to certain vertical practices. Moreover, the authority has been favouring the settlement of agreements in a way that does not contribute to the creation of a trustworthy legal framework. In addition to these challenges, it would be useful to look at another specific challenge that may jeopardize any possibility of reaching optimal level of antitrust enforcement in Brazil: the institutional design of the Brazilian Competition Authority.

When the new Brazilian Competition Law entered into force, one important feature of the reform was the need for additional staff. This is because the lack of staff, added to the high employee turnover, led to an overload situation. Actually, according to OECD Peer Review, CADE has for years been considered as 'one of the most understaffed competition enforcement regimes in the world'.[94] To change this scenario, Law No. 12.529/2011 foresaw the creation of two-hundred new positions, that

92. *Fórum de Operadores Hoteleiros do Brasil v. Expedia do Brasil Agência de Viagens e Turismo Ltda., Decolar.com Ltda. e Booking.com Brasil Serviços de Reserva de Hotéis Ltda*, Case No. 08700.005679/2016-13.
93. Data available in 39th Edition of the research Webshoppers, by E-bit.
94. This is considering technical staff per unit of GDP or population. *See*, OECD, 2019, *supra* note 8, p. 21.

would more than double the previous SDE, SEAE and CADE combined staff. However, the hiring of the new staff did not happen because of government budget cuts.[95]

Nowadays, CADE's General Superintendence is organized into nine main units. Five of these units work on cases related to mergers and unilateral conduct, and four units focus on cartel cases, one of them being specifically related to cartel screening activities.[96] This means that cases involving vertical agreements are handled together with the overload merger cases. Therefore, one can predict that there are significantly fewer resources allocated to investigations of unilateral conduct, including vertical restraints, and more devoted to merger review given the number of filed notifications added to the statutory deadlines.[97]

CADE consisted of 385 employees in 2018, of which 137 are non-administrative staff working on competition enforcement, being 40% lawyers, 25% economists, and the last 28% graduates in other areas.[98] Organisation for Economic Co-operation and Development (OECD) Peer Review also highlights that from all the non-administrative staff, only five are dedicated to antitrust conduct apart from mergers and cartels,[99] which includes the analysis of vertical restraints.

With regard to CADE Commissioners, they often have a background in economics and law because the Competition Law foresees in its Article 6 that such decision-making positions should be filled by lawyers or economists.[100] However, recent appointments have not necessarily respected this procedural requirement. The current President, Alexandre Barreto de Souza, has a background in management and public administration.[101] This fact raises questions regarding the latent political influences behind the process of making appointments. It should be noted that in Brazil, the members of CADE's Administrative Tribunal – the President and the six Commissioners – do not apply themselves for open positions but are rather appointed by the Brazilian President and the Senate.[102]

95. OECD, 2019, *supra* note 8, p. 21.
96. CADE, *Annual Report 2018*.
97. Law No. 12.529/2011 stipulates specific deadlines form the authority to conclude merger cases. The maximum deadline is 240 days that can be extended by CADE's Tribunal to 90 extra days in very complex cases.
98. CADE, *Annual Report 2018*, p. 41.
99. OECD, 2019, *supra* note 8, p. 33.
100. Article 6 of Law No. 12.529/2011: 'Art. 6. The Administrative Tribunal, an adjudicatory body, is comprised of a President and six Commissioners chosen among citizens over thirty (30) years old, who are well reputed for their knowledge of law or economics and who possess a reputation for moral integrity, appointed by the President of the Republic, after being approved by the Federal Senate.'
101. Alexandre Barreto de Souza has a mandate from 22/6/2017 until 21/6/2021. His background can be traced at: http://www.cade.gov.br/acesso-a-informacao/institucional/acesso-a-informacao/institucional/presidencia (15/4/2019).
102. While the Executive Power of the Brazilian government can control CADE by indicating and approving (or disapproving) the mandates of Commissioners and the President of the Authority, the Legislative Power exercises its control by approving the national annual budget, which includes CADE's annual budget. *See* a more extensive analysis on accountability in A. C. Gomes & M. E. A Camargo e Gomes, 'Ouvidoria do CADE: contribuições para o equilíbrio entre autonomia e accountability', *in* C. Campilongo & R. Pfeiffer (eds), Evolução do antitruste no Brasil, São Paulo, Editora Singular, 2018.

To sum up, while considering the state of the art of *ex post* enforcement of vertical restraints in Brazil, we have identified some of the authority's main challenges and threats.

On behalf of the limited jurisprudence, we can conclude that CADE fails in defining objective parameters for assessing vertical agreements (including the definition of whether some practices are per se illegal or not). This behaviour of the Brazilian authority enhances a high degree of obscurity, complexity and subjectivity in its decisions. Moreover, when it comes to the institutional design, CADE does not have enough staff to carry out its work. This means that the authority may have been favouring *ex post* enforcement of vertical agreements in a context where the lack of resources and staff has been the rule.

3.4.4.2 The Judiciary System

The Brazilian judiciary is responsible for two main activities involving antitrust law. The first one is related to damages claims. The second one is related to the judicial review of CADE's administrative decisions. In fact, it is impossible to talk about antitrust enforcement without discussing the possibility of judicial review. The Brazilian Competition Law, the Federal Constitution, and the Brazilian Civil Code provide together the understanding that all decisions taken by the antitrust authority are subject to judicial review.

In Brazil, the evolution of judicial review involving antitrust cases has been quite interesting. Since Law No. 8.884/1994 entered into force, CADE became an independent agency, and, naturally, there have been a growing number of administrative decisions in that matter. The increase in the number of administrative decisions was followed, to some extent, by the increase in the number of requests for judicial review. During this period, CADE's procedures were still quite incipient, and the decisions were contradictory. This scenario gave the companies the opportunity to submit requests for review. While in 1994 there were 7 requests for judicial review filed in courts, this number increased to 161 in 2000, and 480 in 2007.[103] Actually, 2007 was the year with the largest number of judicial review requests involving CADE's decisions throughout the national territory.

Until the mid-2000s, CADE's decisions were not so effective, since most of them were suspended by the judiciary. From 1994 onwards, when the old Competition Law entered into force, until 2005, only 18% of CADE's infringement decisions were essentially confirmed by courts.[104] Between 2002 and 2004, for instance, less than 4% of the fines imposed by the Brazilian authority were actually paid by parties. This scenario started to slowly change after 2008.[105]

The fall in lawsuits involving CADE's decisions from 2008 onwards can be explained by several reasons. First, the Superior Court of Justice started to demand

103. CADE, *Defesa da Concorrência no Brasil: 50 anos*, 2013, p. 130.
104. CADE, 2013, *supra* note 103, p. 132.
105. In 2008, there were 343 new cases for judicial review; in 2009, 150 new cases; in 2010, 62 new cases; and in 2011, 58. CADE, 2013, *supra* note 103, p. 131.

from companies a judicial deposit that amounted to the fine imposed by CADE, in order to proceed with the judicial review. This fact, naturally, discouraged many companies from filing review requests. Second, there was an improvement in the performance and cooperation of the CADE Attorney's Office with the judiciary as a whole. A third important change was the increase in the number of negotiations and settlements signed between the companies and the competition authority.[106] Lastly, the agency's success rate in court disputes started to increase over the following years (which also reflects the quality of CADE Attorney's Office). In a study conducted by the Brazilian Society of Public Law (in Portuguese '*Sociedade Brasileira de Direito Público*' or just *SBDP*) in 2011, it was pointed out that almost 50% of CADE's decisions about administrative proceedings regarding anticompetitive conduct were confirmed by national courts.[107] Another data set presented by CADE in 2013 indicates that almost 80% of CADE's decisions have been upheld by the judiciary.[108]

Despite this significant evolution of the judiciary's performance in matters related to competition law, there are still challenges to be overcome. The first one refers to the length of the judiciary proceedings. The research carried out by *SBDP* indicates that it takes, on average, more than five years for the case to be decided in court, and more than two years to have a ruling at first instance.[109] Moreover, Brazilian magistrates still refrain from applying economic concepts in court decisions either due to lack of knowledge or reluctance. Indeed, judges tend to focus more on the formal issues of the administrative proceedings. However, as we have been addressing throughout this book, in cases of vertical agreements, economic analysis is fundamental to balance economic efficiencies with the potential anticompetitive effects of restrictive agreements in the marketplace. In the *SKF* case involving RPM, exposed in section 3.3.1, the parties were able to reverse CADE's position in the first instance in 2013 (i.e., the court decision interpreted that RPM should not be considered illegal), but the case is still being discussed in higher instances.

3.5 THE CONTEXT OF ANTITRUST POLICY IN BRAZIL: THE INTERACTING GROUP OF AGENTS

This section presents one possible explanation of the above-mentioned legal reform oriented to vertical agreements. It aims to analyse whether the latent interests of private relevant actors (antitrust authorities, lawyers, business people and their lobby groups) help to explain the recent changes in the Brazilian regulation. As discussed in Chapter 2, regulation is often motivated by public interests. Externalities, information asymmetry, market power are often the market failures that give grounds to regulation. However, in certain contexts, the law- and decision-making processes do not advance in the path of what is optimal for society, and therefore they are not able to achieve the public interest goals.

106. CADE, 2013, *supra* note 103, p. 132.
107. SBDP, 2010, *supra* note 57.
108. CADE, 2013, *supra* note 103, p. 136.
109. SBDP, 2010, *supra* note 57.

Historically, the democratic legitimacy in Brazilian public policies has been put in question because only a few interest groups of agents have indeed access to the law- and decision-making processes regarding different kinds of public policies.[110] As for antitrust policies, CADE has foreseen some mechanisms of public participation, such as public consultations that allow different individuals or interested groups - affected by the new regulatory context - to give their opinion on the content of the new regulation.

From 2012, when the new Competition Law entered into force, until 2018, seventeen public consultations were launched in different topics. In practical terms, whenever CADE launches a public consultation, the authority first makes available on its website a first draft of the new proposed regulation ('first draft'). Then the agency opens the public consultation to the public for a couple of weeks or months. After this period of open consultation, CADE publishes the final version of the new regulation ('final version') together with a technical note which contains a brief summary of the contributions and gives some explanation regarding this final result. Taking this background into consideration, the aim of this section is to analyse the interest-groups participation in the recent changes in antitrust policies oriented to vertical agreements.

3.5.1 Behind Resolution No. 17/2016: Identifying Interest Groups of Agents

From all the public consultations issued by CADE in the past years, two of them were devoted to the discussions of vertical agreements: Public Consultation No. 03/2014 and Public Consultation No. 02/2016 (respectively regarding Resolution No. 10/2014 and the Resolution No. 17/2016).[111] The discussions of Public Consultation No. 03/2014 were focused on the definition of agreements and the thresholds for the notification system.

For this first Public Consultation No. 03/2014, CADE received twenty-three contributions: thirteen from law firms/bar association;[112] seven from industry associations and three from companies that opted to send an individual contribution. There was no specific group of consumers that actively participated in this public consultation. Considering the group of lawyers, it is worth noting that, in this scenario, they were not representing any specific client, but simply presenting an individual contribution. In general terms, the main concern brought by those lawyers was the need to clarify concepts and objective criteria for the notification system of contracts since the first draft was considerably broad. In principle, they were all in favour of the notification system to both horizontal and vertical agreements, once an objective criterion was better defined.

110. P. Mattos, 'Regulação econômica e social e participação pública no Brasil', *IX Congreso Internacional del CLAD sobre la Reforma del Estado y de la Administración Pública*, Madrid, Spain, 2004, p. 3.
111. As explained in previous sections, the first regulation that attempted to bring clear rules in respect to the notification of vertical and horizontal agreements was Resolution No. 10/2014. While Resolution No. 17/2016 excluded vertical agreements from the notification system.
112. It is worth noting that the first group identified, i.e., the group of lawyers, involve mostly big law firms, bar association, groups and institutions that are represented by the law firms.

Regarding the industry associations and the companies which have contributed to this public consultation on their own, they were mostly related to regulated sectors. Apart from requesting more objective criteria to the notification system, the business community argued that some of those associative agreements that they engaged in are contracts which are controlled by their own regulatory agency. Therefore, according to them, an extra control from the antitrust agency would not be necessary. It was the case, for example, of network sharing agreements among telecom companies that are tightly controlled by the National Agency of Telecommunication and that would fall into the scope of CADE, bringing additional high costs to those companies.

As a result of this first public consultation, Resolution No. 10/2014 indeed reflected some of the concerns presented by parties, especially in relation to narrowing down the scope of the notification system (e.g., a market share threshold for horizontal and vertical agreements was added in this regulation). However, as shown in section 3.3, the final legal text was not enough to guarantee a legal and safe framework for business people.

The brief description of this first public consultation is important in order to apprehend the role of relevant actors that were interested in this issue since the beginning of the regulatory discussions. The content of this first consultation, however, is not the focus of this section. Indeed, for the objectives of this section, the second round of public consultations turned out to be much more relevant, since it resulted in the exclusion of vertical agreements from the *ex ante* notification system.

Before entering into further detail, it is important to highlight that the 'first draft' prepared by CADE of the Public Consultation No. 02/2016 still considered both horizontal and vertical agreements as part of the pre-merger control policy. This draft aimed at clarifying the notification criteria for commercial contracts. This means that the first idea of CADE was not to exclude vertical agreements of the notification system but merely to define clearer parameters for the *ex ante* monitoring. Table 3.2 describes the changes in legislation proposed by the first draft.

Table 3.2 Public Consultation No. 02/2016: Main Changes Proposed by the 'First Draft'

Resolution No. 10/2014	*Public Consultation No. 02/2016 (First Draft)*
General criteria for notification of commercial agreements	
1. A duration equal to, or longer than, 2 years, or the 2-year period is reached or exceeded through renewals provided for in agreements. 2. Involve 'horizontal or vertical cooperation or sharing of risks entailing inter-dependence'.	1. Duration equal to, or longer than, 2 years, or, *in case of shorter than 2 years or open-ended periods, a notification must be made when such period is reached.* * 2. Whenever the agreement results in horizontal and/or vertical cooperation and the corresponding risks and results are shared.

Resolution No. 10/2014	*Public Consultation No. 02/2016 (First Draft)*
Criteria for notification of horizontal agreements	
The share of the parties to the agreement in the relevant affected market is equal to or higher than 20%.	The share of the parties to the agreement in the relevant affected market is equal to or higher than 20%.
Criteria for notification of vertical agreements	
At least one of the parties holds 30% or more of the relevant markets affected by the agreement, provided that the following conditions are met: (a) the agreement provides for the sharing of revenue or losses between the parties; and (b) an exclusivity relationship derives from the agreement.	*There is an obligation that sets forth or may result in exclusivity and at least two parties to the agreement hold market shares equal to, or higher than, twenty percent (20%) in the potentially affected relevant markets.* *

Note: *emphasis added

Source: Compiled by the Demarest Advogados, based on Resolution No. 10/2014 and first draft of Public Consultation No. 02/2016.

In this second round of public consultation, CADE received - in the period of twenty days -fourteen contributions, nine being from law firms/law bar association; two from Industry Associations and three from companies that opted to send an individual contribution.[113] For this consultation, there was again no specific group of consumers that actively participated in it.

Considering this context, the analysis to be carried out in the coming subsection will consider three main groups of relevant actors: (i) the antitrust authority (CADE), (ii) the law firms that provide advocacy services to companies, and (iii) the business enterprises and their lobby groups (i.e., including their associations). The choice of these three main groups reflects not only their participation in the Public Consultation No. 02/2016, but also the methodology used by previous studies that tried to identify the interest groups who influence antitrust lawmaking processes in other jurisdictions, such as in the EU (Oliver Budzinski and Andt Christiansen; Angela Wigger) and in China (Weng Ng).[114]

113. Among the contributions were: *Sinditelebrasil, ABIQUIM, OAB – SP, Trench Rossi Watanabe, Calcione Advogados; OAB – DF; Petrobras S.A;Claro S.A; ABA; TIM S.A; IBRAC; MC Millan + ICN; VPBG; and CESA*. The full documents of this public consultation can be found at: http://www.cade.gov.br/acesso-a-*informacao/acesso-a-informacao/participacao-social-1/consultas-publicas-concluidas* (7/7/2019).

114. O. Budzinski & A. Christiansen, 'Competence Allocation in the EU Competition Policy System as an Interest-Driven Process', *Journal of Public Policy*, Vol. 25, No. 3, 2005, pp. 313-337; A. Wigger, 'Revising the European Competition Reform: The Toll of Private Self-Enforcement', *Working Papers Political Science of Vrije Universiteit Amsterdam*, No. 07, 2004; W. Ng, *The Political Economy of Competition Law in China*, Cambridge, Cambridge University Press, 2018.

Although our attempt involves complex relations, the proposed outline is still far from exhaustive, as consumer groups and the academic interactions are omitted. One can speculate that consumers (including consumer's representatives) did not contribute to this public consultations because they were not well informed about the existence of the consultation itself. Indeed, the public consultation was not spread in the main channels of national media and CADE opened the discussion for only twenty days, which is not enough time for the news to be well spread in a country with the dimensions of Brazil, and/or for specialists to do a full assessment of the proposed first draft.

3.5.2 Main Assumptions about the Behaviour of Relevant Actors

This subsection starts addressing the relevance of the basic premise that public interest goals are not enough to explain certain antitrust policies and therefore that private interests also play a role in the lawmaking process. This premise will be further analysed taking into consideration the identified set of relevant actors: the business enterprises that are directly affected by the competition rules, the lawyers that represent their firms, and the antitrust authority (in this case, CADE).

Taking into account the business community and their lobby groups, we assume that their self-interest is related to the minimization of compliance costs that include the costs associated with the lengthy administrative and judicial proceedings (and therefore high costs with lawyers), the notification requirements, and indirect costs of having erratic decisions. Therefore, they would consistently argue in favour of clear rules and simplified notification systems, so that they could count on the legal certainty and predictability of an *ex ante* control and with the green flag from the authority that would protect them from future litigation costs. This means that business enterprises, when contributing to the public consultation, would argue in favour of a limited scope of the notification system both for horizontal and vertical agreements, including the possible exemption system for certain agreements (following the EU model of Block Exemptions), in order to minimize their compliance costs.

As for the law firms (and bar associations), it could be assumed that they would follow a similar pattern as the business community. This is because the analysis of the content of public consultations usually requires a degree of expertise that many clients (illustrated here by the business community) do not have.[115] This means that the lawyers, in theory, participate in those public consultations to represent their clients who do not have the expertise in the field. They would therefore contribute to the consultation in favour of a limited scope for a notification system to both horizontal and vertical agreements, and also because this notification system guarantees to those law firms a great number of legal services to be provided. However, the exact behaviour of law firms is not always easy to predict. There is some literature that suggests, for example, that lawyers have an interest in keeping the law complex, so that

115. R. Van den Bergh, 'Towards Efficient Self-Regulation in Markets for Professional Services', *in* C. D. Ehlermann & A. Atanasiu (eds), *European Competition Law Annual*, Oxford, Hart Publishing, 2004.

they may benefit from the increased demand for legal services.[116] If we take this into account, law firms, in this case, would not contribute to make the law clearer but would rather leave it with legal gaps.

Finally, as for the antitrust authority, it is supposed that CADE would first observe the goals of the country and specific constitutional principles when drafting specific rules. Meaning that the lawmaking process carried out by CADE would respect the constitutional principles of human dignity and social justice, by proposing new rules that preserve an environment in which companies have effective incentives to compete, innovate and satisfy the demands of consumers; protect competition and prevent markets from being harmed by agents with a high degree of economic power.[117] Second, CADE would seek to minimize the enforcement costs of the agency. In this case, the enforcement costs would be the administrative costs of the notification system (i.e., having enough staff to prepare competition assessments for all notified contracts), and/or the investigation costs of potential administrative procedures. Third, antitrust agencies would give high importance to their reputation and credibility in their policy and decision-making process. It is likely that CADE would want to guarantee the delivery of good policymaking with good policy results, in order to guarantee its reputation as a serious and capable antitrust agency. The perception of the competition agency's quality directly influences not only the judicial or legislative decisions but also the willingness of companies to comply with the law.[118] The international recognition of the competition agency also plays a major role in its reputation. Actually, William Kovacic argues that agencies' reputations can be compared to brands since having a well-respected brand is an extremely valuable asset.[119]

In practical terms, the observation of the goals of the country, the willingness to minimize enforcement costs and to maintain a good reputation could be achieved by CADE by drafting clear rules, and limiting the scope of the notification system for both horizontal and vertical agreements, without leaving apart situations that might lead to abuse of market power. It is also supposed that in the lawmaking process, the formulation of the content of regulation would indeed consider the arguments and justifications presented by the contributions of interested actors. And more than that, the agency would present the reasoning of its decisions, by justifying why the final version of the norm was done in one way and not the other.[120]

Figure 3.1 summarizes the main assumptions about the behaviour of main actors.

116. *See*, for example, A. Ogus, 'The Economic Basis of Legal Culture: Networks and Monopolization', *Oxford Journal of Legal Studies*, Vol. 22, No. 3, 2002, pp. 419-443.
117. Forgioni, 2016, *supra* note 3.
118. W. Kovacic, H. Hollman & P. Grant, 'How Does Your Competition Agency Measure Up?', *European Competition Journal*, Vol. 7, No. 1, 2011, p. 28.
119. W. Kovacic, 'Rating the Competition Agencies: What Constitutes Good Performance?', *George Mason Law Review*, Vol. 16, No. 4, 2009, p. 905.
120. Mattos, 2004, *supra* note 110.

Figure 3.1 The Context of Public Consultation No. 02/2016: Main Assumptions about Different Actors

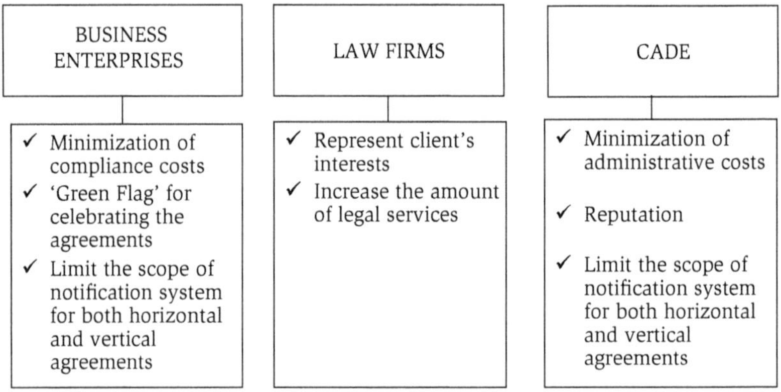

Source: Compiled by the author.

3.5.3 Qualitative Analysis of the Context of Public Consultation No. 02/2016

From a qualitative analysis of Public Consultation No. 02/2016, it is possible to confirm some of the above-mentioned assumptions, mainly in relation to the interests of the business community. The group named as 'business enterprises and their lobby groups' was represented by five contributions. These manifestations were made by companies or associations of highly regulated markets, such as telecom (three contributions) and the oil and chemical industry (two contributions). As assumed, all these contributions aimed at requesting a better limitation on the scope of the notification system of horizontal and vertical agreements. Moreover, some of them suggested the introduction of exemption systems for specific agreements that are already controlled by sector regulators. For example, SindiTelebrasil, the association that represents all telecom companies in Brazil, asked for exemption from the interconnection networks agreements:

> Attention must be given to the General Interconnection Regulation, approved by ANATEL[121] (Resolution No. 410, of July 11, 2005), which establishes the basic rules for the mandatory interconnection networks among telecommunications services. According to this sector regulation, telecommunications operators are obliged to engage in different agreements with each other, in accordance with parameters defined by ANATEL. It should be clear that those contracts foster competition as they enable different companies to have access to a greater amount of infrastructure necessary to provide their services (infrastructure which would be too costly to maintain alone).[...] Thus, to settle the discussion, SindiTelebrasil suggests the inclusion of a legal provision clarifying that regulated contracts

121. ANATEL is the Brazilian National Telecommunications Agency.

> should not be subject to CADE's notification system. This, of course, wouldn't prevent the authorities (both CADE and ANATEL) to open an investigation in cases of abuses of market power.[122]

In contrast with what was initially supposed, the contributions from law firms and the final version of the regulation prepared by CADE indicated some interesting results that require further analysis. Starting from the contributions of law firms, it was possible to identify that the majority of them are big and international and argued, among other issues, in favour of the strict exclusion of vertical agreements from the notification system.

If we carefully assess the reasons that underlined those contributions, we can conclude that no party brought economic-oriented arguments to the discussion. For instance, most of the submissions justified the exclusion of vertical agreements by observing the 'best international practices', such as the policies in the US and the EU. However, they have not considered the different institutional realities and experience when treating competition law and cases related to vertical agreements (as seen in the previous sections, they are very limited in Brazil). Considering the international landscape, national competition agencies design their policies based on similar grounds, for instance, the promotion of market efficiency. This does not mean that antitrust rules will be the same in all jurisdictions, or even that the enforcement of competition law in different countries is free of tensions.[123] Countries are at different stages of implementation of antitrust policies and different policies are required for each of those stages. The pure legal transplant (meaning, the copy of a foreign legislation), without any understanding of local social, political and cultural reality, should not be the main motivation or explanation to a change in the law.

Taking one step further in the analysis of these legal contributions, the suggestion regarding the exclusion of vertical agreements makes sense when analysing it under the public choice theory. As explained in Chapter 2, the main idea of the public choice theory is that an individual's preferences are reflected in the lawmaking process and therefore affect the social welfare. For the purpose of this section it is important to note that the big law firms (including the bar associations and other legal institutions run by those firms) represented around 65% of the total number of contributions and they were the only group to suggest the exclusion of vertical agreements from the *ex ante* notification system. In this case, big law firms may earn more profits from lengthy litigations/investigations raised in the *ex post* enforcement than the simple preparation of filings to the notification system. This can be a reason that explains their submissions to the public consultation.

Several law and economics scholars have pointed out that the private interest of lawyers might seek to shape laws in ways that follow their own interests rather than the public interest.[124] For instance, Roger Van den Bergh pointed out the serious

122. SindiTelebrasil contribution on Public Consultation No. 02/2016, at 4. Free translation.
123. A. Ezrachi, 'Sponge', *Journal of Antitrust Enforcement*, Vol. 5, No. 1, April 2017, pp. 49-75.
124. *See*, for instance, F. Cross, 'The Role of Lawyers in Positive Theories of Doctrinal Evolution', *Emory Law Journal*, Vol. 45, 1996, pp. 523-527.

information asymmetries in the market for professional services, such as legal services.[125] The author explains that, in these markets, there is a high risk of principal-agent problem occurring (in this case, the big law firms instead of representing the interest of clients, might indicate their own interest), therefore affecting an optimal regulation. Wigger, when analysing the change for *ex post* control of agreements in the EU, has also indicated that the ones to profit from the new regime and long-run increased litigations are law companies providing advocacy services to companies.[126]

Taking these manifestations into account, some peculiarities should be highlighted with respect to the final version of the regulation and the technical note prepared by CADE as a result of the public consultation. Even knowing that the first draft of the regulation kept the mandatory notification system for vertical agreements, the final version adopted the suggestions from the lawyers' group, excluding vertical agreements from the *ex ante* control. Table 3.3. shows the summary of the new rules, when compared to the previous resolution.

Table 3.3 Resolution No. 17/2016: Main Changes Proposed by the 'Final Draft'

Public Consultation No. 02/2016 (First Draft)	*Resolution No. 17/2016 (Final Draft)*
General criteria for notification of commercial agreements	
1. Duration equal to, or longer than, 2 years, or, in case of shorter than 2 years or open-ended periods, a notification must be made when such period is reached. 2. Whenever the agreement results in horizontal and/or vertical cooperation and the corresponding risks and results are shared.	1. The duration of the agreement must be of two years or more or, *if they are valid for less than two years or for an indefinite term, CADE must be notified before their renewal, and the continued effectiveness of the agreement for two (2) or more years will depend on CADE's prior approval.* * 2. The agreement must involve horizontal cooperation (between competitors) as well as the sharing of risks and results.
Criteria for notification of horizontal agreements	
The share of the parties to the agreement in the relevant affected market is equal to or higher than, 20%.	The market share criterion was excluded. Only the general criteria will apply.
Criteria for notification of vertical agreements	
There is an obligation that set forth or may result in exclusivity and at least two parties to the agreement hold market shares equal to, or higher than, twenty percent (20%) in the potentially affected relevant markets. *	*The criterion of notification to CADE based on vertical relations between the parties was also excluded.* *

Note: * emphasis added

Source: Compiled by Demarest Advogados, based on Public Consultation No. 02/2016 and Resolution No. 17/2016.

125. Van den Bergh, 2004, *supra* note 115.
126. Wigger, 2004, *supra* note 114, p. 18.

The choice for the exclusion of vertical agreements, however, was also not justified by the authority, either in terms of economic arguments or in terms of the goals and constitutional principles of the country. The only general explanation given by CADE was the following:

> After analysing all the contributions and with *the aim of improving legal provisions,* a final version of the Resolution is found annexed. This final version: [...] (iii) defined as associative contracts only the ones signed among competitors, withdrawing the vertical contracts, *again privileging the best legal provision taking into consideration the goals of the Law.*[127] (Emphasis added)

The expressions 'the aim of improving legal provisions' or the choice of the 'best legal provision taking into consideration the goals of the Law' are rather too general as the main justification for the change in legislation. Moreover, CADE did not explore the main reasoning or rationale adopted in its lawmaking process.[128] In contrast to what was supposed, the technical note did not present the reasons for its decisions in order to justify why the final formulation was in favour of the exclusion of vertical agreements from the notification system. Moreover, there was no explicit reference to welfare-oriented arguments, and there was no explanation of how the new policy trends followed the goals of the law.

The above-mentioned discussion brought by Wigger also identified that the *ex post* control of agreements increases the duties of business people in carefully complying with the competition rules.[129] The author emphasizes that under the *ex post* rule, undertakings must pay special attention to self-assessing their agreements before their consummation, while competition authorities are free from this task.[130] This means that, under the public choice theory, one possible explanation is that the agency aimed at simplifying the legislation in the most convenient way, by simply excluding vertical agreements, as suggested by the big law firms, instead of putting more effort into analysing the most efficient regulation. The exclusion of vertical agreements from the notification system positively impacts the administrative costs to be borne by the authority and therefore justifies even more the change in legislation.

The decision concerning an *ex post* control of vertical agreements is also somehow justified by the need to guarantee good reputation. Usually, the performance of a good agency is evaluated by its substantive results and processes.[131] These results and processes are closely linked to the initiation and judgment of high-profile cases. It means that a case-related activity pattern is the main index that designates the value of an agency. For instance, the *Global Competition Review* publishes an annual ranking of the most recognized antitrust agencies around the world, named as Rating Enforcement, and CADE is often ranked among the leading competition authorities in Latin

---

127. Free Translation from Technical Note No. 1/2016/SGA1/SG/CADE, at 4. Public Consultation No. 02/2016.
128. Kochan explains what is expected from agencies to be accountable during public consultations. *See* D. Kochan, 'The Commenting Power: Agency Accountability Through Public Participation Public Participation', *Oklahoma Law Review*, Vol. 70, No. 3, pp. 601-622.
129. Wigger, 2004, *supra* note 114, p. 17.
130. Wigger, 2004, *supra* note 114, p. 17.
131. Kovacic, 2011, *supra* note 118, p. 905.

America and worldwide.[132] Its criteria are very much related to the number of new mergers and cartel cases. Cases related to vertical agreements are not often taken into account in those rankings. This fact can possibly explain CADE's decision to leave out the vertical agreements from the notification system, as they lead to high administrative costs and do not contribute to the reputation of the agency.[133]

Some literature reaffirms that CADE has as its priority the fight against cartels, especially after the advent of leniency policies.[134] This highlights here the work of Salomão Filho who challenges the way CADE has been defining its enforcement priorities that are 'focused exclusively or primarily on the fight against cartels, forgetting that the enforcement should also be focused on fighting against other abuses of economic power'.[135] The author even mentions that the priority given to leniency policies might have negative effects in the long run, since the information given by business people might not always be trustworthy.

It is worth noting that case-driven measures ignore other non-litigation activities (such as advocacy, quality control mechanisms, transparency, accountability) that should also be taken into account when examining the quality of enforcement and stages of implementation of antitrust law and reputation. However, this is not the focus of this chapter.

The proposed analysis suggests that the choice of favouring *ex post* control of vertical agreements may be explained by interest-driven arguments, since welfare economic oriented arguments, and the goals of the Brazilian law were not necessarily considered in this lawmaking process.

3.6 CONCLUDING REMARKS

From an economic point of view, vertical agreements should be assessed case by case. The legal framework of vertical agreements should not be seen as fixed and immutable, since markets are in constant development, and the economic assessment of these business practices depends to a large extent on the dynamics of a given market. Therefore, it cannot be accepted that the rules in Brazil are simply transplanted from other jurisdictions, disregarding the economic and institutional conditions of the country, as well as its goals and constitutional principles. This is the case because the level of development and maturity of markets such as in the US or in many EU countries are very diverse from the level of the Brazilian one. Consequently, the tolerance of vertical agreements in Brazil should be the object of further reflection.

---

132. For more information, *see* globalcompetitionreview.com/series/rating-enforcement (20/2/2018).
133. Moreover, according to the OECD, 2019, *supra* note 8, p. 38: 'CADE has the autonomy to open investigations into any sector or markets that might potentially harm competition. That said, cartel enforcement, and bid rigging in particular, has been a clear priority since the enactment of the new Law.'
134. *See*, for example, Gonçalves, 2016, *supra* note 75, p. 307.
135. C. Salomão Filho, 'Evolução ou Involução do direito antitruste?', *in* C. Campilongo & R. Pfeiffer (eds), *Evolução do antitruste no Brasil*, São Paulo, Editora Singular, 2018, p. 213.

Chapter 2 showed that vertical agreements can bring to markets one of the most harmful effects of business practices: market foreclosure. It is therefore necessary to discuss the position of CADE with regard to these practices, considering that the authority has been concentrating its resources almost exclusively for cartel investigations, and for the merger control system. The sub-optimal enforcement of vertical agreements in Brazil may encourage in the short and/or in the long-run deleterious effects on social welfare.

This chapter argued that the legal framework in Brazil that excluded vertical agreements from the notification system and favoured the *ex post* control presents several limitations. This chapter demonstrated that these limitations can be observed in different ways. They are expressed through (but not exclusively): (i) CADE's non-consolidated antitrust jurisprudence, and lack of clear parameters for an effect-based assessment of vertical agreements; (ii) CADE's institutional design and its enforcement priorities; (iii) the neglected way in which the goals of the Competition Law in Brazil are being considered in the decision and lawmaking process; and (iv) the incomplete regulatory impact assessment of the current policies.

In more detail, when analysing case law under CADE's *ex post* enforcement, the antitrust jurisprudence is not consolidated enough to guarantee greater levels of legal certainty to parties when assessing their vertical agreements. For instance, it highlighted the case of RPM, where there is no clear rule or clear jurisprudence regarding the topic. Besides, CADE's Tribunal is also not completely sure of whether to define such practice as a per se illegality.

Previous sections showed that one of the goals of competition policies in Brazil is to protect competition and prevent markets from being harmed by agents with a high degree of economic power, by preserving an environment where companies have effective incentives to compete, innovate and attend to consumers' demands. The use of the presumption of illegality in RPM cases does not necessarily respect these goals, and this happens to be because RPM can bring economic efficiencies to markets, such as solving the double markup problem, preventing free-riding, or reducing transaction costs. These economic efficiencies can help to create a level playing field among competitors that are intrinsically expressed in the constitutional principles, and therefore should be carefully assessed by the Brazilian authority in the analysis of any vertical cases, even when it involves price restrictions.

Moreover, CADE relies heavily on settlements. The downsides of settlement agreements are also the reduction of legal certainty in the marketplace and the slow development of the jurisprudence in Brazil towards the economic assessment of vertical agreements. With the settlements, there is no effect-based assessment and/or decision published by CADE and legal cases are not reviewed by national courts.

Even considering all the achievements of the authority in the last decade, mostly in terms of merger control and cartel policies, CADE still fails in defining objective parameters for assessing vertical agreements (including the definition of whether some practices are per se illegal or not) and also has not enough staff to do such work (the authority counts only five people to assess all the antitrust cases other than cartels and mergers). This means that CADE has favoured *ex post* enforcement with a lack of staff to do so. Actually, nowadays, the trust in CADE's precedents has become a real problem for business people. In this sense, the enactment of guidelines could be a good example of measures aimed at stabilizing and improving this legal environment.

This discussion leads us to another important topic of this chapter: the identification of the self-interest of relevant actors as a possible explanation to the enactment of Resolution No. 17/2016. As CADE did not include in its policy assessment document any reference to the goals of the country, nor did it give clear reasoning to the choice of this specific regulation, one could hypothesize that the exclusion of vertical agreements from the notification system has been based on private interests of relevant agents. Moreover, Schuartz's theory of 'deconstitutionalization' of the Brazilian competition rules is somehow confirmed. This is because the application of rule of reason in vertical cases seems to be neglected and the lawmaking process and the implementation of competition law have not been observing the constitutional principles of the country.

All these issues embrace two main problems to be overcome in the country. The first one is related to the unstable learning process of the enforcer and business community with regard to the assessment of vertical restraints that leads to great legal uncertainty. The second one is the prevalence of private-interest grounds in the lawmaking process. Both problems lead to sub-optimal regulations and lower levels of antitrust enforcement.[136]

For these reasons, a comparative law and economics analysis makes sense. We started this chapter indicating that both Brazil and the EU passed through a similar change in policy applicable to vertical restraints: from an *ex ante* notification system of agreements to an *ex post* control of restrictive practices, although with some crucial differences. The comparison between the two legal systems, specifically on policies applicable to vertical restraints, is one of the contributions of this book.

Therefore, the following Chapter 4 will describe in further detail the EU policies. Afterwards, Chapter 5 will identify the enforcement costs for each legal system. The comparative law and economics analysis of information, incentive and administrative costs will allow a deeper understanding of policy design and enforcement among countries with different institutional realities and stages of implementation of antitrust law.

136. I briefly highlight here the current discussion on the Federal Senate's decision of the new Commissioners to take over CADE's Tribunal. From June to October 2019 CADE's activities were suspended because of the uncertainty of the nominations, which resulted in more than 80 (eighty) transactions paralysed, including mergers, and other joint ventures. According to information released by the press, the late nominations of CADE's Commissioners were due to friction between the Executive and the Legislative Branches. For more information, *see* J. Basile, 'Vagas no Cade viram moeda de troca', *Jornal Valor Econômico*, 6 August 2019.

CHAPTER 4

Vertical Agreement Policy and Enforcement in the European Union

Historically, Regulation 1/2003 replaced the centralized *ex ante* notification system of vertical agreements to a decentralized ex post control of these business practices in the European Union. Important lessons can be drawn from the European experience in favouring the *ex post* control of vertical agreements, from their consistent jurisprudence, to their successful Vertical Block Exemption Regulation. The aim of this study is to explore the legal framework and case law in Europe when it comes to enforcing anticompetitive vertical agreements. The chapter investigates the evolution of the legal rules in the EU under a historical perspective from the period of 1957 – when the internal market was established – until the late 1990s; the current rules related to vertical agreements; and the challenges that law enforcers might face in the upcoming years, including the different outcomes of case law across the EU Member States when it comes to cases involving digital economies.

4.1 INTRODUCTION: THE CHOICE OF THE EU IN THE COMPARATIVE STUDY

This book aims at identifying an optimal mix of antitrust policies oriented to vertical agreements. The previous chapters explained that the regulation of vertical agreements constitutes one of the most animated disputes in competition law. This is because vertical agreements can bring efficiencies to markets (in the form of cost savings to companies) but can also excite anticompetitive practices (e.g., market foreclosure). Because of this regulatory dilemma, countries have different approaches towards this topic. In this book, a comparative law and economics analysis of antitrust policies in Brazil and in the EU was conducted. This specific chapter aims at analysing the evolution of the EU competition law related to vertical agreements, as well as its current challenges.

Several reasons encouraged this choice of the EU policies as a framework in this comparative law and economics study. First and more generally, Brazil has historically followed the EU civil law legal traditions.[1] Second, and now referring specifically to competition law, both legal systems passed through a change in policies oriented to vertical agreements: from an *ex ante* notification of agreements to an *ex post* control of anticompetitive practices, although with some crucial differences. Briefly speaking, Chapter 3 discussed the change in the Brazilian Competition Law oriented to vertical agreements. It showed that the recent Resolution No. 17/2016 removed vertical agreements from the notification system, leaving the enforcement of vertical restraints in Brazil solely dependent on *ex post* control. Fourteen years before, EU Regulation 1/2003 installed the *ex post* control of vertical contracts putting an end to the centralized notification system among EU Member States. As it will be explained in this chapter, in contrast with Brazil, in the EU, the change from an *ex ante* to an *ex post* control happened after forty years of having a notification system of agreements, and the reform was complemented by Block Exemption Regulations and Guidelines to help business people self-assessing the potential anticompetitive effects of their contracts.

Third, the political, social and economic reality in Brazil can be directly compared to some less developed EU countries, e.g., CEE countries. This means that the challenges encountered by these jurisdictions, mainly related to late development of market economies and late implementation of competition law – and the way they are overcoming them – can also be considered comparable to the Brazilian reality.

Lastly, a lot of new facts and discussions have been happening in the EU in relation to vertical agreements and it is worth having a closer look. The new realities of a more globalized, technology-driven, and digitalized competitive environment may suggest that the current rules adopted by the European Commission are outdated and require adjustment. The following years will be dynamic in the discussion of online and offline vertical agreements, since more enforcement action is expected regarding sales restrictions and digital conduct. Moreover, the VBER is now under review,[2] and the Geo-Blocking Regulation 302/2018 is also applicable. The recent attempts of the Commission in discussing the competitive outcomes of digital economies, as part of the 'Digital Single Market Strategy', certainly broaden the views on the new forms of market power that can be transferred to other countries, such as Brazil.[3]

The chapter is organized into four main sections, apart from this introduction and the concluding remarks. Section 4.2 presents the evolution of policies oriented to vertical agreements/vertical restraints in the EU in the period of 1957 – when the internal market was established – until the late 1990s. The section briefly describes the origins of antitrust policy in Europe, the Council Regulation 17/1962 that introduced the centralized notification system of agreements, and the first sector exemptions for vertical agreements. Subsequently, section 4.3 describes the modernization of the EU

1. The law in Brazil law was mainly influenced by Roman law and the law of contemporary European countries, such as Portugal, France, Italy and Germany. G. Angelozzi, *História do Direito no Brasil*, Rio de Janeiro, Freitas Bastos Editora, 2009.
2. The current Vertical Block Exemption Regulation (Commission Regulation 330/2010), will expire in 2022.
3. European Commission, *A Digital Single Market Strategy for Europe*, 2015.

competition policies introduced by Regulation 1/2003. Section 4.4 identifies the main components (pillars) that made this legal reform possible. Then, section 4.5 focuses on the current challenges of EU competition law and policies to enforce anticompetitive vertical agreements. Two main challenges are identified: a substantive one related to the uncertainties on the outcomes/effects of digital economies in vertical relations, and an institutional one linked to the different levels of enforcement and institutional designs among the Member States.

4.2 HISTORY AND FRAMEWORK OF EU COMPETITION LAW

The legal framework of competition policies in the EU is based on the treaties which have further developed over the years, as a result of legal amendments and successive negotiations.[4] The evolution of competition policies oriented to vertical agreements in Europe allows us to make some interesting reflections. History has a great impact on the outcomes of the EU competition policies, and its deep understanding might help us to have a 'solid view on the future',[5] by predicting and proposing adequate normative discussions.

If we look at the origins of competition law in the EU, it is possible to say that the initial movements started before the 1957 Rome Treaty, meaning before the growth of the European Economic Community (EEC).[6] Over the decades, several main events have influenced the fundamentals and the framework of the EU antitrust policies. First, one can highlight the earlier national rules throughout Europe that were frequently intended to promote orderly competition and often pre-dated the Second World War.[7] Second, influenced by the emergence of the post-war economic order of Germany, the German Ordoliberal school which promoted the principle of free competition.[8] Third, the development of antitrust laws in other jurisdictions, such as the Sherman Act in the US. Fourth, after the Second World War, the evolution of national sources, such as the 1957 German Act against restraints of competition (*Gesätz gegen Wettbewerbsbeschrankungen*). Finally, one can highlight other sources that formed part of efforts of market integration in Europe, notably the fight against cartels and the regulation on merger control in the European Coal and Steel Community Treaty, also called the Paris Agreement, in 1951.[9]

Considering these influences, the competition regime in Europe was introduced to eliminate trade restriction in the internal market. The challenge for law enforcement at that time was massive since the Commission had to start from scratch, a policy in a

4. W. Souter, *Coherence in EU Competition Law*, Oxford, Oxford University Press, 2016, p. 31.
5. W. Schreuders, 'Welcome in Brussels on the Rhine: A Positive Perspective on the EU', *in* M. Faure, W. Schreuders & L. Visscher (eds), *Don't Take It Seriously: Essays in Law and Economics in Honours of Roger Van den Bergh*, Cambridge, Intersentia, 2018.
6. The Treaty of Rome was signed on 25 March 1957 by Belgium, France, Italy, Luxembourg, the Netherlands and West Germany and corresponds to the creation of the European Economic Community (EEC).
7. Souter, 2016, *supra* note 4, p. 34.
8. *See* R. Van der Bergh, *Comparative Competition Law and Economics*, Cheltenham, Edward Elgar, 2017, p. 105.
9. Souter, 2016, *supra* note 4, p. 34.

continental scale that aimed at integrating different domestic economies into a single economic area and developing competition as the major driver of the economic order.[10]

Because this book is focused on policies oriented to vertical agreements, this section will present a closer look to the application and implementation of Council Regulation 17/1962, as well as to its consequences for the competition within markets. Actually, the Council Regulation 17/1962 was the first regulation that oriented and brought specific antitrust norms to the Members States in relation to commercial agreements, both the horizontal and vertical ones. It was also the first regulation to address the centralized enforcement powers on the EU level. Regulation 17/1962 was created to prevent restrictive arrangements between producers and distributors from harming the process of market integration and/or even promote the exclusion of new rivals that might both enhance competition and generate pressure to reduce prices.[11] This regulation created an enforcement system that the Commission has applied for almost forty years without significant changes.

Regulation 17/1962 gave the monopoly to the European Commission in assessment of the potential anticompetitive effects of vertical agreements and therefore the monopoly in granting exemptions. According to Articles 85 and 87 of the EEC Treaty, the exemption of agreements was granted solely by the European Commission, based on a system of prior notification.[12] Actually, Article 85(1) (current Article 101 TFEU) provided for a prohibition on trade-related agreements that may have the purpose or effect of preventing, restricting or distorting competition. This kind of agreements could be exempted by Article 85(3) whenever they generated procompetitive outcomes, such as efficiency gains.

Consten-Grundig[13] was the first case of vertical restraints under the application of Article 85. Briefly speaking, the case discussed the validity of *Grundig's* system of absolute territorial protection in the market for electronic goods, that used to bar all *Grundig* purchasers, German and foreign, from exporting or re-exporting its products.[14] The Court of Justice decided that:

> an agreement between producer and distributor which might tend to restore the national divisions in trade between Member States might be such as to frustrate the most fundamental objections of the Community. The Treaty, whose preamble and content aim at abolishing the barriers between States, and which in several

10. European Commission, *White Paper on Modernisation of the Rules Implementing Articles 85 and 86 of the EC Treaty*, 1999.
11. European Commission, *Green Paper on Vertical Restraints in EC Competition Policy*, 1997, p. 2.
12. One interesting fact is that recent historical research holds that the text of the old Article 85 reflected both French and German thinking: the French thinking in respect to the decentralization and their views on legal exceptions; and the German on regarding the exemption system and centralization in the hands of the Commission. For example, *see* Souter, 2016, *supra* note 4; S. Pérez & S. Scheur, 'The Evolution of the Law on Article 85 and 86 EEC: Ordoliberalism and Its Keynesian Challenge', *in* K. K. Patel & H. Schweitzer (eds), *The Historical Foundations of EU Competition Law*, Oxford, Oxford University Press, 2013.
13. Joined Cases 56 and 58/64 *Établissements Consten S.à.R.L. and Grundig Verkaufs- GmbH v. Commission* (1966) ECR 429.
14. A detailed history and analysis of the case can be found at L. Ebb, 'The *Grundig-Consten* Case Revisited: Judicial Harmonization of National Law and Treaty Law in the Common Market', *University of Pennsylvania Law Review*, Vol. 115, No. 6, 1967, pp. 855-889.

> provisions gives evidence of a stern attitude with regard to their reappearance, could not allow undertakings to reconstruct such barriers. Article 85(1) [now Article 101(1) TFEU] is designed to pursue this aim, even in the case of agreements between undertakings placed at different levels in the economic process.[15]

The *Grundig* case guided the decisions and position of the European Commission in the following decades in this topic. In fact, this worry related to keeping uniform and equilibrated conditions in the internal market led the Commission to over-enforce vertical restraints. This extreme concern in fighting against vertical restraints was not always in line with their potential harmful nature in a more objective economic sense,[16] but it could be explained by the influence of the Ordoliberal school of thought.[17]

Moreover, several historical, institutional and cultural reasons justified the choice of a centralized notification system of agreements. By the time Regulation 17/1962 entered into force, the Commission was in the best position (i) to access anticompetitive conducts; (ii) to ensure the comprehensive interpretation of Article 85; (iii) to ensure the necessary information for NCAs; and (iv) to guarantee legal certainty to undertakings.

Actually, in the 1960s, only six countries were part of the Community (Belgium, France, Italy, Luxembourg, the Netherlands and West Germany) and therefore the Commission could easily guarantee the correct implementation of the existing Regulation. In the 1970s and 1980s, countries such as Denmark, Ireland, United Kingdom (UK),[18] Greece,[19] Portugal and Spain,[20] and later in the 1990s Austria, Finland and Sweden also joined the Community,[21] some of which had a background of dictatorial periods, with no experience whatsoever in enforcing competition law. Because most of these countries had limited or even no experience in applying competition policies, the centralized authorization system showed itself to be essential and effective in setting up a 'culture of competition'.[22]

However, as an unintended side effect of the centralized authorization and notification system, the eventual result was the submission of thousands of agreements for consideration by the Commission services. As a result of that, from the 1960s until the 1980s, several measures were taken by the Commission to reduce notifications and/or speed up the assessments: starting from comfort letters, then *de minimis* notice, and the creation of sectoral block exemptions. In more detail, the Commission first started giving comfort letters to companies. However, the undertakings were still not completely covered by legal certainty as they did not give a formal 'green flag' to the proposed agreements. With regard to the *de minimis* notice, in the *Völk v. Vervaecke* case,[23] the Commission declared that, in the scope of Article 85, a threshold of 5%

15. *Consten-Grundig v. Commission* [1966] ECR 429, p. 340.
16. *See* discussion on the economic analysis of vertical agreements in Chapter 2.
17. Souter, 2016, *supra* note 4, p. 38.
18. Treaty of Accession of Denmark, Ireland and the United Kingdom (1972).
19. Treaty of Accession of Greece (1979).
20. Treaty of Accession of Spain and Portugal (1985).
21. Treaty concerning the accession of Austria, Finland and Sweden to the European Union of Accession (1994).
22. European Commission (1999), *supra* note 10, paragraph 4.
23. *Franz Völk v. S.P.R.L. Ets J. Vervaecke* [1969] Case No. 5/69.

market share (and a turnover threshold of 20 million accounting units) should be used to determine the scope for agreements of minor importance. It means that companies that had such a market share did not have to notify their agreements to the Commission anymore.

Another important measure to decrease the number of notifications was the creation of block exemptions. The core idea was that if an agreement fulfilled all the conditions in a particular block exemption, it was automatically cleared, and therefore did not have to be notified. These block exemptions were issued for standard types of agreements, notably (i) vertical agreements, such as exclusive distribution agreements or exclusive purchasing agreements,[24] respectively licensing and franchising;[25] (ii) sectoral agreements, e.g., motor vehicle distribution[26] and insurance;[27] as well as (iii) horizontal arrangements, e.g., specialization agreements and research and development agreements.[28] It is worth noting that some of these exemptions have been the subject of intensive industry lobbying.[29] The various block exemptions, however, were originally highly specific. Undertakings were forced to choose a particular business model (specific contract) and stick to that in order to obtain an exemption under the competition rules, even if for commercial reasons a mixed form or even a wholly new format would have been preferred.

By the late 1990s, fifteen Member States were part of the Community, which meant eleven different languages and more than 350 million people having to respect those Treaties.[30] Indeed, the Community grew significantly and the role of the Commission in guaranteeing uniform conditions in the internal market also changed. Moreover, the world became globalized, speeding up the internationalization of the European economy and therefore all the transactions (including the number of commercial contracts). This reality brought into question the procedural rules from the 1960s.

24. Commission Regulation (EEC) No. 1983/83 of 22 June 1983 concerning exclusive distribution agreements, OJ 1983, L173/1; Commission Regulation (EEC) No. 1984/83 of 22 June 1983 concerning exclusive purchasing agreements, OJ 1983, L173/55.
25. Commission Regulation (EEC) No. 2349/84 of 23 July 1984 concerning patent licensing agreements, OJ 1984, L219/15; Commission Regulation (EEC) No. 4087/88 of 30 November 1988 concerning franchising agreements, OJ 1988, L359/46; Commission Regulation (EEC) No. 556/89 of 30 November 1988 concerning know-how licensing agreements, OJ 1989, L61/1.
26. Commission Regulation (EEC) No. 123/85 of 12 December 1984 concerning motor vehicle distribution and servicing agreements, OJ 1985, L15/16.
27. Council Regulation (EEC) No. 1534/91 of 31 May 1991 on the application of Article 85(3) of the Treaty to certain categories of agreements, decisions and concerted practices in the insurance sector, OJ 1991, L143/1.
28. Commission Regulation (EEC) No. 417/85 concerning specialization agreements, OJ 1985, L53/1; Commission Regulation (EEC) No. 418/85 of 19 December 1984 concerning research and development agreements, OJ 1985, L53/5.
29. *See*, for instance, discussion of Chapter 7 in C. R. Swaak, *European Community Law and the Automobile Industry*, Deventer, Wolters Kluwer, 1999.
30. Information given by the European Commission, 1999, *supra* note 10, paragraph 5.

4.3 THE MODERNIZATION OF EU COMPETITION LAW

Several decades of notification system proved to be somehow effective to create a 'culture of competition' among the Member States, especially considering the different historical and political backgrounds among them. However, several reasons encouraged the revision of Regulation 17/1962, and new rules started to come up as an option.[31] In the late 1990s, there were two main initiatives from the Commission in respect of evaluating competition policies. The first one was the 1997 *Green Paper on Vertical Restraints in EU Competition Policy*[32] (hereinafter called the 'Green Paper') and the second one was the 1999 *White Paper on Modernization of the Rules Implementing Articles 85 and 86 of the EC Treaty* (hereinafter called the 'White Paper').[33]

The first one focused exclusively on policies oriented to vertical agreements, while the second one focused on the modernization of competition policy in Europe, including the need to revise the notification system of agreements and the monopoly of the Commission in analysing antitrust cases. Moreover, the documents also showed alternative policies to guarantee the enforcement of vertical restraints that - although not applied in the EU - could be implemented in other countries. The following subsections intend to show the view of the European Commission in deciding on new policies for vertical agreements, taking into consideration the goals of the Community and the self-interest of parties. The analysis and the outcome of these policy-evaluation documents are very rich in terms of setting the grounds of this comparative analysis and later normative conclusions.

4.3.1 The Green Paper and the White Paper

The Green Paper first identified the progress that had been made in the EU during the 1980s and 1990s in respect of *de minimis* notice and other block exemptions. The Green Paper acknowledges the advantages of the notification system, such as: the guarantee of full economic assessment of those agreements, the better promotion of market integration, the consistency among the decisions, and the legal certainty offered to business people.[34] The economic assessment of vertical agreements was also included in the document. The Green Paper recognized that some legal and procedural changes needed to be considered, not only because of the growth of the Community and the rise in administrative burdens but also to enable the Commission to concentrate on more severe antitrust cases.

The Green Paper mentions that the process of globalization and market expansion changes the dynamics of markets,[35] making contracts among business more complex in a scenario where technology starts playing a new role in the market

31. In the late 1990s, several scholars started to point out the need of a reform of policies oriented to vertical restraints. I highlight the work of B. Hawk, 'System Failure: Vertical Restraints and EC Competition Law', *Common Market Law Review*, Vol. 32, No. 4, 1995, pp. 937-989.
32. European Commission, 1999, *supra* note 10.
33. European Commission, 1999, *supra* note 10.
34. European Commission, 1997, *supra* note 11, Chapter III.
35. European Commission, 1997, *supra* note 11, paragraphs 244-247.

dynamics.[36] The document also identifies several pitfalls in the former policy applicable to verticals. It identifies, for instance, that the existing block exemptions did not contain any market share limits to address the market power of undertakings and they were rather too strict, as a high percentage of vertical agreements that could not bring any anticompetitive concerns to market was outside their scope.[37]

As alternative policies brought by the Green Paper, one can highlight the adoption of wider block exemptions (wider interpretations), or even more focused block exemptions (covering other types of contracts), in order to lower the number of notifications to be assessed by the Commission.[38] The market share limits in block exemptions and other objective parameters for the application of Article 85(1) were also presented as alternative policies. In this context, a couple of years later, not only Regulation 2790/99[39] – the 1999 VBER – but also the White Paper was published, incorporating somehow the concerns brought by the Green Paper and also adding some new insights to the reform that was about to happen.

With regard to the White Paper, succinctly, the document presents three main justifications for the legal reform. First, as anticipated before, the growth of the Community and the globalization of the market economies. According to the Commission, within the decades of implementation of Regulation 17/1962, the NCAs had also slowly acquired better knowledge, and more than that, they developed some infrastructure and human and legal resources in order to be able to take action in their territories. The 1999 White Paper describes that by 1998, there were more than a thousand agents working for the national authorities of all Member States, as opposed to around one hundred and fifty officials in the Commission.[40]

Second, the Commission also identified that there was a need to prioritize cartels and abuse of dominant position. According to the White Paper, the enlargement of the EU led to an increase in restrictive practices and in the abuse of dominant positions that needed to be tackled, especially considering those cartels in concentrated markets and in markets that were about to be liberalized.[41] Even knowing that the notification system was necessary to acquire the knowledge required to assess anticompetitive practices, the Commission ended up shifting its attention from other important cases. For example, from 1988 to 1998, only 13% of the cases were ex officio investigations and about 6% of the cases were actually closed,[42] since most of the staff were focused on handling a large number of notifications.

Third, the high administrative burden was also highlighted by the Commission. The notification and authorization system – the way it was proposed by Regulation 17/1962 – created over the years a burden both to the Commission and to business

36. European Commission, 1997, *supra* note 11, paragraphs 223-225.
37. F. Wijckmans & F. Tuytschaever, *Vertical Agreements in EU Competition Law,* 3rd ed., Oxford, Oxford University Press, 2018, p. 17.
38. Wijckmans & Tuytschaever, 2018, *supra* note 37, *see* Chapter VIII.
39. The Commission adopted the block exemption on Vertical Agreements and Concerted Practices on 22 December 1999. The Regulation entered into force on 1 January 2000, and the new block exemption conferred by it applies with effect from 1 June 2000.
40. European Commission, 1999, *supra* note 10, paragraph 44.
41. European Commission, 1999, *supra* note 10, paragraph 45.
42. European Commission, 1999, *supra* note 10, paragraph 44.

people and their legal advisors. This burden was reflected, for instance, in the drafting and preparation of notifications, the collection of information requested in the forms, and the analysis itself of all those cases by the Commission.[43]

Having this background, the White Paper's main suggestion was that the Commission should face a reform based on the decentralization of competition rules, and the termination of the notification system of agreements. Under a legal exemption system, vertical restraints are valid under certain conditions defined by law. There were, of course, other alternative policies presented by the White Paper, such as: (i) changing the interpretation of Article 85 to a rule of reason approach; (ii) decentralizing the application of Article 85 to national authorities (but keeping the notification) - and, in this case, it would not reduce the total number of notifications but rather redistribute them among the national authorities; (iii) broadening the waiver of the notifications; (iv) simplifying procedures by, for example, abolishing the requirement to translate into all the languages, among others.[44] These alternative policies would undoubtedly have attacked some of the issues identified by the Commission; however, other difficulties would have remained in place, such as the lack of resources of the Commission and the non-focus on dealing with the most serious restriction cases. For these reasons, the reform brought by Regulation 1/2003 kept the main suggestions of the White Paper, that is, the end of the notification system for vertical agreements and the decentralization of competition law.

In May 2004, Regulation 1/2003 came into effect in all Member States (and therefore is hereinafter called '2004 Reform'). It replaced the old centralized *ex ante* authorization system of commercial agreements (including vertical agreements) to a decentralized *ex post* control.[45] It means that companies do not have to notify their agreements and wait for the approval from the Commission but have to self-assess their arrangements instead. The Reform also changed the allocation of responsibilities, and the Commission somehow lost its monopoly in applying former Article 85 and in granting exemptions to the agreements. Actually, Article 3 of Regulation 1/2003 lays down the responsibilities to the national authorities to apply Articles 101 and 102 (formerly Articles 81, 82 and, before that, Articles 85 and 86) of the TFEU alongside their national rules.[46] It means that the decentralization not only needed a coherent

43. European Commission, 1999, *supra* note 10, paragraph 76.
44. For more details on the alternative policies, *see* European Commission, 1999, *supra* note 10, paragraphs 56-68.
45. Council Regulation (EC) No. 1/2003 of 16 December 2002 on the implementation of the rules on competition laid down in Articles 81 and 82 of the Treaty.
46. Article 101 TFEU (ex Article 81 TEC). *1. The following shall be prohibited as incompatible with the internal market: all agreements between undertakings, decisions by associations of undertakings and concerted practices which may affect trade between Member States and which have as their object or effect the prevention, restriction or distortion of competition within the internal market, and in particular those which: (a) directly or indirectly fix purchase or selling prices or any other trading conditions; (b) limit or control production, markets, technical development, or investment; (c) share markets or sources of supply; (d) apply dissimilar conditions to equivalent transactions with other trading parties, thereby placing them at a competitive disadvantage; (e) make the conclusion of contracts subject to acceptance by the other parties of supplementary obligations which, by their nature or according to commercial usage, have no connection with the subject of such contracts. 2. Any agreements or decisions prohibited pursuant to this Article shall*

implementation of competition rules among Member States and their national authorities but also close cooperation among them. It should be noted that 1 May 2004 also marked a shift in the EU's history since ten new Member States entered the Community on that occasion: Cyprus, Czech Republic, Estonia, Hungary, Latvia, Lithuania, Malta, Poland, Slovenia, and Slovakia. Consequently, Regulation 1/2003 turned out to be a requirement for these countries' accession to the EU.[47]

4.3.2 The Context of the EU Modernization of Competition Law: A Public Choice Perspective

As discussed in Chapter 2, political economy discussions allow us to have an alternative look at the European experience when regulating vertical agreements. This section aims at reviewing some literature that explains the context in which the 2004 Reform of EU Competition Law happened. It questions, for instance, the main argument of the White Paper regarding the workload of the Commission with the notifications of agreements. It discusses the possibility that private interests also may have justified part of the reform.[48] For instance, it shows that, contrary to appearances, the Commission has benefited from the decentralization and has not lost its central position in the development and implementation of European competition policies. This is not necessarily the case for other stakeholders, such as NCAs.

As we have discussed in the previous subsection, the Commission's justification for the 2004 Reform was a combination of overload of the notification system and a need for simplification to adapt to the enlargement of the EU. From the viewpoint of the Commission, the notification system was also ineffective in identifying anticompetitive conduct since anticompetitive agreements were not being notified anyway, but instead left as secret.[49] Indeed, one of the main arguments of the White Paper was that the Commission's resources could be better spent on more severe antitrust cases. This is the case because the Commission was overloaded with the notifications of agreements and the end of such a policy – together with the decentralization – permitted the

be automatically void. 3. The provisions of paragraph 1 may, however, be declared inapplicable in the case of: – any agreement or category of agreements between undertakings, – any decision or category of decisions by associations of undertakings, – any concerted practice or category of concerted practices, which contributes to improving the production or distribution of goods or to promoting technical or economic progress, while allowing consumers a fair share of the resulting benefit, and which does not: (a) impose on the undertakings concerned restrictions which are not indispensable to the attainment of these objectives; (b) afford such undertakings the possibility of eliminating competition in respect of a substantial part of the products in question.

47. B. M. Chiritoiu, 'Convergence Within the European Competition Network: Legislative Harmonization and Enforcement Priorities', *in* A. Almăşan & P. Whelan (eds), *The Consistent Application of EU Competition Law: Substantive and Procedural Challenges*, Cham, Springer International Publisher, 2017, p. 5.
48. In Chapter 3 there is a more extensive discussion (both on literature review and analysis) of public choice and antitrust, in which Brazil is taken as a case study.
49. P. Nicolaides, 'Development of a System for Decentralised Enforcement of EC Competition Policy', *Intereconomics*, Vol. 37, No. 1, 2002, pp. 42-44. *See also* J. Venit, 'Brave New World: The Modernization and Decentralization of Enforcement under Article 81 and 82 of the EC Treaty', *Common Market Law Review*, Vol. 40, No. 3, 2003, pp. 545-580.

European authority to focus its resources on cartels and other more severe antitrust cases. The recital 3 of Regulation 1/2003 indicated that the notification of agreements 'hampers application of the Community competition rules by the courts and competition authorities of the Member States, and the system of notification it involves prevents the Commission from concentrating its resources on curbing the most serious infringements'.

However, some statistics show that the number of notifications of agreements, by the time Regulation 1/2003 entered into force, was not that significant. Alan Riley suggests that the notification was already an 'irrelevant procedure with marginal impact on the enforcement of EU competition law' and therefore there was almost no cost to the Commission in abandoning this policy.[50] Indeed, even though in the late 1960s the Commission was receiving more than 30,000 notifications a year, this amount was substantially reduced by the introduction of comfort letters, block exemptions (mainly the 1999 Block Exemption Regulation), and notices. For instance, only seventy-one agreements were actually notified in 2003, before the new regulation entered into force.[51]

Actually, Phedon Nicolaides suggested that if the work overload was indeed the main problem for an effective enforcement of competition policies in the EU, then 'an increase in the Commission's resources would have been the first-best solution'.[52] Damien Neven, argued that the change in systems was not necessary, but, instead, the Commission should have decided to use its resources more efficiently in its internal working process, since the number of individual exemption notifications was naturally going to be reduced with the changes to the substantive law (block exemption regulations for vertical restraints).[53] Neven also stressed that the Commission's notification system was also very costly due to the time spent in several informal lengthy such as unnecessary pre-notification discussions with firms.[54]

Riley also supported the argument that the end of notification system of agreements was not necessary, and suggested that dealing with one-hundred or so notifications a year would be less burdensome to the Commission than dealing with the

50. A. Riley, 'EC Antitrust Modernization: The Commission Does Very Nicely – Thank You! Part One: Regulation 1 and the Notification Burden', *European Competition Law Review*, Vol. 11, 2003a, p. 604.
51. According to the *XXXIII Report on Competition Policy 2003*, 216 agreements were notified in 1998, followed by 162 in 1999, 101 in 2000, 94 in 2001 and 101 in 2002.
52. Nicolaides, 2002, *supra* note 49, p. 44.
53. D. Neven, 'Removing the Notification of Agreements: Some Consequences of Ex-post Monitoring', *in* A. Bogdandy, P. Mavroidis & Y. Meny (eds), *European Integration and International Cooperation: Studies in International Economic Law in Honour of Claus-Dieter Ehlermann*, The Hague, Kluwer Law International, 2002. In this paper, Neven also argued that the merger task force was doing a good job, while the staff combatting anticompetitive behaviour have been frustrated in carrying out their tasks. He also mentioned in his paper that the German Federal Cartel Office have used a system of prior notification for more than forty years without having management problems.
54. According to Neven, almost 70% of all notifications passed through a pre-notification discussion with the authority. *See* D. Neven, P. Papandropoulos & P. Seabright, *Trawling for Minnows: European Competition Policy and Agreements Between Firms*, London, Center for Economic and Policy Research (CEPR), 1998, p. 112.

cooperation and supervision of Regulation 1/2003.[55] Indeed, the decentralization unsurprisingly created huge transaction costs related to the coordination of responsibilities, an item that was not considered in the official policy evaluation documents.[56] This argument is particularly important considering that Regulation 1/2003 is equally applied to countries with different economic and political backgrounds, different experience in applying competition law, different levels of resources,[57] and cultural diversities, which inevitably raises such coordination costs.

This political economy reading on the 2004 Reform suggests that the Commission had the interest of ending the notification system of agreements so that the officials could focus on the more high-profile cases (and therefore save the administrative costs of the notification).

As part of this interest-driven discussion, other authors demonstrate how the Commission has benefited from the 2004 Reform. According to David Gerber, the agenda of the Competition Directorate (DG Comp) was a central point in the modernization analysis, since it had developed the proposals and lead the implementation of it.[58] Some commentators indicate that (because of self-interests) the Commission did not lose its central role in the enforcement of EU competition law, and that the 'decentralization' can somehow be questioned. Indicated here are some of the relevant supporters of this view. Oliver Budzinski and Arndt Christiansen argued that the competence allocation in the EU competition policy brought by Regulation 1/2003 was not clear or welfare-enhancing since self-interested actors had an important role in shaping the policy reform.[59] Their point was that when the competence allocation is not clear in a multilevel system of competition policies, there is more space for the self-interest of agents to prevail. The authors argued that the vagueness and lack of clarity of the delimitation of competences between the European and national levels were mainly ignored by the reform and therefore 'brought a rather complicated mixture of explicit decentralization (of enforcement) and more implicit centralization (of substantial rules)'.[60]

They identify, for instance, that not only the Commission but also the European Courts (Court of First Instance and Court of Justice) historically have enjoyed this role in the law-and decision-making process, and that competition law has provided them with status and power.[61] Therefore, the vagueness of the 2004 Reform in relation to the

55. Riley, 2003a, *supra* note 50, p. 615.
56. For instance, no cost-benefit analysis was published by the Commission as policy evaluation documents.
57. Riley's analysis provides an insight into the inadequacy resources, knowledge and independence of many of the NCAs and the associated courts. *See* Riley, 2003a, *supra* note 50.
58. D. Gerber, 'Modernizing Competition Law: A Developmental Perspective', *European Competition Law Review*, Vol. 4, 2001, p. 125.
59. O. Budzinski & A. Christiansen, 'Competence Allocation in the EU Competition Policy System as an Interest-Driven Process', *Journal of Public Policy*, Vol. 25, No. 3, 2005, pp. 313-337.
60. Budzinski & Christiansen, 2005, *supra* note 59, pp. 318-319.
61. This argument is also brought by Gerber, 2001, *supra* note 58, p. 126.

competence allocation could be seen as an opportunity to not change this scenario or take this centralized power from them.[62]

The Commission, however, was not the only stakeholder that benefited from the change in policy in Europe. According to Angela Wigger, law firms providing antitrust advocacy to the undertakings also profited from the decentralized *ex post* control of Regulation 1/2003.[63] Indeed, with the 2004 Reform, companies have to privately self-assess their agreements (to minimize antitrust risks and to know better how to deal with competitors) and private damage actions were also facilitated.[64] It means that law companies became extremely important in this context, since they are the ones who will measure the antitrust risks of potential restrictive agreements.[65] It is worth remembering that with the end of the notification system of agreements, parties lost part of their legal certainty, and therefore have additional responsibilities in this process.

When it comes to the national authorities in Europe, the effects of the 2004 Reform were not all positive, since they now face greater responsibilities (and therefore costs) and, at the same time, too little freedom when it comes to defying their rules and legal proceedings. In this context, Stephen indicates that instead of 'decentralizing' the EU competition policy, Regulation 1/2003 'Europeanized' the national antitrust regimes and extended the powers of the Commission. The author presented four main arguments that support his claim.[66] First, Article 3's provision marginalizes national law by saying that all the national authorities should apply Articles 101 and 102 TFEU, whatever their current legal framework.[67] Second, Regulation 1/2003 provided a system of close monitoring, in which the Commission, at any time, can replace the cases of national authorities by its own proceedings. In third place, the European Competition Network (ECN) is somehow controlled by the Commission, and therefore the competence allocation is controlled by the Commission as well. Lastly, Regulation

62. Budzinski also explains that the ECJ historically has explicitly affirmed the priority of European Competition rules over the national ones in cases of conflict, for example in the Walt Wilhemen judgment of 1969 (Case 14/68), Delimitis case regarding beer supply agreements in 1991 (Case C-234/89), Materfoods case in 2000 (Case C-344/98), among others. *See* the author's explanation in O. Budzinski, *The Governance of Global Competition: Competence Allocation in International Competition Policy*, Cheltenham, Edward Elgar Publishing, 2008, p. 126.
63. A. Wigger, 'Revising the European Competition Reform: The Toll of Private Self-Enforcement', *Working Papers Political Science of Vrije Universiteit Amsterdam*, No. 07, 2004.
64. Wigger, 2004, *supra* note 63, at 14-15.
65. For instance, Chapter 3 shows that in Brazil, law companies are the agents that participate more in public consultations and therefore have an impact in the lawmaking process.
66. S. Wilks, 'Agency Escape: Descentralization or Dominance of the European Commission in the Modernization of Competition Law?', *Governance: An Institutional Journal of Policy, Administration and Institutions*, Vol. 18, No. 3, 2005, pp. 431-452.
67. About this specific point, Roger Van den Bergh questions whether, in the case of Germany, the rules of Regulation 1/2003, mainly in respect to vertical restraints, reflected indeed a better approach than the ones that were already in force in the country. According to the author, the old German Competition Law (*Gesetz gegen Wettbewerbsbeschrankungen*, or GWB) used to differentiate the rules applicable for vertical agreements from the ones applicable to horizontal ones, which was a good rule, since vertical agreements require a more economics-based approach than the horizontal ones. *See* discussion in R. Van den Bergh & P. Camesasca, *European Competition Law and Economics: A Comparative Perspective*, 2nd ed., London, Sweet & Maxwell, 2006, pp. 227-229.

1/2003 extends the Commission's powers of investigation, the size of the fines, and even its abilities to negotiate biddings settlements with the parties.[68]

In addition, Budzinski explains that larger Member States - such as Germany, France and the UK - were against the decentralization since their national laws were in this context further marginalized,[69] and their national authorities were corralled.[70] Also, in later works, the same author suggests that the ECN was unequivocally implemented 'to heal' some of the deficits of the competence allocation discussions, and to a certain extent to guarantee that the Commission's rule interpretation is not affected by the decentralization.[71] The author also discusses political economy aspects of the EU merger control policies, although he recognizes that in the case of merger control, the delimitation of competences is much more specified than in the case of cartel policies (or vertical restraints).[72]

Riley used the expression 'political masterstroke' to characterize the 2004 Reform, as the Commission gave the impression of radical reform, when it actually had not lost its central role in the development and implementation of European competition.[73] By setting the outline of Regulation 1/2003, the author argued, for instance, that the Commission's powers of decision and investigation were actually extended with Regulation 1/2003 (e.g., power to obtain information; to take statements; to start their own procedure; among others). Finally, the author concluded that the Commission was the 'sole beneficiary' of the new regulation, since undertakings did not benefit greatly from the removal of the notification system (legal uncertainty increased) and the NCAs also did not benefit since they had to incur extra costs of adjusting their legislation to the EU context.[74]

Apart from the above-mentioned literature, several other authors - such as Suzanne Kingston,[75] Jeremy Lever,[76] Ian Forrester,[77]

68. Wilks, 2005, *supra* note 66, p. 439.
69. Budzinski, 2008, *supra* note 62, p. 320.
70. *See also* Wilks, 2005, *supra* note 66, pp. 431-452.
71. Budzinski, 2008, *supra* note 62.
72. *See*, for instance, O. Budzinski, 'Towards an International Governance of Transborder Mergers? Competition Networks and Institutions Between Centralism and Decentralism', *NYU Journal of International Law and Politics*, Vol. 36, No. 1, 2003, pp. 1-52. Also, O. Budzinski, 'An Economic Perspective on the Jurisdictional Reform of the European Merger Control System', *European Competition Journal*, Vol. 2, No. 1, 2006, pp. 119-140.
73. Riley, 2003a, *supra* note 50, p. 604.
74. A. Riley, 'EC Antitrust Modernization: The Commission Does Very Nicely - Thank You! Part Two: Between the Idea and the Reality: Decentralization under Regulation', *European Competition Law Review*, Vol. 12, 2003b, p. 671.
75. S. Kingston, 'A "New Division of Responsibilities" in the Proposed Regulation to Modernize the Rules Implementing Article 81 and 82 EC? A Warning Call', *European Competition Law Review*, Vol. 22, No. 8, 2001, pp. 340-348.
76. J. Lever, 'The German Monopolies Commission's Report of the Problems Consequent upon the Reform of the European Cartel Procedures', *European Competition Law Review*, Vol. 23, No. 7, 2002, pp. 321-325.
77. I. Forrester, 'Modernization: An Extension of the Powers of the Commission?', *in* D. Geradin (ed.), *Modernization and Enlargement: Two Major Challenges for EC Competition Law*, Antwerp, Intersentia, 2004.

John Fingleton,[78] and René Smits[79] – also explored the political economy perspective to the 2004 Reform, among other points, the discussion regarding the implicit centralization of the Commission on the institutional side and/or the fear that, within this policy design, the NCAs (even the traditional ones, such as the German authority) became 'automaton satellites' of the Commission.

4.4 THE 2004 REFORM: THE THREE ENFORCEMENT COMPONENTS

Despite the political economy discussion brought by section 4.3, there are still very important lessons to be drawn from the evolution of antitrust policy in the EU and the 2004 Reform. These lessons are mainly related to the instruments that are still used by the NCAs to guarantee the enforcement of vertical agreements, in the *ex post* control scenario. Three of these instruments, also called 'pillars', that made this massive reform possible, can be identified. The identification of these pillars is one of the main contributions of this chapter.[80]

First, the consolidated antitrust jurisprudence: After almost four decades of a notification system, the jurisprudence of restrictive agreements was clear enough to allow a decent degree of legal certainty to parties and to guide national authorities to decide upon restrictive practices. Second, the cooperation among national authorities: Regulation 1/2003 created the ECN to guarantee cooperation among authorities and a coherence and uniform application of Article 101 TFEU. Third, the intensification of *ex post* control: Since parties no longer have to notify their potential restrictive practices, the strengthening of *ex post* control via both public and private enforcement was necessary. The following subsections describe in detail these three pillars.

4.4.1 The Consolidated Antitrust Jurisprudence, the VBER and the Guidelines

Over the years, the decisions and notices established by the Commission, and also the role of the Court of Justice sometimes in upholding or annulling decisions, were fundamental to the understanding of existing rules (including the complex assessment of Article 101 TFEU) and the goals of the Community. After almost forty years of enforcement of Resolution 17/1962, the rules on vertical agreements became more predictable for undertakings. In other words, several decades of a notification system contributed to a good knowledge acquaintance on how to assess the potential

78. J. Fingleton, 'The Distribution and Attribution of Cases among the Members of the Network: The Perspective of the Commission/NCAs', *in* C. Ehlermann & I. Atanasuy (eds), *Constructing the EU Network of Competition Authorities*, Oxford, Hart Publishing, 2005.
79. R. Smits, 'The European Competition Network: Selected Aspects', *Legal Issues of European Integration*, Vol. 32, No. 6, 2005, pp. 175-192.
80. Chapter 5 will take a closer look into these three pillars from a Law and Economics perspective, and the theories of enforcement. For this specific chapter, the intention is to merely describe them as important factors that permitted the enforcement of vertical restraints in Europe, after Regulation 1/2003.

anticompetitive effects of vertical agreements taking into consideration the particularities of the Community, the entire legal system and its policy priorities.[81] We can mention, for example, the *Metro SB-GroBmarkete GmbH v. Commission*[82] for selective distribution cases, and the *Yamada*[83] case for resale prince maintenance, among others.[84]

The Commission itself indicated that the choice for alternative policies oriented to vertical agreements was only possible due to the legal certainty carried out by decades of antitrust jurisprudence and the decision-making process, and more recently by the block exemption regulation, notices and guidelines.[85] The White Paper highlighted:

> *In a directly applicable exception system, the legislative framework is of primary importance.* The application of the rules must be sufficiently reliable and consistent to allow businesses to assess whether their restrictive practices are lawful. The Commission would keep the sole right to propose legislative texts, in whatever form – regulations, notices, guidelines etc. – and would act whenever necessary in order to ensure consistency and uniformity in the application of the competition rules.[86] (Emphasis added)

Indeed, the 1999 VBER, and later on notices and guidelines, gained strength and importance.[87] In the absence of a notification system, those hard and soft law instruments became fundamental tools to business people to self-assess their contractual relations, and also to national authorities when investigating anticompetitive practices. Actually, as highlighted by Alison Jones and Brenda Sufrin, most of these notices and guidelines were 'crucial to complete an overall picture of a particular competition rule and in practice they influence the way in which firms conduct business'.[88] The authors also mention that although the notices and guidelines are soft law instruments, and do not have a legislative force, the EU decision makers are constantly referring their decisions to it.

81. Souter, 2016, *supra* note 4.
82. *Metro SB- GroBmarkete GmbH and Co KG v. Commission*, Case No. 26/76.
83. *Yamaha Corporation Japan, Yamaha Europa GmbH, Yamaha Musica Italia, s.p.a., Yamaha Musique France S.A. and Yamaha Scandinavia AB v. Commission*, Case No. IP/03/1028.
84. The Commission's Guidelines on Vertical Restraints bring several other examples of consolidated jurisprudence related to vertical restraints.
85. According to the White Paper, paragraph 70. 'While there were legitimate doubts in 1960 as to the scope of the conditions for exemption under Article 85, the Commission's decision-making practice, the case-law of the Court of Justice and the Court of First Instance and the various block exemption regulations and general notices have made the conditions governing exemption much clearer. Furthermore, the national authorities and courts, undertakings and their legal advisers have progressively gained a better knowledge of Community competition law. These changes now make it possible to overcome obstacles which, at the time when Regulation No 17 was adopted, prevented the establishment of a system of ex post control and stemmed essentially from uncertainties as to the precise scope of the exemption conditions provided for in Article 85(3).' *See* European Commission, 1999, *supra* note 10.
86. European Commission, 1999, *supra* note 10, paragraph 84.
87. It is worth noting that in the EU law, Treaties are known as primary law, and all the body of law that comes from the principles and objectives of the treaties is known as secondary law. This includes Regulations (such as Regulation 1/2003 and the Vertical Block Exemption Regulation), directives, decisions, recommendations and opinions.
88. A. Jones & B. Sufrin, *EU Competition Law: Text, Cases and Materials*, 5th ed., Oxford, Oxford University Press, 2014, p. 118.

Regulation 2790/99 addressed some innovative aspects when compared to the previous group of (sector) block exemptions, such as (i) the introduction of an umbrella block exemption applied to a broad variety of supply and distribution contracts; (ii) the implementation of market share thresholds for producers and distributors, for instance, in the case of exclusive supply; and (iii) the adoption of a blacklist approach, that included, *inter alia*, bans on vertical price-fixing and on geo-blocking provisions.[89] The 1999 VBER was also accompanied by explanatory guidelines to help enforcers and mainly business people to better understand the types of agreements and/or clauses they could or could not be engaged in.[90] Actually, in view of the fact that Regulation 1/2003 abolished the notification system, the rationale for the exemption system changed. Instead of being used as a policy tool to reduce the number of notifications, the VBER has proved to be the most relevant tool for businesses and lawyers to carry out the self-assessment demanded by Article 101(3) TFEU.[91]

It is worth noting that the most updated version of the VBER entered into force in June 2010.[92] Regulation 330/2010 (or 2010 VBER) brought about two main developments to the policies applicable to vertical restraints when compared to Regulation 2790/99: (i) a double market share limit and (ii) a brief assessment over internet sales. In the current system, an agreement benefits from the legal exemptions in a situation where the market share held by both the supplier and the buyer does not exceed 30%, and if the contract does not include a number of blacklisted clauses (hardcore restrictions). As blacklist clauses, Regulation 330/2010 highlights, for instance, in its Article 4, RPM clauses, territorial and consumer restrictions (including selective distribution systems).

The Regulation 330/2010 is currently under review since a new VBER is expected to enter into force in 2022. Since October 2018, the European Commission has launched an evaluation phase of the current regulation, followed by an evaluation roadmap and public consultation. By following these steps, the Commission wishes to collect 'in-depth and high-quality evidence on the key competition issues arising in vertical relationships from the perspective of the businesses, consumers and EU competition law enforcers'.[93] Indeed, 164 stakeholders have contributed in the first phase of the public consultation.

The consolidated antitrust jurisprudence, the VBER and the Guidelines are therefore the first pillars that permitted the change from a notification system of vertical agreements to a system of legal exception in Europe without parties encountering too much legal uncertainty. The next section analyses the role of the ECN in guaranteeing

89. Wijckmans & Tuytschaever, 2018, *supra* note 37, p. 18.
90. European Commission, *Guidelines on Vertical Restraints*, 2010 (updated version).
91. Wijckmans & Tuytschaever, 2018, *supra* note 37, p. 16.
92. Commission Regulation (EU) No. 330/2010 of 20 April 2010 on the application of Article 101(3) of the Treaty on the Functioning of the European Union to categories of vertical agreements and concerted practices.
93. European Commission, *Consultation Strategy for the Evaluation of the Vertical Block Exemption Regulation*, 2019, p. 1.

cooperation and consistency in the enforcement of Article 101 TFEU among the Member States.

4.4.2 The ECN: Cooperation among EU Member States

The ECN was established in 2004 as a forum for discussion on the application of EU competition policies, mainly Articles 101 and 102 TFEU. In detail, Article 11 and Article 14 of Regulation 1/2003 and the ECN Cooperation Notice establish the principle of close cooperation between national authorities and the Commission.[94] The network is supported by the allocation of cases[95] and information exchange,[96] including the exchange and use, across ECN members, of confidential information. This network was created to help national authorities to enhance cooperation and the coherence, consistency and uniform application of the competition rules, given the diverse experience among the NCAs in applying competition law.[97] It means that the national authorities and courts themselves had (and still have) an active role in supporting one another to apply competition rules to restrictive practices, and therefore this close cooperation is identified as the second pillar that sustains the 2004 Reform. Indeed, one of the main differences of Regulation 1/2003 and Regulation 17/1962 was the cooperative provisions.

Given the complexity of assessing antitrust cases (as in vertical agreements cases) and the deficiencies of the competence allocation of EU competition policies brought by Regulation 1/2003, the ECN showed up as an important pillar for the national authorities. Also, the ECN has developed guidance for the more effective distribution of competences.[98] In this respect, the ECN has been capable of overcoming certain weaknesses and conflicts of the current system, by establishing additional and more informal internal procedures. According to Budzinski and Christiansen and 'In the absence of a mutual consent on a clear-cut delimitation of competences, however, this only represents a makeshift/emergency solution.'[99]

It should be noted that in the hierarchical structure of the ECN, the European Commission functions as a manager to ensure that EU regulations are applied uniformly.[100] In other words, the ECN offers cooperative support for NCAs, so they can consistently apply Articles 101 and 102 TFEU, and also commit to the creation and establishment of a prevalent competition culture across Europe.[101] The idea of having the support of the Commission and of more experienced competition authorities,

94. European Commission, *Commission Notice on Cooperation Within the Network of Competition Authorities*, 2004.
95. European Commission, 2004, *supra* note 94, paragraphs 5-15.
96. European Commission, 2004, *supra* note 94, paragraphs 16-19.
97. K. Cseres, 'Comparing Laws in the Enforcement of EU and National Competition Laws', *European Journal of Legal Studies*, Vol. 3, No. 1, 2010a, pp. 7-44.
98. Budzinski, 2008, *supra* note 62, pp. 132-133.
99. Budzinski & Christiansen, 2005 *supra* note 59, p. 322.
100. Cseres, 2010a, *supra* note 97, p. 19.
101. F. Cengiz, 'Multi-Level Governance in Competition Policy: The European Competition Network', *European Law Review*, Vol. 35, No. 5, 2010, p. 662.

mainly for the new Member States with no tradition whatsoever in implementing competition rules, certainly characterizes the second pillar of the reform.

4.4.3 Intensification of *Ex Post* Control

Finally, a crucial item of the reform was the intensification of enforcement and monitoring by the Commission, NCAs and national courts to ensure that restrictive practices (including anticompetitive vertical agreements) were not taking place and competition rules were respected among all the Member States. Because the law became more predictable to undertakings over the years of the notification system, the *ex post* control of vertical agreements turned out to be the alternative policy to simplify the administration of these practices. Actually, the Commission acknowledged that – without the mandatory system of notifications – the better level of enforcement of anticompetitive agreements could only be accomplished when the *ex post* enforcement has been guaranteed.[102]In this context, it is important to differentiate between the two instruments of *ex post* control to be considered in this analysis: the public and the private enforcement.

Regarding the public enforcement, the strengthening in the *ex post* control means guaranteeing a larger power to the Commission (but also to national enforcers) to start their own cases (ex officio) and a larger power of enquiry (e.g., power to seal premises, request for information, ask questions during investigations). Within the new legal framework, both the Commission and the national authorities could start their own investigation on vertical infringement founded on external complaints. In this context, one can say that private parties are also protagonists in the enforcement of competition law, since any interested individual or any firm may be able to file a legitimate complaint against restrictive contracts.[103]

Law and economics theory discusses that the increase in *ex post* control, not only through the increase of fines but also through more focused and powerful investigatory powers, would ultimately lead to an increase in the costs of businesses to engage in restrictive practices. For example, Gary Becker explains that the offenders eventually stop committing crimes (or lower the number of crimes), according to the severity of the enforcement (e.g., probability of detention, size of fines).[104] The increase in the level of fines is indeed a basic enforcement tool in order to tackle anticompetitive practices. In 2006, new guidelines[105] with specific methodologies to set fines for antitrust infringements were adopted by the European Commission. These guidelines increased the deterrent effect of fines by determining, for instance: (i) that fines may be

102. European Commission, 1999, *supra* note 10, paragraph 108.
103. Wijckmans & Tuytschaever, 2018, *supra* note 37, p. 21.
104. G. Becker, 'Crime and Punishment: An Economic Approach', *Journal of Political Economy*, Vol. 76, No. 2, 1968, pp. 169-217. Although the author focused his analysis on criminal law, most of the insights can be applied to other law infringements, such as anticompetitive conducts. A more extensive law and economic analysis of *ex post* enforcement instruments will be carried out in Chapter 5.
105. European Commission, *Guidelines on the Method of Setting Fines Imposed Pursuant to Article 23(2)(a) of Regulation No 1/2003*, 2006.

based on up to 30% of the company's annual sales to which the infringement relates, multiplied by the duration, in years, of the infringement; (ii) that an 'entry fee' may be applicable regardless of the length of the infringement; (iii) that fines for undertakings that continue to repeat the infringement may be increased by up to 100%.

Some current developments in EU law have also contributed to the strengthening of the *ex post* control in the field of private enforcement, meaning the application of EU antitrust legislation in conflicts between private parties before the judiciary. Frank Wijckmans and Filip Tuytschaever discuss the importance of considering private actions also (and mainly) in vertical cases: 'more than cartels, vertical restraints give rise to autonomous private litigation before national courts because vertical practices are more a contractual matter and also because there is simply less public enforcement activity in the field of verticals'.[106] Over the years, the Commission actively promoted some actions with the aim of harmonizing and promoting the relevant national rules on damages actions. Towards the end of 2014, the EU Private Damages Directive entered into force,[107] containing rules which assist any individual who has been harmed – including harm originated by vertical restraints – to exercise a right to claim full compensation. Some of the obstacles to effective compensation were removed by the new directive, guaranteeing therefore better protection for citizens and businesses.

Without these three main pillars – that is to say, the consolidated jurisprudence, the ECN cooperation and the intensified *ex post* control – the optimal enforcement of restrictive commercial practices in Europe, mainly related to vertical agreements, would have been impaired. The understanding of these three enforcement pillars is fundamental to the next step of this chapter that aims at identifying the current challenges of the EU policies applicable to vertical restraints and to formulating lessons for other jurisdictions. Among the current challenges, it is believed that two of them can be seen as a threat to the optimal enforcement of vertical restraints among the Member States. The first challenge is the new interpretation of the current regulation when applied to vertical restrictions in online markets. Because these new cases are not completely covered by the existing regulation and case law, enforcers and firms are encountering greater levels of legal uncertainties in this matter. The second challenge is related to the different procedural and institutional realities among Member States, which affect greater levels of enforcement. These challenges are better explained in the following section.

4.5 THE CHALLENGES OF THE CURRENT EU ENFORCEMENT OF VERTICAL AGREEMENTS

The contribution of this section is not only to identify the evolution of EU competition policies oriented to vertical agreements but also to categorize the main challenges faced

106. Wijckmans & Tuytschaever, 2018, *supra* note 37, p. 27.
107. Directive 2014/104/EU of the European Parliament and of the Council of 26 November 2014 on certain rules governing actions for damages under national law for infringements of the competition law provisions of the Member States and of the European Union Text with European Economic Area (EEA) relevance.

by the Commission and the EU Member States. Highlighted here are some authors who have discussed specific challenges of EU competition law in terms of the optimal enforcement of vertical restraints.

First, and more generally, Damien Gerard identifies some paradoxes which resulted from the modernization process and the effects-based approach of Article 101TFEU.[108] He identifies, for instance, a drop-in enforcement level, beyond cartels. He argues that after Regulation 1/2003, vertical agreements have 'disappeared from the EU antitrust enforcement radar' and, apart from Germany and France, this anticompetitive conduct is hardly prosecuted at national level either. He also says that after Regulation 1/2003, enforcement and justification costs rose, instead of dropping. This is because parties now have to encounter extra costs of self-assessing their contracts under this effects-based approach to avoid future litigation. Gerard lastly criticizes the paradox of having, on the one hand, Article 101 TFEU that requires the competitive analysis to be tailored to the specific case and markets, and on the other hand a reliance on abstract guidance found in the Block Exemption Regulation and Guidelines.

Also, Roger Van den Bergh argues that the policies oriented to vertical agreements in Europe are characterized by a high degree of regulatory intervention and the excessive role of technical legal distinctions.[109] The author recognized that designing an optimal legal system for vertical agreements is not an easy process due to their uncertain effects in the markets. However, he stresses that EU competition law – different from US antitrust law – does not allow a full efficiency economic assessment of the positive and negative outcomes of vertical restraints. His main criticism is that: (i) market share thresholds of the VBER are not always a best proxy for market power and therefore they are not good indicators for identifying anticompetitive practices; (ii) the guidelines on vertical restraints do not pay sufficient attention to the particularities of buying power and (iii) the guidelines do not consider the dynamic efficiencies that might arise mainly in e-commerce transactions.[110]

Miguel de la Mano and Jones, similarly, emphasize that the antitrust analysis of vertical restraints has not evolved towards a more 'effects-based' approach, as was expected.[111] First, they argued that the economic rationale of vertical agreements is still not properly reflected in the current legal framework, since it continues to strongly depend on broad presumptions of illegality that are not necessarily sustained by economic theory or evidence. Second, they criticized the shortage of decided cases – mainly related to digital markets – which indicated the lack of transparency for assessing and judging the pro- and anticompetitive effects of vertical agreements. According to the authors, these factors increase the uncertainty and turn out to

108. D. Gerard, 'The Effects-Based Approach under Article 101 TFEU and Its Paradoxes: Modernization at War Itself?', J. Bourgeois & D. Waelbroeck (eds), *Ten Years of Effects-Based Approach in EU Competition Law Enforcement*, Brussels, Bruylant, 2012.
109. R. Van den Bergh, 'Vertical Restraints: The European Part of the Policy Failure', *The Antitrust Bulletin*, Vol. 61, No. 1, 2016, pp. 167-185.
110. Van den Bergh, 2016, *supra* note 109, pp. 172-175.
111. M. de la Mano & A. Jones, 'Vertical Agreements under EU Competition Law: Proposals for Pushing Article 101 Analysis, and the Modernization Process, to a Logical Conclusion', *King's College London Law School Research Paper*, No. 23, 2017.

instigate disparities in the approaches to enforcement emerging at the national level.[112] Indeed, most of the cases involving vertical agreements in Europe are cases of hardcore restrictions, such as RPM cases, and not cases involving a deep economic effect-based analysis.[113]

Paul Dobson discusses that the end of the notification system of vertical agreements placed a severe regulatory burden on companies, since they mainly rely on the self-assessment of potential restrictive practices.[114] Wolfgang Kerber and Simonetta Vezzoso, on their terms, reinforced that the general features of EU competition policy on vertical restraints mainly rely on neoclassical concepts on market competition, while neglecting the relevance of innovation.[115] The authors propose the development of an analysis based on a dynamic or evolutionary framework for vertical agreements' assessment where they use theories of evolutionary economics, dynamic competition and innovation economics. However, they acknowledged that the implementation of the rule of reason methodology in Europe looks deeply troublesome, since it assumes the existence of a specific knowledge and expertise that companies and competition authorities often do not have. In particular, the lack of staff that is able to conduct a full economic analysis of restrictive agreements is a problem often faced by national authorities with lower experience regarding the enforcement of competition law.

In addition to what has been discussed in the literature, this section proposed to take a closer look at two important challenges for improving the European enforcement: one that invokes a debate of concepts and another one related to institutional matters. These identified challenges directly put into question the three main pillars that were discussed in section 4.4: consolidated jurisprudence, networks among authorities and an intensified *ex post* control.

The first challenge refers to the controversies among the different Member States on the application of regulations and soft law instruments to cases involving the digital economy. Briefly speaking, some examples show that NCAs, as in France, Germany and the UK, are taking different approaches towards vertical restraints. This means that the classic European case law that has been uniform and consolidated in the past decades does not necessarily cover new forms of abuse of market power - mainly due to the new transactions coming from the digital economy. Vertical restraints, such as exclusive distribution, selective distribution, and RPM, are now intrinsic to digital platforms, e-commerce, and online marketplaces, and the current legal instruments in

---

112. de la Mano & Jones, 2017, *supra* note 111, pp. 26-27.
113. In the 15th Annual Conference organized by Global Competition Law Centre in January 2020, entitled: 'Vertical Restraints in the Digital Economy: VBER Reform and the Future of Distribution', Professor Alice Jones (Kings College London) discussed that fifty-nine of the seventy-six cases involving vertical agreements in the EU were by object restriction, meaning that they did not required an effect-based analysis from the authority. Presentation available at: https://www.coleurope.eu/system/tdf/uploads/event/alison_jones.pdf?&file=1&type=node&id=53465&force= (7/3/2020).
114. P. Dobson, 'Vertical Restraints Policy Reform in the European Union and United Kingdom', *Loughborough University Business School Research Series*, No. 2, 2005.
115. W. Kerber & S. Vezzoso, 'EU Competition Policy, Vertical Restraints, and Innovation: An Analysis from an Evolutionary Perspective', paper presented at *10th International Joseph A. Schumpeter Society Conference (ISS)*, Milan, 9-12 June 2004.

the EU do not always bring a clear answer on how to tackle the outcome of these practices. In other words, there are some substantive gaps relating to the interpretation of Article 101 TFEU.[116] The objective of a careful look at these cases has a normative importance, since the Block Exemption Regulation is about to expire in 2022 and this is an opportunity to reflect upon this topic.

The second challenge is related to different levels of enforcement of Article 101 TFEU among the EU Member States. This is explained by a diversity of historical perspectives, different institutional backgrounds, different stages of implementation of antitrust policies and a very diverse access to information for business people and law enforcers. The legal diversity of national laws and procedures, and moreover, the diversity of institutional designs remain a challenge when it comes to the capacity of establishing adequate *ex post* enforcement systems and to achieve consistency in the implementation of competition policies across the Member States.

4.5.1 Challenge #1: Uncertainties of the Digital Economy

The first challenge to be discussed refers to the limits of the current jurisprudence and the silence of the VBER and guidelines with regard to most vertical restraints involving digital markets. Over the past decade, the NCAs have been essentially entrusted with the scrutiny of vertical agreements. In the absence of uniform guidance, the NCAs have dealt with some of the numerous challenges that emerged from digital markets and their decisions led to the adoption of heterogeneous approaches towards vertical restraints across the EU. It has been seen that in the EU, a number of vertical restraints have also been categorized as hardcore restraints, which include RPM, geo-blocking clauses, bans on online selling and certain selective distribution systems. However, there is still the debate whether some other new restraints (especially certain online practices) also fall within this category.[117] The revision of the VBER will face some of these open questions.

Competition authorities across the EU have received various complaints about online sales restrictions set by brand manufacturers. As we will see in the next paragraphs, the decisions by the NCAs so far do not make it clear whether the EU competition law is moving towards a more or less strict approach to restrictions on online sales. As the Commission has not adopted consistent infringement decisions with regard to the different vertical restraints in online markets, national enforcers and businesses have to rely on jurisprudence which is relatively sparse (and old) for such guidance.

There might be reasons to justify diverge decisions among the different Member States, since countries encounter different market dynamics and therefore different assessments might occur. However, such considerable disparities among NCAs add uncertainty to the already complicated debate about vertical restraints on e-commerce.

116. P. I. Colomo, *The Shaping of EU Competition Law*, Cambridge, Cambridge University Press, 2018, p. 281.
117. de la Mano & Jones, 2017, *supra* note 111, p. 25.

In this context, the publication of the E-commerce Sector Inquiry[118] indicated the Commission's desire to provide coherence and legal certainty in order to prevent market fragmentation that might hinder the achievement of one of the main the goals of the EU competition law, that is, the internal market.[119] Even though the Sector Inquiry suggested that the updated VBER (to enter into force in 2022) does not have to be adjusted with regard to abuses of e-commerce restrictions, an extensive research was conducted to better assess the agreements that result in online markets.

This chapter aims at illustrating, via case studies, the need for better consistency in applying Article 101 TFEU across the EU. It must be acknowledged that the following subsections present a non-exhaustive list of cases.

4.5.1.1 Selective Distribution in Online Marketplaces

A first example emphasizes the different positions among authorities with regard to restrictions to advertising or selling on third-party platforms can be considered. As a general rule, suppliers may require certain quality standards of their distributors in order to resell their products online, and they may impose quality standards on products intended to be sold offline.[120] It has been a common practice among suppliers operating selective distribution systems to impose quality criteria on the conditions or the types of online platforms on which they can advertise and/or sell the suppliers' products. Paragraph 54 of the Vertical Restraints Guidelines explicitly allows such restrictions:

> [A] supplier may require that its distributors use third party platforms to distribute the contract products only in accordance with the standards and conditions agreed between the supplier and its distributors for the distributors' use of the internet. For instance, where the distributor's website is hosted by a third-party platform, the supplier may require that customers do not visit the distributor's website through a site carrying the name or logo of the third-party platform.

This excerpt has two main messages. First, that a supplier is indeed entitled to impose quality standards in respect of distributors that use online marketplaces such as *Amazon* or *eBay*. Second, it concerns a ban on buyers' sales via online marketplaces, for instance by requiring that the website on which the supplier's products are sold must be operated by the buyer. By the time the guidelines were enacted, there was no consideration that, in the future, a consumer would not even know that he/she was on a third-party platform.[121]

118. European Commission, *Final Report on the E-commerce Sector Inquiry*, 2017.
119. M. B. S. Cardenal, 'Vertical Restraints on E-commerce in the Context of the Single Digital Market Initiative of the European Commission', *Stanford-Vienna European Union Law Working Paper*, No. 23, 2017.
120. OECD, *Vertical Restraints for Online Sales*, 2013.
121. Wijckmans & Tuytschaever, 2018, *supra* note 37, p. 329.

The Commission does not take the online marketplace ban into consideration as a hardcore restriction when it concerns a marketplace which is visible to the customer.[122] The Commission has noted in its E-commerce Sector Inquiry[123] that bans on sales on marketplaces do not constitute hardcore restrictions per se, as in principle their object is not to prevent, restrict, or distort competition:

> Such an approach is in line with the Vertical Guidelines which specify that marketplace restrictions requiring the retailer to use third party platforms (e.g. marketplaces) only in accordance with the quality criteria agreed between the manufacturer and its retailers for the retailer's use of the internet are not considered a hardcore restriction. They concern the question of how the distributor can sell the products over the internet and do not have the object to restrict where or to whom distributors can sell the products.[124]

However, the Commission has admitted that these platform bans might not always comply with the existing rules. For instance, they might amount to hardcore restrictions when the suppliers and distributors exceed the market share threshold in Article 3 VBER.[125] For instance, the position of the German and the French NCAs in relation to restrictions originating from online platforms, such restrictions to sell on certain websites, have not always been clear. In some cases, their approaches were shown to be different even from those rooted in the EU competition law.

For example, in 2013, the French Competition Authority (FCA) opened administrative proceedings against Adidas,[126] while the German Federal Cartel Office (FCO, or, in German, *Bundeskartellamt*) opened administrative proceedings against several sports clothing and running shoes manufacturers, including Adidas and ASICS, on account of their distribution policies.[127] The FCO adopted an infringement decision in August 2015, concluding that the conditions imposed by ASICS on its authorized retailers could lead to a restriction of intra-brand competition. In the *ASICS* case, the company was limiting the use of its trademark on price-comparison websites. The FCO also found that this specific restriction could be predominantly harmful to medium and small-sized distributors.[128]

In the view of the FCO, ASICS' distribution system contained provisions that qualified as restrictions of competition by object pursuant to Article 101(1) TFEU. Those provisions were non-exemptible under Article 2 VBER, as they were deemed

122. Z. Georgieva, 'Competition Soft Law in French and German Courts: A Challenge for Online Sales Bans Only?', *Maastricht Journal of European and Comparative Law*, Vol. 24, No. 2, 2017, p. 179.
123. European Commission, 2017, *supra* note 118.
124. European Commission, 2017, *supra* note 118, paragraph 509.
125. Article 3 VBER: '1. The exemption provided for in Article 2 shall apply on condition that the market share held by the supplier does not exceed 30 % of the relevant market on which it sells the contract goods or services and the market share held by the buyer does not exceed 30 % of the relevant market on which it purchases the contract goods or services.'
126. Judgment of 2 February 2016 in Case No. 15/01542, the Paris Court of Appeal.
127. Decision of the German FCO, *ASICS* no B2-98/11, 26 August 2015. Decision of the German Competiton Authority, *Adidas*, no B3-137/12, June 2014.
128. *See* Cardenal, *supra* note 119, for a full assessment of this case.

hardcore restrictions within the meaning of Article 4(c) VBER.[129] Likewise, in the *Adidas* case, the FCA confirmed the *Pierre Fabre*[130] doctrine and concluded that manufacturers could organize their distribution networks freely, as long as they do not unjustifiably restrain competition.

In contrast with what has been decided by German and French enforcers, by the end of 2017, the European Court of Justice (ECJ) decided that no antitrust violation has been verified in a selective distribution case against the luxury cosmetics company *Coty Germany GmbH* ('*Coty*'). This case started with a complaint from the distributor *Parfümerie Akzente GmbH*, an authorized distributor, who was banned from selling Coty's products in online platforms such as Amazon or eBay.[131] The ECJ, based on Article 101(1) TFEU, assessed whether there were indeed any restrictions to competition imposed by *Coty* and moreover, whether *Metro-criteria* applied to selective distribution systems were verified.[132] In practice, commercial restrictions initiated by companies with less than 30% of market shares are exempted by Article 3 of the VBER. In this case, the Court clarified that marketplace bans such as the ones observed in the *Coty* case do not constitute hardcore restrictions under Article 4(b) or 4(c) VBER.[133]

The *Coty* case sets an important precedent when it comes to platform bans in the scope of luxury goods. However, several questions remain unanswered when it comes to platform bans involving other highly differentiated and complex products. Because of that, the scope of platform bans is one of the main topics that requires more clarification from the European Commission and shall be addressed by the new regulation.

4.5.1.2 MFN Clauses and Price Parity Arrangements

The MFN clauses that appear in vertical agreements between suppliers and distributors generally consist of an offer by the supplier of a price or rate to a client no higher than the lowest offered to other clients. For instance, in the online hotel booking sector, an MFN clause obligates the hotels to always give to the platform the best price for online hotel bookings, among other most favoured conditions. They can be considered 'wide clauses' or 'narrow clauses' depending on the scope of their conditions. Indeed, because of the nature of these clauses, and because parity clauses are not addressed in

129. Article 4 (c) VBER 'The exemption provided for in Article 2 shall not apply to vertical agreements which, directly or indirectly, in isolation or in combination with other factors under the control of the parties, have as their object [...](c) the restriction of active or passive sales to end users by members of a selective distribution system operating at the retail level of trade, without prejudice to the possibility.'
130. *Pierre Fabre v. L'Autorité de la concurrence*, Case No. 439/09. In this case, the European Court of Justice ruled that a prohibition on internet sales in the framework of selective distribution systems represents an infringement of competition by Article 101(1) TFEU.
131. *Coty Germany GmbH v. Parfümerie Akzente GmbH*, Case C-230/16, decision Luxembourg Court of Justice of the European Union on 6 December 2017.
132. *Metro SB- Großmarkete GmbH and Co KG v. Commission*, Case No. 26/76.
133. European Commission, 'EU competition rules and marketplace bans: Where do we stand after the Coty judgment?', *Occasional discussion papers by the Competition Directorate–General of the European Commission*, 2018.

the current vertical guidelines, the online hotel booking sector has attracted significant interest throughout the EU competition enforcers.

In 2012, the Office of Fair Trading (OFT)[134] opened a formal investigation against the OTAs *Booking.com, Expedia,* and *InterContinental Hotels Group* (or simply *IHG*). The case examined whether certain arrangements between hotels and OTAs infringed British Law and Article 101TFEU. The OFT sustained that *Booking.com* and *Expedia* had 'each entered into separate agreements with *IHG* that restricted the OTAs' ability to discount the headline rate at which room-only hotel accommodation bookings were offered to consumers'.[135] The OFT also held these commercial restrictions constituted a form of RPM that could limit price competition and also increase entry barriers and prevent the growth of established online agencies.

The British authority, in early 2014, accepted formal commitments from *IHG, Booking.com,* and *Expedia.* The parties agreed, among other things, to allow OTAs to offer discounts on room rates, but these discounts could be exclusively offered to certain groups of consumers who were members of the OTA in question and who had previously booked a room on that platform. Irrespective of the removal of all the discounting restrictions, the OFT recognized that enabling hotels to have certain control over the headline rate for their rooms generated efficiencies. In September 2014, the British Competition Appeal Tribunal upheld the appeal presented by Skyscanner, a price comparison website, against the OFT's decision of January 2014. Skyscanner claimed that the OFT had failed to assess the impact of the decision on inter-brand competition, and the company questioned the accepted commitments.[136] The Tribunal sent the case back to Competition and Markets Authority (CMA) (OFT's successor), in order to reconsider the matter. In the light of the new judgment, in September 2015, the CMA closed its investigations alleging 'administrative priority grounds'. The OFT's approach in this online booking case – meaning the acceptance of certain types of narrow MFN clauses – was in line with the approach developed by the French, Swedish, and Italian NCAs. However, this approach was quite different from the one taken by the FCO in Germany, who had adopted a stricter position towards the topic.

In 2012, the FCO initiated an action against Hotel Reservation Service (HRS), an online hotel booking platform, alleging that *HRS's* MFN clauses restricted competition between online hotel booking platforms and foreclosed the market.[137] In December 2013, the FCO prohibited *HRS* from enforcing MFN clauses and ordered the company to delete them from its contracts with hotel partners, since such clauses remove the hotel portals' incentives to offer lower prices on other OTAs.[138] Moreover, the FCO argued that the market entry conditions of new online hotel booking platforms or the expansion of the number of smaller competitors was considerably more difficult since

134. In April 2014, the Competition and Markets Authority (CMA) was established and combined many of the functions of the OFT and the Competition Commission in the UK.
135. OFT Case CE/9320/10.
136. Case 1226/2/12/14 *Skyscanner Ltd v. CMA* (2014) CAT 16.
137. *See* Cardenal, *supra* note 119, for a full assessment of this case.
138. *Bundeskartellamt* Case B 9 – 66/10.

MFN provisions prohibit hotels from providing reduced prices for their accommodation.

The FCO decided that not only should booking's MFN clause be removed from its website by 31 January 2016 but also that such a clause could not be replaced by a 'narrow MFN' clause, since limiting the scope of the MFN clause was 'insufficient to allay competition concerns'.[139] In January 2015, the FCO's decision against *HRS* was upheld on appeal by the Düsseldorf Higher Regional Court that reached a decision on June 2019. Different from the FCO, the German Court found that 'narrow MFN clauses' are compatible with competition law, since they are proportional commercial practices to guarantee a fair service exchange between the hotels and the online platforms.[140]

In short, it seems like there is a unanimous acceptance that wide MFN clauses are hardcore restrictions of competition pursuant to the VBER and, therefore, they fall under the prohibition set by Article 101(1) TFEU. However, over the last years, there was no consensus with regard to narrow MFN clauses. There is also a lack of economic literature that tries to assess and/or estimate the effects of such clauses.[141] Some authors have emphasized that MFN clauses generate serious anticompetitive effects simply because it makes low-price entry less likely, since parties (in this case hotels) that have engaged in contracts with such price parity clauses would not allow this lower-price setting.[142]

The E-commerce Sector Inquiry indicates the position of the Commission: parity clauses, both narrow and wide ones, are not hardcore restrictions and therefore are block exempted:

> In the absence of a hard-core restriction under Article 4 of the VBER, parity clauses in vertical agreements are covered by the VBER if the parties' market shares do not exceed 30 %. Should market shares exceed 30 % an individual assessment of parity clauses will be required.[143]

These perceived differences in the interpretation and application of the EU law across jurisdictions create challenges for business and may even prevent firms from expanding within the internal market. Since the economic literature regarding the effects of MFNs is also very limited, it is also very difficult to authorities relying on a specific criterion for the assessment of these clauses. The result is a shortage of guidance on how assessment is to be conducted in relation to the new vertical models

139. The Bundeskartellamt's prohibition decision was adopted in December 2015 and took effect in February 2016.
140. Information found on free English translation of the Press Release, *see* http://www.olg-duesseldorf.nrw.de/behoerde/presse/Presse_aktuell/20190604_PM_booking/index.php (26/7/2019). Since the decision of the Düsseldorf Higher Regional Court is not yet available, it is not possible to see whether the approach taken by the German court was different from the ones taken by the FCO, or even by the other countries that reached similar outcomes.
141. An example of recent literature is A. Boik & K. Corts, 'The Effects of Platform Most-Favored-Nation Clauses on Competition and Entry', *The Journal of Law and Economics*, Vol. 59, No. 1, 2016, pp. 105-134.
142. *See*, for instance, N. Sahuguet, J. Steenbergen, T. Verge & A. Walckiers, 'Vertical Restraints: Towards Guidance to Iron Out Perceived Enforcement Discrepancies Across Europe?', *Journal of European Competition Law & Practice*, Vol. 7, No. 4, 2016, pp. 274-279.
143. European Commission, 2017, *supra* note 118, paragraph 621.

of distribution and practices that have been emerging online, such as agency arrangements, online RPM, parity clauses, restrictions on inclusion in price comparison tools and marketplace restrictions.

4.5.2 Challenge #2: Different Procedural and Institutional Realities among the EU Member States

The second identified challenge is related to different levels of enforcement of Article 101 TFEU, more specifically anticompetitive vertical agreements, among the EU Member States. It is expected that different Member States (i.e., different NCAs, courts, tribunals) will vary in the speed, competence, and effectiveness of the manner in which they apply competition law, since regimes respond to differing sets of pressures.[144] This section argues, therefore, that for different reasons, not all the authorities developed adequate enforcement procedures over the time to guarantee *ex post* control of vertical agreements. It pretends to present some aspects - without being exhaustive - of this institutional discussion that jeopardize the optimal antitrust enforcement of vertical restraints in Europe.

Before entering into the institutional discussion, it would be best to highlight that comparing enforcement activities of vertical agreements among the Member States is a very difficult task. Several Commission's publications and statistics show only the general number of cases held by NCAs or by the Commission over time. They also show information about enforcement of Article 101 TFEU, but again without a clear definition of which cases refer to cartels, or which cases refer to vertical restraints or other anticompetitive agreements. Figure 4.1 shows some of the information available at the Commission's website. It shows precisely that, since the 2004 Reform, the NCAs have decided on average forty-seven cases under Article 101 TFEU.

144. Wilks, 2005, *supra* note 66, p. 441.

Figure 4.1 Cases in Which an Envisaged Decision under Article 101 TFEU Has Been Submitted by NCAs (2005-2018)

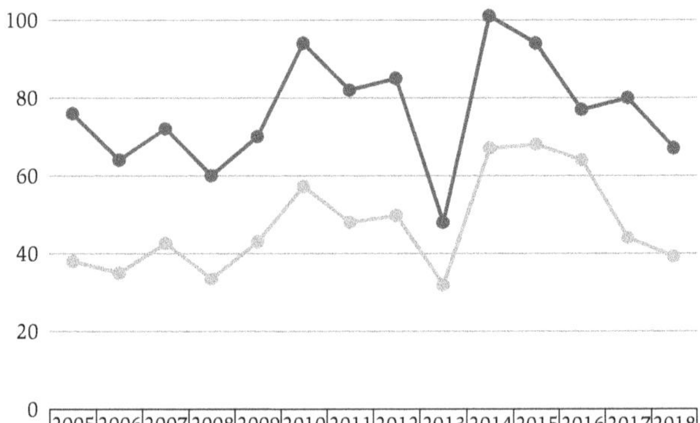

	2005	2006	2007	2008	2009	2010	2011	2012	2013	2014	2015	2016	2017	2018
Cases in which an envisaged decision has been submitted by NCAs	76	64	72	60	70	94	82	85	48	101	94	77	80	67
Envisaged Decision under Article 101 TFEU	38	35	43	34	43	57	48	50	32	67	68	64	44	39

Source: Compiled by the author. Data from European Commission Statistics.

In addition to this information, the Commission also published the number of cases held by the different countries, when applying Articles 101 and 102 TFEU (Figure 4.2). It is worth highlighting that since Regulation 1/2003 entered into force, the countries that carried out the highest number of investigations and/or envisaged decisions, are the countries with long-standing traditions in competition law – such as France, Germany and Italy. Actually, the three countries together represent 32 % of all new investigations and almost 40% of all envisaged decisions. Even though this information is not exclusively related to the enforcement of vertical restraints, it is possible to expect that this proportion also applies for the verticals. Even though there are a number of factors that affect the volume of cases and enforcement decisions, such as the budget of each country, or the time invested in complex cases, Figure 4.2 demonstrates that there is still room for more effective enforcement in some of the Member States.

Figure 4.2 New Antitrust Cases and Envisaged Decisions under Articles 101 and 102 TFEU by Country[145] *(May 2004-December 2018)*

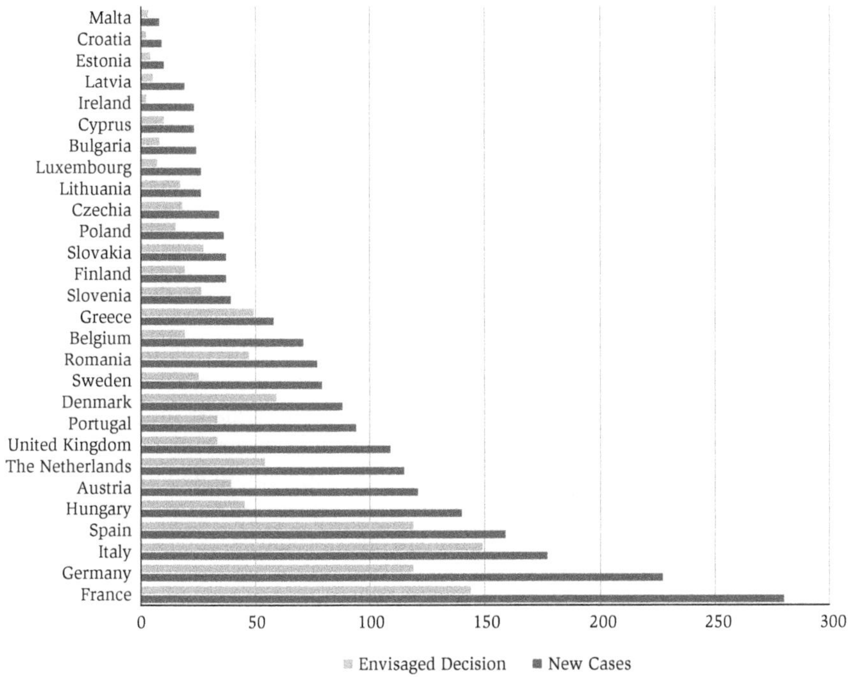

Source: Compiled by the author. Data from European Commission Statistics.

Indeed, in order to find more detailed information specifically about the level of enforcement of vertical agreements among the different Member States, an extensive analysis of the Annual Reports from 2004 until 2018 from all NCAs was carried out.[146] The main purpose of this analysis was identifying the number of cases in which vertical agreements were assessed by each authority, mostly at the administrative level. From this analysis, there are some findings:

- The Annual Reports indicate that, in the past five years, some NCAs have also launched their own guidelines, notices and studies to support the assessment of vertical agreements. For instance, in 2014, the Federal Competition Authority in Austria (AFCA) produced an official opinion regarding RPM called

145. Investigations of which the European Competition Network has been informed.
146. The analysis of Annual Reports was limited to the countries that indeed publish their Annual Report online, and that had information in English, Portuguese, French, Italian or Spanish. The Annual Reports of all NCAs are available at: http://ec.europa.eu/competition/ecn/annual_reports.html (2/3/2019).

'Standpoint on Resale Price Maintenance', that also orientates society regarding the possible scenarios in which these price restrictions can negatively affect competition. In 2016, with the same purpose, the British CMA issued the study 'Vertical Restraints: New Evidence from a Business Survey'. Also in 2016, the Authority for Consumers and Markets (ACM) in the Netherlands, published the document 'ACM's Strategy and Enforcement Priorities with Regard to Vertical Agreements'. Although the Dutch authority did not actively enforce too many cases of vertical agreements in the past years, the ACM recognizes the need for a careful look at these practices. In 2017, the Germany competition authority (*Bundeskartellamt)* launched a note on RPM in the food sector, called 'Guidance Note on the Prohibition of Vertical Price-Fixing in the Brick-and-Mortar Food Retail Sector'.

- Several countries hardly ever explicitly discuss the enforcement of vertical restraints in their Annual Reports, including Bulgaria, Cyprus, Estonia, Finland, Ireland and the Netherlands.[147] It means that they do not indicate any case in which the authority started an investigation or reported a decision.
- Other countries have very incomplete and not systematic information about their enforcement of vertical agreements. For example, in their Annual Reports, Austria and Germany discuss the same investigation over different years (e.g., the RPM in the food market in Germany or Austria),[148] and France reports in its Annual Reports only few high-profile cases.[149] These facts give the reader the impression that only a few cases are being assessed by the authority, which may not be the reality.
- Very few countries present in their Annual Reports complete information of all vertical cases including the ones subjected to judicial review (e.g., Poland).

The fact that there is incomplete and unparalleled information among the Annual Report of the national authorities, also makes it difficult to create a fair picture of the level of enforcement regarding vertical agreements and the problems associated to it. If we do not know where the problem is in the first place, it becomes harder to suggest policy that guarantees better levels of enforcement. Despite these methodological limitations, Table 4.1 summarizes the findings. Because of the incomparable type of information provided among the different EU Member States, Table 4.1 simply indicates with the sign 'X' when new cases and/or new decisions related to the

147. Even though the Dutch Authority (ACM) did not present any information regarding specific cases of vertical agreements, in the 2016 Annual Report, the Authority indicated that the topic will be more carefully analysed considering the new cases that have been popping up in the EU level.
148. The 2015 Annual Report from the *Bundeskartellamt* indicated fines of 50, EUR 8 million. According to the 2017 and 2016 Annual Reports, the *Bundeskartellamt* imposed fines amounting to EUR 260.5 million on twenty-seven companies for having engaged in price-fixing agreements between retailers and manufacturers in the food sector.
149. For instance, while the French Annual Reports of 2017 and 2018 do not indicate any enforcement regarding vertical agreements, information provided by the legal platform 'Getting the Deal Through: Vertical Agreements', indicated that in the same period, the French Authority ruled 9 decisions which relate to vertical agreements. For more information, access: https://gettingthedealthrough.com/area/41/vertical-agreements (20/4/2019).

enforcement of vertical agreements were mentioned in the documents, and with the sign '-' when no enforcement activity oriented to vertical agreements was mentioned in the same documents.[150]

Table 4.1 Enforcement of Vertical Agreements Across the EU Member States, According to NCAs' Annual Reports (2004-2018)

	04	*05*	*06*	*07*	*08*	*09*	*10*	*11*	*12*	*13*	*14*	*15*	*16*	*17*	*18*
Austria	-	X	-	-	-	-	X	-	X	X	-	-	X	-	X
Belgium												-	-	-	-
Bulgaria								-	X	X	-	-			
Croatia															
Cyprus	-	-	-	-	-	X	-	-	-	-	-	-			
Czech Republic	-	-	X	X	X	X	-	-	-	X	X	X	X	X	X
Denmark	-	-	-												
Estonia						-	-	-	-	-	-	-	-	-	-
Finland								-					-	-	
France	-	X	X	-	-	-	-	-	X	-	-	-	-	-	-
Germany										X	X	X	X	X	X
Greece	-	X	X	-	X	X	X	-	-	X	-	-	X	X	X
Hungary	-	X	X	-	X	X	X	-	-	X	-	-	X	X	-
Ireland	-	-	-	-	-	-	-	X	X	-	-	-	-	-	-
Italy	-	X	-	X	-	X	X	-	X	-	X	X	-	X	X
Latvia															-
Lithuania	X	X	X	X	-	-	X	X	-	-	X	-	-	-	-
Luxembourg															
Malta															
The Netherlands										-	-	-	-	-	-
Poland								X	X	X	X	X	X	X	X
Portugal	X	-	X	-	X	-	-	-	X	X	-	X	X	X	X
Romania	X	-	-	X	X	X	X	X	X						
Slovakia	-	-	-	-	-	X	X	X	-	-	X	-	X	X	X
Slovenia															
Spain															X
Sweden										-	-	X	X		
UK										-	-	-	X	X	-

Source: Compiled by the author.

150. In addition, the grey cells were indicated when there was no published Annual Report in that year. It is important to reinforce that the sign '-' does not necessarily mean that there was no case within each national law, but that the agency did not indicate it in its Annual Report.

In this context, an important point to be made in this subsection is that the different level of enforcement might be explained by historical perspectives, and different experiences related to market economies and therefore also to competition law. By the time Regulation 1/2003 entered into force, some EU Member States (mainly the ones from CEE countries) had just left the socialist regime and were having to establish a market economy with trade liberalization and privatization within a short period of time.

There are indeed several differences that distinguish the CEE NCAs from the Western NCAs. Actually, the CEE NCAs have been created in a very distinct institutional set-up compared to the Western Europe NCAs. As a result of the Soviet influence and the ideology of state planning and intervention, CEE's economies presented a high degree of market concentration, low technological development and only marginal growth of consumer markets.[151] Moreover, the state bureaucracy had limited knowledge of the functioning of the market economy and favoured direct control and regulation of economic activities.

As a result, in the aftermath of the collapse of the Soviet system and the creation of a market system in those countries, the CEE NCAs had a huge task to support and enhance the emerging competition regimes. The NCAs had to cope with the reality that they needed to shape markets following the rules of free enterprise, market competition and efficiency. In this scenario, the NCAs played a significant advocacy role across all government ministries to guarantee that government regulation and decision-making would not fragilize the dynamics of the market economy.[152] This historic perspective gives us some grounds to think about the reasons why some of the NCAs might not take the enforcement of vertical restraints as a priority, and it also puts into question whether government agencies and courts, at the national level, may not have the ability to judge and make decisions about complex market situations.

With the 2004 Reform of competition policies in Europe, some Member States faced the implementation of completely new competition laws and also the creation of a competition culture. Other Member States had to completely modify the legislations to the new EU reality. With the Regulation 1/2003 in place, not only was the change in legislation a reality among the EU Member States but also the direct involvement of national courts or tribunals in the application of Article 101 TFEU. In this new context, judges (and not expert officials) ended up being the ones to solve antitrust issues. One of the ECN Reports of ten years of Regulation 1/2003 demonstrated that less than ten Member States had a specialized judiciary that handled competition cases, among them Belgium, Denmark, France, Germany, Italy, Poland Spain, and the UK.[153] Most of these selected countries turn out to be the ones with long-standing traditions in antitrust cases and the ones with the greater levels of antitrust enforcement (*see* Table 4.1). This

151. Riley, 2003b, *supra* note 74, p. 661.
152. Riley, 2003b, *supra* note 74, p. 661.
153. European Competition Network, *Results of the questionnaire on the reform of Member States (MS) national competition laws after EC Regulation No. 1/2003*, 2013.

means that the other Member States still counted on civil courts that might have no knowledge whatsoever to deal with complex competition cases, such as vertical restraints that require a specific expertise to assess and balance the efficiencies and the potential anticompetitive effects of business practices.

Taking these different historical perspectives into consideration, another point of controversy that also contributes to the different levels of enforcement (of vertical restraints) in the EU was the lack of guidance from the Commission's side on how to enforce anticompetitive practices. As briefly described above, in the context of the modernization of antitrust policies, Regulation 1/2003 set legal obligations on the Member States to enforce Article 101 TFEU (Article 3).[154] Over the years, the Commission has not clarified the institutional elements to be observed by the Member States other than the obligations to apply Articles 101 and 102 TFEU uniformly.

The Commission's report of ten years of implementation of Regulation 1/2003[155] acknowledges that the EU law tended to leave to Member States a large degree of flexibility ('procedure autonomy')[156] in the design of their competition enforcement regimes.[157] Therefore, even though the same rules are applied to all NCAs, their institutional set-ups vary significantly. The Commission also reported that the divergences among the Member States' enforcement systems refer to important aspects to guarantee *ex post* control via public enforcement. Among these aspects, it highlighted the ability of NCAs to set adequate sanctions, including criminal ones, to impose structural remedies, and to set enforcement priorities.[158] Given these different procedural and institutional realities, this section raises the question whether this decentralized enforcement system, where national authorities operate under different procedural rules, could endanger the effective enforcement of EU public and private law.[159]

Moreover, Article 35 of Regulation 1/2003[160] generally foresees that Member States should appoint the competition agencies responsible for applying EU competition rules in such a manner as to comply with the provisions of the regulation.[161] Since this article was obviously intended to ensure the efficient implementation of EU

154. K. Cseres, 'The Impact of Regulation 1/2003 in the New Member States', *Competition Law Review*, Vol. 6, No. 2, 2010b, pp. 145-182.
155. European Commission, *Ten Years of Antitrust Enforcement under Regulation 1/2003*, 2014.
156. Expression used by D. Geradin, A. Layne-Farrar & N. Petit, *EU Competition Law and Economics*, Oxford, Oxford University Press, 2012, p. 327.
157. *See also* W. Wils, 'Ten Years of Regulation 1/2003: A Retrospective', *Journal of European Competition Law and Practice*, Vol. 4, No. 4, 2013, pp. 293-301.
158. K. Cseres, 'Multi-Jurisdictional Competition Law Enforcement: The Interface Between European Competition Law and the Competition Laws of the New Member States', *European Competition Journal*, Vol. 3, No. 2, 2007, p. 466.
159. Although this Chapter does not focus on the challenges of private enforcement of EU competition law, this analysis cannot be forgotten. *See*, for instance, C. Cauffman & N. J. Philipsen, 'Who Does What in Competition Law: Harmonizing the Rules on Damages for Infringements of the EU Competition Rules', *in* B. Akkermans, J. Hage, N. Kornet & J Smits (eds), *Who Does What in European Private Law?*, Ius Commune Europaeum No. 137, Cambridge-Antwerp-Portland, Intersentia, pp. 245-287.
160. Article 35(1) of Regulation 1/2003: 'The Member States shall designate the competition authority or authorities responsible for the application of Articles 81 and 82 of the Treaty in such a way that the provisions of this regulation are effectively complied with.'
161. European Commission, 2017, *supra* note 118, paragraph 9.

competition rules in each Member State, it again refrained from imposing any specific requirements concerning the institutional setup of the NCAs. Souza Ferro, for instance, explains that this principle of effectiveness brought by Article 35 did not facilitate the exercise of the rights granted by Articles 101 and 102 TFEU, as well as the fundamental rights associated with their enforcement. The author describes that, in some cases, national authorities might be influenced by lobbying groups and/or other political or economic pressure groups, and this situation could frustrate the full efficient application of the EU law.[162] For instance, Brook and Cseres demonstrated that the decentralized enforcement system provided room for the national authorities to promote their own specific domestic interests.[163] This is not necessarily a problem, but it might justify the focus of certain competition authorities on high-profile cartel cases, rather than on complex vertical agreements cases.

Indeed, political factors can justify inconsistent decisions on vertical restraints among the Member States, or even the enacting of national law that somehow circumvents Article 101 TFEU. For instance, Van den Bergh discusses that in certain industries, the pressure of lobbying groups influenced national legislation to make RPM a legal practice, even though it is not clear whether these practices enhance economic welfare. In this case, the author explains that when prices of certain industries are regulated by law, Article 101 TFEU is no longer applied.[164] An important example of that is the market for books. Several countries around the world have adopted legislation fixing the retail prices for book, even though the economic theory and even empirical evidences fail to provide welfare-oriented justification for such practices.[165]

If we go back to the argument that several NCAs have encountered difficulties in establishing a proper institutional background to tackle vertical restraints, one can say that this point is reinforced by the recent efforts of the Commission to publish new directives in the topic. The *ex post* policy evaluation of Regulation 1/2003 indeed recognized several ways in which the NCAs can enhance a more effective enforcement. Having a closer look at the policy tools and actions that directly affect the enforcement of vertical restraints, the Commission highlights (i) the general lack of instruments to enforce competition law; (ii) the lack of powers to effectively set fines; and (iii) the lack of safeguards which guarantee the independence of national authorities with regard to the enforcement of EU competition rules.[166]

162. M. S. Ferro, 'Institutional Design of National Competition Authorities: EU Requirements', *Competition Law Review*, Vol. 13, No. 2, 2018, p. 120.
163. O. Brook & K. Cseres, 'Member States' Interest in the Enforcement of EU Competition Law: A Case Study of Article 101 TFEU', *in* M. Varju (ed.), *Between Compliance and Particularism: Member State Interests and European Union Law*, Cham, Springer Publishing, 2019.
164. Van den Bergh, 2016, *supra* note 110.
165. Van den Bergh, 2016, *supra* note 110, p. 183.
166. These items are further described in: European Commission, *Impact Assessment on Enhancing Competition in the EU for the Benefit of Businesses and Consumers* – Reinforcement of the application of EU competition law by national competition authorities, 2017. Available at: http://ec.europa.eu/competition/antitrust/im qpact _assessment_summary_en.pdf (30/1/2019).

The Commission recently took an important step by publishing the Directive (EU) 2019/1 'to empower the competition authorities of the Member States to be more effective enforcers and to ensure the proper functioning of the internal market'.[167] In more detail, the Directive aims at ensuring a minimum common toolkit to foster effective enforcement powers for the authorities, such as the rights: (i) to act independently when enforcing EU competition law, without being influenced by public or private entities (Article 4); (ii) to have sufficient necessary financial resources and staff to be able to lead the substantive cases (Article 5); (iii) to have power to collect evidence, even in complex cases (Article 6); (iv) to impose adequate sanctions to deter anticompetitive practices in accordance with EU competition policies and (e) to have adequate leniency programmes that discourage undertakings from engaging in illegal cartels (Article 20).[168] Although not all these enforcement powers are directly related to the enforcement of vertical restraints, they confirm the relevance of the institutional challenge that has been faced by the Commission.

4.6 CONCLUDING REMARKS

This chapter analysed the evolution of EU competition law in relation to vertical restraints, as well as its current challenges. Historically, Regulation 1/2003 replaced the centralized *ex ante* notification system of vertical agreements with a decentralized *ex post* control of these business practices. The chapter shows some alternative literature that suggests that behind the 'decentralization', the Commission has not lost its central position in the development and implementation of European competition policies, since it kept (and even expanded) most of its investigatory and lawmaking powers.

Despite the political economy discussions and the suggested alternative readings, this piece of work shows that there are still very important lessons to be drawn from the European experience and the 2004 Reform. These lessons are mainly related to the instruments that are still used by the NCAs to guarantee the enforcement of vertical restraints, in the *ex post* control scenario. Among the sections three of these instruments called 'pillars' were picked out: (i) the existence of a consolidated antitrust jurisprudence, a VBER and guidelines to support firms and law enforcers in self-assessing the economic effects of vertical agreements; (ii) the creation of a network among authorities that permitted some coordination, the sharing of experiences and a more effective allocation of competences among the NCAs and the Commission; and (iii) the intensification of *ex post* control instruments.

The chapter also recognized that over the years, even with the presence of the three enforcement pillars, there are still open questions to be considered when thinking about optimal enforcement of vertical restraints in the EU context. Therefore, two challenges were identified. The first challenge refers to the controversies about the application of regulations and soft law instruments to cases involving the digital

167. Directive (EU) 2019/1 of the European Parliament and of the Council of 11 December 2018 to empower the competition authorities of the Member States to be more effective enforcers and to ensure the proper functioning of the internal market.
168. For further analysis of the Directive 2019/1, *see* Ferro, *supra* note 162, pp. 109-137.

economy. The two chosen case analyses (selective distribution and price parity arrangements) illustrate that the authorities of countries such as in France, Germany, and the UK are facing important controversies and are presenting different interpretations of Article 101 TFEU and of the content of the VBER. The new realities of a more globalized, technology-driven and digitalized competitive environment may suggest the need for a clearer framework for assessing and balancing the anti- and procompetitive effects of such restrictive practices.

The second challenge is related to the different levels of enforcement of Article 101 TFEU among the Members States. This chapter argued that not all the national authorities developed adequate enforcement procedures over time. The analysis suggests that the institutional disparities remain a challenge to be overcome by the Commission in the coming years.

From what has been discussed, one can note that the challenges faced by several EU countries - even with the support of the Commission - are also faced by several developing countries around the world. The difficulties of establishing a proper competition authority, with sufficient resources to enforce all antitrust topics (including the complex cases of vertical restraints), with specialized courts, among other items, are not a problem encountered only in the European reality. For this reason, the understanding of the EU experience and its challenges are valuable for this comparative study.

This chapter started by indicating that both Brazil and the EU passed through a similar change in policy applicable to vertical restraints: from an *ex ante* notification system of agreements to an *ex post* control of restrictive practices, although with some crucial differences. In the EU the change from an *ex ante* notification system to an *ex post* monitoring regime happened after forty years of notification system of agreements, and it was accompanied by the VBER and guidelines to help business people self-assessing the potential anticompetitive effects of their contracts. In Brazil, Resolution No. 17/2016 excluded vertical agreements from the notification system, leaving the enforcement of vertical restraints in Brazil solely dependent on *ex post* control. It means that, unlike in Europe, the Brazilian authority did not publish any guidelines to better inform companies and/or took specific measures to strengthening the *ex post* control.

Considering the relevance of the institutional set-up to policymaking and enforcement, the next step of this chapter is to identify the enforcement costs for each legal system. The comparative analysis of information, incentive and administrative costs will allow a deeper understanding about the design and policy implication among countries which are at different stages of implementation of antitrust law.

CHAPTER 5

Enforcement Costs of Vertical Agreements: A Comparative Law and Economics Analysis

When discussing the international trends in antitrust policies concerning vertical agreements, regulators have several policy options to choose from. In contrast with other antitrust illegal practices that are more easily characterized, such as cartels, an adequate antitrust assessment of vertical agreements requires deep knowledge of specialized economic concepts that might not be well established among businessmen, or even lawyers, judges, or other public officials. Experience and knowledge of how to handle complex antitrust cases (especially on the side of antitrust authorities) tend to be crucial pillars to be considered when the regulator is making a decision about the adequate policy to enforce the anticompetitive vertical agreements. In this context, a policy framework is proposed, that seeks welfare maximization by minimizing enforcement costs. To design this conceptual framework, three important dimensions of enforcement costs were studied: information costs, incentive costs and administrative costs. The goal of this study is to reintroduce the discussion about the enforcement of vertical agreements from a comparative perspective in order to see what can be learned from it.

5.1 INTRODUCTION: THE POLICY OPTIONS FOR VERTICAL AGREEMENTS

This chapter aims to provide a normative analysis of antitrust policies applicable to vertical agreements. For this analysis, the antitrust enforcement cost framework and a comparative approach to the experiences from Brazil and the EU are considered. Previous chapters showed that the regulation of vertical agreements can be a challenging exercise to antitrust agencies around the world since such agreements have mixed consequences in the marketplace. It also investigated the legal framework and context of the Brazilian and the European experiences in trying to regulate these commercial practices. Even though both experiences favoured the *ex post* control of vertical restraints over the *ex ante* notification system – the EU through Council Regulation 1/2003, and Brazil via CADE's Resolution 17/2016 – some differences were identified, which will be elaborated upon in the next sections.

When discussing the international trends in antitrust policies concerning vertical agreements, regulators have several policy options to choose from. Regulators can choose among a notification system for vertical agreements, pure *ex post* enforcement of restrictive practices or mixed policies, for instance, legal exemption regimes. In their decisions, regulators should take into consideration several aspects, such as the costs of enforcement under each policy option, the existing capabilities and resources, as well as the institutional aspects of the country. For example, jurisdictions with limited experience of enforcing competition law and with less qualified staff (in respect to assessing restrictive agreements) might opt to choose (or to begin with) a notification system of agreements and prohibiting a narrow range of vertical restraints.[1]

Regulators should also carefully assess the behaviour of firms under different enforcement regimes. Companies, on the one hand, have better legal certainty when they notify their agreements and receive the 'green flag' from the authority. On the other hand, they might engage in more anticompetitive agreements in the *ex post* enforcement system if the chances of being caught by the law enforcers and the fines are too low.

In contrast with other antitrust illegal practices that are more easily characterized, such as cartels, an adequate antitrust assessment of vertical agreements requires deep knowledge of specialized economic concepts that might not be well established among businessmen, or even lawyers, judges, or other public officials. Experience and knowledge of how to handle complex antitrust cases (especially on the side of antitrust authorities) tend to be crucial pillars to be considered when the regulator is making a decision about the adequate policy to enforce the anticompetitive vertical agreements. Within this framework, the following questions are proposed to the readers: *Does a change in antitrust policies from* ex ante *to* ex post *control of vertical agreements always enhance the efficiency of the enforcement of competition law? What are the direct and indirect enforcement costs in a notification system of vertical agreements and in an* ex post *monitoring system? Which elements affect those different costs? What are the lessons to be learned from the Brazilian and the European experiences in regulating vertical agreements?*

In the attempt to find an answer to the proposed questions and to expand on the existing literature, this chapter is organized into nine sections, including this introduction and the concluding remarks. Section 5.2 presents a relevant literature review. Section 5.3 introduces a general theoretical background about the economic analysis of antitrust enforcement systems. The main goal is to prepare the reader for the proposed normative analysis. In sequence, the chapter looks at three main types of costs faced by the antitrust agency when enforcing vertical agreements. Section 5.4 focuses on the

1. Kovacic develops similar argumentation in a more general context, not applied to vertical agreements. *See* W. Kovacic, 'Institutional Foundations for Economic Legal Reform in Transition Economies: The Case of Competition Policy and Antitrust Enforcement', *Chicago Kent Law Review*, Vol. 77, 2001, pp. 265-306.

information costs involved in the assessment of vertical agreements. As information costs, we consider the costs of gathering relevant information for an antitrust assessment and the costs of assessing the complex effects of vertical agreements. Section 5.5 describes incentive costs, which are costs related to the legal uncertainty of parties in a given framework. These costs are measured by analysing the level of fines of different jurisdictions, the probability of error, the role of private enforcement, and the general trust in institutions. Section 5.6 describes the administrative costs of enforcement practices. To illustrate the cost analysis, comparative elements from Brazil and the EU that have been previously discussed in this book are presented. Following the cost analysis, section 5.7 presents a normative discussion of efficient policies of vertical agreements taking into consideration different enforcement costs scenarios. Finally, section 5.8 presents policy prepositions for the EU and Brazil and the last section indicates concluding remarks.

5.2 LITERATURE REVIEW

Prior attention has been given in the literature about the economic analysis of competition policies applicable to restrictive agreements, mainly in the European context, when Regulation 1/2003 was being formulated.[2]

Verena Hahn, for instance, by using a game theory framework, discusses that the choice between notification of agreements and *ex post* control relies on the 'pre-commitment' of the competition authority to an enforcement probability.[3] In other words, the author claims that if companies cannot know for sure the probability of detection when deciding to engage in anticompetitive agreements (e.g., when the authority faces considerable discretion in its decisions), the notification system is preferred; however, when the pre-commitment is possible (e.g., when the authority announces an enforcement probability), then the *ex post* control is preferred, since companies will tend not to sign agreements with restrictive clauses.

Damien Neven emphasizes that the notification system and the *ex post* monitoring are not necessarily substitutes. He argues that if an agency (in his paper, the Commission) decides upon ending a notification system of agreements and leaving the *ex post* monitoring system unchanged, this change in policy may encourage the implementation of unlawful agreements.[4] According to the author, when the *ex ante* system is removed, it is expected that the *ex post* system is 're-calibrated and strengthened'[5] by, for instance, having a better screening of investigated cases,

2. Regulation 1/2003 entered into force in 2004, and substitutes the old centralized *ex ante* authorization system of agreements (including vertical ones) to a decentralized *ex post* control. For more details, *see* section 4.3 of Chapter 4.
3. V. Hahn, 'Antitrust Enforcement: Abuse Control or Notification?', *European Journal of Law and Economics*, Vol. 10, No. 1, 2000, pp. 69-91.
4. D. Neven, 'Removing the Notification of Agreements: Some Consequences of Ex-post Monitoring', *in* A. Bogdandy, P. Mavroidis & Y. Meny (eds), *European Integration and International Cooperation: Studies in International Economic Law in Honour of Claus-Dieter Ehlermann*, The Hague, Kluwer Law International, 2002.
5. Neven, 2002, *supra* note 4, p. 351.

increasing the probability of enforcement of restrictive agreements and re-evaluating the amount of fines.

In a similar way, Pedro Pita Barros proposes a model that looks at how firms react in the context of *ex ante* notification and *ex post* monitoring of agreements.[6] He shows that even in the case of an overall decrease of enforcement of restrictive agreements, two possible effects could be observed. On the one hand, in the absence of *ex ante* notification, firms may start engaging in more anticompetitive agreements, since they will hardly ever be prosecuted. On the other hand, firms may also engage in less restrictive agreements, since they may be less likely to take risks. This is also the case because the costs of being prosecuted and fined under an *ex post* monitoring regime tend to be more expressive than the costs related to the disapproval of the authority in the scope of a notification system.

Barros concludes that, in Europe, this last effect was more likely to be observed. According to the author, agreements that are restrictive to start with (such as cartels that probably would not be notified in the first place) may get worse in the *ex post* monitoring, whereas agreements that have mixed consequences may become even less restrictive. This happens because of the different adjustment costs (of contracts) that business people experience in the scope of *ex post* system. To reach these conclusions, the author considers that the EU enforcement capabilities are evenly spread among the different Member States, which may not always be the case.

Finally, Frédéric Loss et al. investigate the optimal antitrust policy for restrictive agreements based on the competition authority's accuracy of judgment.[7] The authors look not only to the *ex ante* versus *ex post* efficiency trade-off but also to mixed policies such as block exemptions regimes and blacklists. They conclude that the policy change from a notification system to an *ex post* control regime is relevant only if the quality of judgment of the competition authority is sufficiently high. This happens because, according to the authors, when the accuracy and quality of the assessment is high enough, it is possible to deter anticompetitive agreements by simply applying adequate fines in the *ex post* regime. However, if the quality of antitrust assessments of restrictive agreements is low, the notification system can thus be more effective than a legal exception or *ex post* regime in preventing anticompetitive agreements from being signed. The authors conclude that *ex ante* notification systems are the optimal policy when there is a high probability of errors, for instance, in the case of young competition authorities that have less experience in applying adequate antitrust assessments. According to them, an authority should only move away from a notification system and impose an *ex post* control when the decisions reach more accurate levels. The paper from these authors is the one that most closely relates to the analysis of this chapter.

This existing literature, however, has some limitations. First, the contributions mainly refer to the context of modernization of the European Competition rules, not

6. P. Barros, 'Looking Behind the Curtain: Effects from Modernization of European Union Competition Policy', *European Economic Review*, Vol. 47, No. 4, 2003, pp. 613-624.
7. F. Loss, E. Malavolti-Grimal, T. Verge & F. Berges-Sennou, 'European Competition Policy Modernization: From Notifications to Legal Exception', *European Economic Review*, Vol. 52, No. 1, 2008, pp. 77-98.

expanding the analysis to other jurisdictions. Second, restrictive agreements are considered as the unique anticompetitive problem, without paying too much attention to the differences among vertical agreements, cartels, and so on. Third, none of the authors systematically identified the different costs related to the enforcement of restrictive agreements which directly affect the policy options. It is also important to point out that the above-discussed theoretical contributions have not been updated to cope with the fundamental changes in the dynamics of contemporary markets. Therefore, the goal of this chapter is to reintroduce the discussion about the enforcement of vertical agreements from a comparative perspective in order to see what can be learned from it.

5.3 MULTIPLE DIMENSIONS OF ANTITRUST ENFORCEMENT

Shavell's contribution on law enforcement describes three main dimensions that help characterizing the enforcement of the law.[8] First, there is the 'timing of legal intervention', which can happen either before (preventive-based measure) or after (act-based or harm-based) the act happens. In more detail, the *ex ante/ex post* parameters mainly depend on the combination of some variables, such as the design of the sanctions together with the probability of its application, the ability of law enforcers (also in terms of resources) in prosecuting illegal practices, and the quantity of information held by law enforcers and by the parties in respect to a specific misconduct. At this respect, Shavell says:

> The knowledge that individuals have about the dangerousness of their acts is also germane to answering the question about the optimal stage of legal intervention. The more information that individuals have about the dangerousness of their acts, the more appealing will be later intervention. [...] Nevertheless, individuals who do not recognize the dangerousness of an act might be unaware that committing the act could result in an act-based sanction or a harm-based-sanction – so that prevention would be required to control their behaviour.[9]

Second, another dimension of enforcement of the law is the 'form of sanctions', which can be monetary or non-monetary (such as imprisonment), depending on the severity of the infringement.[10]

Finally, the third dimension explained by Shavell is the 'role of private and public agents' in the enforcement of the law. A so-called private-oriented enforcement system occurs when private parties provide the most relevant information regarding the case. Public enforcement, in its turn, stands when public agents have or are capable of having more information about the given situation. These three dimensions can also be studied in the context of competition enforcement, especially, within the framework of policies applicable to vertical agreements as it is shown in the following subsections.

8. S. Shavell, 'The Optimal Structure of Law Enforcement', *Journal of Law & Economics*, Vol. 36, No. 1, 1993, pp. 255-287, p. 257.
9. Shavell, 1993, *supra* note 8, p. 265.
10. For this topic, *see also* G. Becker, 'Crime and Punishment: An Economic Approach', *Journal of Political Economy*, Vol. 76, No. 2, 1968, pp. 169-217.

5.3.1 Timing of Legal Intervention

The optimal choice between *ex ante* and *ex post* policies, in the traditional theory of law and economics, is also discussed by Kaplow's approach towards the trade-off 'rules versus standards'.[11] The author describes both a rule and a standard as legal commands, and emphasizes that 'the only distinction between rule and standards is the extent to which efforts to give content to the law are undertaken before or after individuals act'.[12] According to his theory, a legal norm might be precise in the sense that it is an outline for action by a judge and civil servants or might be imprecise when it simply indicates the direction in which the law requires decisions to be made. These precise norms (rules) allow simple and mechanical decisions, while vague norms (standards) require complex and policy-oriented decisions.

Considering the systematic approaches adopted by Shavell and Kaplow, and applying it to the peculiarities of antitrust law and enforcement of vertical agreements, some remarks can be added. First, it is questioned in this book whether an *ex ante* notification system of vertical agreements (precise rules; preventive oriented policy) is a more efficient policy than an *ex post* monitoring (vague norms; act/harm-oriented policy) and under which conditions. Within an *ex ante* notification regime, firms are required to notify to antitrust agencies the agreements that they are intending to sign (meaning, the practices they are contemplating) before they put them into practice. The *ex post* control of vertical restraints, in contrast, attempts to reach an optimal level of deterrence by sanctioning parties after the harm is caused by a certain agreement. *Ex post* control of restrictive agreements is induced by general antitrust legal criteria that can sometimes be unclear and require complicated interpretation. As explained in the previous chapter, both in Brazil and in the EU the *ex post* enforcement of vertical agreement was favoured by the authorities, but with certain differences. In the EU, for instance, the current legal framework applicable to vertical agreements is based on both precise norms (e.g., Article 101 TFEU) that describe the general rule applicable to restrictive agreements, and vague norms or standards, which correspond to the soft-law instruments, such as the existing guidelines on the application of Article 101 TFEU, that was based on previous jurisprudence of the authority.

5.3.2 Form of Sanction

As for the 'form of sanctions', antitrust agencies around the world tend to use monetary sanctions or other behavioural restrictions (such as termination of contract) for condemned cases of restrictive agreements. Usually, in terms of antitrust policies, imprisonment is an option applied often for hardcore cartels and just in a few countries, such as in the US.

The form of sanction can directly affect the incentive of parties to engage or not in restrictive agreements. If the sanction over anticompetitive vertical agreements is

11. L. Kaplow, 'Rules Versus Standards: An Economic Analysis', *Duke Law Journal*, Vol. 42, No. 3, 1992, pp. 557-629.
12. Kaplow, 1992, *supra* note 11, p. 560.

very severe (massive monetary fines or even imprisonment), it may discourage companies from engaging in these commercial practices. Under a notification system of agreements, the form of sanction chosen by the antitrust authority can actually determine whether companies will indeed comply with the law or not (meaning, whether they will notify or not the agreements). In the EU level, antitrust sanctions are mostly monetary, and only a few Member States still consider imprisonment as an option for antitrust sanctions. In Brazil, for instance, even though the law foresees imprisonment for some antitrust illegalities, in practice, this sanction has never been used.

5.3.3 The Role of Public and Private Agents

Regarding Shavell's third dimension of antitrust enforcement, the 'role of private and public agents', one can say that like many other areas of the law, competition enforcement practices also frequently rely on a mix of public and private enforcement mechanisms.

In the case of public enforcement, the law enforcers, by means of their joint activities, can determine the probability of detection as well as the severity of penalties to produce the correct incentives to deter violations.[13] Arlen Duke[14] describes two forms of public antitrust enforcement models: the prosecutorial model, under which the antitrust agency undertakes the investigatory and enforcement functions and must prove its case by bringing a complaint before a generalist court or specialist adjudicative body; and the administrative model, in which the investigative and adjudicatory powers are entrusted to one authority or group of agencies.[15] The administrative model can be seen in most of the antitrust agencies around the world, and it is also the model chosen by Brazil and by the EU (as well as by most NCAs).

The literature on competition law and economics points out various advantages of public enforcement. Public authorities are sometimes more qualified to acquire and analyse relevant information, particularly when vast amounts of information are involved.[16] Also, public enforcement regimes provide public agencies with a wider range of detection and means of investigation, as well as alternative sanctioning possibilities, which may provide an optimal level of deterrence. Finally, public servants are, in theory, appointed to pursue social goals dictated by public policy, rather than private objectives.[17] A system of private enforcement, in its turn, involves actions of

13. W. Schwartz, 'An Overview of the Economics of Antitrust Enforcement', *Georgetown Law Journal*, Vol. 68, 1980, p. 1083.
14. A. Duke, 'Public Enforcement', *in* J. Duns, A. Duke, & B. Sweeney (eds), *Comparative Competition Law*, Cheltenham, Edward Elgar Publishing, 2015, p. 271.
15. Although a party found by the enforcement agency to have breached the law will almost always have a right to challenge the agencies' decision in the courts.
16. *See* R. Van den Bergh, 'Should Consumer Protection Law Be Publicly Enforced? An Economic Perspective on EC Regulation 2006/2004 and Its Implementation in the Consumer Protection Laws of the Member States', *in* W. van Boom & M. Loos (eds), *Collective Enforcement of Consumer Law*, Groningen, Europa Law Publishing, 2007.
17. Chapters 3 and 4 discusses that under certain circumstances, authorities might also act in favour of their own interest.

private parties in civil courts that claim compensation for personal losses. That is to say, private enforcement, within the scope of competition law, also contributes to achieve complementary deterrence and corrective justice.[18]

If competition law is efficiently applied, then the literature also suggests that public enforcement can be preferred to private enforcement. Wouter Wils, for instance, justifies the superiority of antitrust public enforcement through three main arguments.[19] In the first place, the author argues that public law enforcers have more effective powers of investigation and sanction. Second, because private enforcement is motivated by private profit, it naturally deviates from the overall public interest that gives grounds to competition law. Lastly, private enforcement can be very expensive for parties, as many additional resources are needed to be able to correctly allocate the damages. In the same sense, Hannah Buxbaum points out that the expansive use of private lawsuits, especially in the US, triggers the development of competition law in a 'somewhat inefficient and piecemeal fashion', as the majority of the issues brought before courts merely reflect the choices of individual plaintiffs and not a coherent enforcement strategy of public agencies.[20]

Public and private enforcement are expensive procedures, yet each model has its own advantages. The question of how best to combine public and private enforcement to guarantee optimal welfare outcomes, invariably arises due to the strengthening of private rights.[21] Also, the choice in favour of public or private enforcement, or most likely in favour of some mixed policy, is very much associated with the analysis of the goals of competition law in a certain jurisdiction, or even in broader terms, to the goals of the country itself. The goal of competition policies can vary considerably from country to country. As examples of goals, one can highlight the promotion of total welfare, consumer welfare and/or market integration. For instance, if the tools to apply competition law are not sufficient, and/or if the goal of another competition national law is pursuing corrective justice through compensation, then private enforcement may be preferred.[22]

In their policymaking process, antitrust agents must consider both the welfare effects of anticompetitive practices, and the enforcement costs related to it. In practice, the competition agency chooses the optimal dimensions of antitrust enforcement by wisely allocating its resources. In certain circumstances, an *ex ante* notification of vertical agreements may be preferred to an *ex post* monitoring policy or even public enforcement may be preferred to a more private-oriented policy so as to reduce the enforcement costs and the abuse of economic power.[23]

18. Van den Bergh, 2007, *supra* note 16.
19. W. Wils, 'Should Private Antitrust Enforcement Be Encouraged in Europe?', *World Competition*, Vol. 26, No. 3, 2003, pp. 472-488.
20. H. Buxbaum, 'Private Enforcement of Competition Law in the United States: Of Optimal Deterrence and Social Costs', *in* J. Basedow (ed.), *Private Enforcement of EC Competition Law*, International Competition Law Series, Zuidpoolsingel, Wolters Kluwer, 2007, p. 48.
21. Wils, 2003, *supra* note 19.
22. Wils, 2003, *supra* note 19.
23. More recent contributions to the literature of antitrust enforcement analyse the effects of private enforcement on public enforcement, for instance, in cartel cases, where the question arises whether the possibility of damage claims discouraging companies to sign leniency agreements in

5.3.4 Considerations on Enforcement Costs

Competition authorities around the world are often subject to two main constraints, the first one being limited resources and the second one information asymmetries.[24] Both constraints are somehow related, since it would be too costly to control every firm or market, and also because markets are rarely transparent. This information problem reduces the efficiency and directly influences the level of enforcement of certain antitrust policies.

When thinking about policies applicable to vertical agreements, if a given antitrust authority chooses to allocate greater resources to the notification control, the probability of detecting anticompetitive agreements increases. The authority, consequently, gathers more information about the markets and on how to correctly assess the potential anticompetitive effects in those situations. However, this option could be too costly, and the authority eventually must face the trade-off of having a more extensive number of investigations or of having more effective results in fewer cases. In the case of *ex post* monitoring of antitrust practices, a smaller number of interventions happens, and these interventions leave more markets without monitoring.[25]

When choosing a methodology that balances welfare effects and enforcement costs, one approach that underlies the choice of antitrust enforcement policy is oriented towards welfare maximization by seeking to *minimize enforcement costs*.[26] This minimization of costs is attributed not only to administrative costs of authorities but also to error costs in the decision-making process, legal uncertainties, and disincentives imposed to parties.

In more detail, costs can be defined as 'any item that makes someone worse-off, or reduces a person's well-being'.[27] Costs can often be categorized according to different parameters. Costs can be monetary or non-monetary, they can be one-off costs and/or recurring costs; they can be described as economic or social costs, or even as indirect costs when related to the inefficiencies, regulatory uncertainty, distrust in institutions, and so on.[28]

---

the first place. However, since most of these contributions are mainly oriented to cartel cases, they fall outside the scope of this book. *See*, T. Reuter, 'Private Antitrust Enforcement and the Role of Harmed Parties in Public Enforcement', *European Journal of Law and Economics*, Vol. 41, 2016, pp. 479-507; W. Wils, 'Private Enforcement of EU Antitrust Law and Its Relationship with Public Enforcement: Past, Present and Future', *World Competition*, Vol. 40, No. 1, 2017, pp. 3-46.

24. S. Souam, 'Optimal Antitrust Policy under Different Regimes of Fines', *International Journal of Industrial Organization*, Vol. 19, No. 1, 2001, p. 2.
25. Souam, 2001, *supra* note 24, p. 2.
26. Wright researched welfare maximization by seeking the minimization of the sum enforcement costs. *See*, J. Wright, 'Evidence-Based Antitrust Enforcement in the Technology Sector', *CPI Antitrust Chronicle*, Volume March, 2013.
27. CEPS, *Assessing the costs and benefits of regulation: Study for the European Commission*, 2013, p. 22.
28. CEPS, 2013, *supra* note 27, p. 22.

This study takes as main cost parameters the ones defined by Roger Van den Bergh.[29] The author discusses that the economic analysis of the switch from an *ex ante* authorization system of contracts to an *ex post* monitoring system involves the assessment of two main types of enforcement costs: the information costs and the incentive costs. To this analysis can be added the assessment of administrative costs. The next sections aim at exploring and expanding this classification by identifying the elements that compose these three enforcement costs.

5.4 INFORMATION COSTS

Generally speaking, when it comes to antitrust cases, the term 'information' refers to 'the knowledge about the occurrence of anti-competitive actions, evidence to support the case, and the technique required to assess whether business practices are anti-competitive or not'.[30] In an ideal world, all market players and law enforcers have full information about market conditions, and the existence of restrictive practices, and they can all fully understand the existing legal rules. This means that both authorities and firms can easily recognize whether a restrictive agreement is an infringement to competition law. However, this scenario is unlikely to happen. In practice, firms often have the detailed information about their business practices (i.e., the content of the contracts) and law enforcers can face high costs in obtaining this relevant information.[31]

As anticipated before, one fundamental problem of formulating competition policies is related to the lack of information regarding market dynamics, price conditions, relevant data on firms' cost curves, market shares, and most importantly, lack of information about the legality of business practices, which means the existence of coordination activities. Information costs can take different forms in the context of antitrust policies. When analysing the economic effects of vertical agreements, information costs refer to the costs of having access to enough information on the content of those agreements as well as on their potential anticompetitive effects on the market dynamics. For this study, these information costs are divided into two different types: (1) costs of gathering market information and (2) costs of assessing the competitive effects (efficiencies and potential harms).

5.4.1 Cost of Gathering Market Information

There are several questions that law enforcers and firms encounter when assessing a vertical agreement, such as: How is the competition dynamic in the upstream and downstream markets? Who are the main market players? Do these players have market

29. R. Van den Bergh, *Comparative Competition Law and Economics*, Cheltenham, Edward Elgar, 2017, p. 430.
30. A. Gonzales & A. Micco, 'Private Versus Public Antitrust Enforcement: Evidence from Chile', *Journal of Competition Law & Economics*, Vol. 10, No. 3, 2014, p. 699.
31. M. Pirrung, 'EU Enlargement Towards Cartel Paradise? An Economic Analysis of the Reform of European Competition Law', *Erasmus Law and Economics Review*, Vol. 1, 2004, p. 89.

power? What are the barriers to entry in the upstream and downstream markets? What are the potential efficiencies and anticompetitive effects of these agreements?

The literature recognizes that companies, as market players, tend to be better qualified to give answers to these questions, since they can more easily detect the anticompetitive contracts that affect their daily activities.[32] An antitrust authority, by default, supervises all economic sectors, and therefore, is not always able to match the firm's ability to identify the most restrictive contracts. The authorities frequently use government statistical records to get information about the markets, or use complaints of other market players to identify anticompetitive behaviour.[33] However, gathering public data and information provided by third parties is often very difficult and costly, and the results are not always accurate enough to guarantee the assessment of market dynamics.

When discussing policies to vertical agreements, one can say that the *ex ante* notification system creates lower costs of gathering market information than the *ex post* control regime. This happens because, under a notification system of agreements, firms should voluntarily reveal the dynamics of their markets and the possible existence of a vertical restraint and the authorities have access to the information that would probably be very costly or even impossible to obtain under an *ex post* regime. Moreover, under the *ex post* monitoring regime, firms must self-assess the effects of their restrictive practices and, therefore, they collect a higher amount of information about the market dynamics. As stated in previous paragraphs, third-party information regarding market dynamics might also be difficult and costly to obtain and, therefore, the firm's information costs for gathering market information tend also to be higher under an *ex post* regime.

This was indeed a concern expressed by some scholars over the years. Wernhard Moschel, in one of his speeches, talked about the risks faced by Europe when Regulation 1/2003 was being discussed:

> For competition policy, such a change is extremely risky. A system of directly applicable exceptions is clearly inferior to a prior notification system, again for a number of reasons: The cartel offices do not receive any information; It leads to a complete lack of transparency for interested third parties, competitors, subcontractors, and customers, including consumers; Self-assessment by the undertakings and their respective attorneys cannot guarantee the public interest in the protection of competition. There are three reasons for this. First, undertakings often lack the necessary data concerning the market. It is simply asking too much

32. *See*, for instance, Hahn, 2000, *supra* note 3; Pirrung, 2004, *supra* note 31.
33. Neven et al., for instance, explored in their research the fact that 'complaint procedure' is a very useful and relevant form to provide the authority (in their research, the European Commission) with relevant information about markets. According to them, in the 1990s, 55% of infringement decisions were related to cases of restrictive agreements that started with a complaint procedure. *See* D. Neven, P. Papandropoulos & P. Seabright, *Trawling for Minnows: European Competition Policy and Agreements Between Firms*, London, Center for Economic and Policy Research (CEPR), 1998, p. 130.

> to ask them to apply Article 81(3) EC. Potential sinners are invited to exonerate themselves. This can hardly be described as a happy arrangement [...].[34]

The passage above suggests that a notification system may be a preferred policy whenever the companies have difficulties in gathering market information and when the competition agency has restricted data on the real impacts of certain types of contracts with vertical agreements. This could be the case, for instance, of less experienced competition agencies, since companies and their lawyers may be unwilling to provide a public authority with accurate information, as a matter of distrust. For instance, Kovacic exemplifies that where the institutionalization of public law enforcement is fragile, antitrust officials may be threatened by business people who do not want to cooperate with the authority when providing market information.[35]

This lack of information of the competition authority might cause errors in the decision-making process. For instance, the lack of information can persuade an authority to set an infringement decision with regard to a RPM case that is related to a procompetitive agreement, or, the lack of information can encourage the authority to dismiss a case of price-fixing that actually creates harm to the marketplace in the form of market foreclosure. An important judgment of a RPM case in Brazil, the *SKF* case, allows us to explore this problem.[36] Although CADE's Commissioners, in their majority, voted to consider the vertical restraint illegal, the two minority votes (from Commissioner Olavo Chinaglia and Commissioner César Mattos) argued that, in the case files, there were insufficient information of the market conditions. Therefore, this fact made it difficult to infer that the conduct was indeed anticompetitive. In the words of Commissioner Olavo Chinaglia:

> It is clear the various gaps observed in the case file in order to prepare a conclusive judgment on the illegality of the investigated conduct can be formed. It is striking, for example, the lack of information to allow me in better analysing the market structure and rationale of the sectors affected by the conduct, in particular the vertical relationships between manufacturers and distributors. It is impossible to confirm, from the evidences, how is the competitive dynamic in the distribution markets for SKF-manufactured products, and it is impossible to infer whether or not the distribution strategies in the affected markets include exclusivity relationships, exclusive territory provision to the distributors, whether the company is worried about the quality of customer service etc.[37]

If that is really the case, if there were not enough evidences of the market conditions to conclude that the SKF's agreements were illegal, then the consequences to society of the potential error in the decision may have been very detrimental. As discussed in Chapter 2, balancing pro- and anticompetitive effects in cases of vertical agreements turns out to be crucial to avoid errors in competition authorities' decisions.

---

34. Speech transcribed from W. Moschel, 'Change of Policy in European Competition Law?', *Common Market Law Review*, Vol. 37, No. 3, 2000, p. 496.
35. Kovacic, 2001, *supra* note 1, p. 308.
36. For more details of the case, *see* section 3.4.1.
37. Free translation from Olavo Chinaglia's Vote on Case *SKF v. Procon-SP*, Case No. 08012.001271/2001-447, from 31 August 2011, case file p. 932.

The discussion concerning the consequences of antitrust errors will be explored in section 5.5.

5.4.2 Cost of Assessing the Effects of Vertical Agreements

Information costs can also be discussed in terms of the lack of knowledge related to the assessment of pro- and anticompetitive effects of vertical agreements. These costs are perceived not only by the law enforcers but also by businessmen and their legal advisors. In practice, companies often engage in certain commercial agreements, as distribution agreements with subtle restrictive clauses, drafted by lawyers, without being fully conscious of the potential negative outcomes of them in the markets.

A precise antitrust evaluation of vertical agreements, most of the time, involves the study of complex economic concepts, which can be done by highly educated people who have specific knowledge on antitrust rules and economic concepts. Chapter 2 discussed the complex nature of vertical agreements. It showed, for instance, that certain vertical restraints can be justified by efficiency arguments, as they can solve the double markup problem, prevent free-riding and reduce transaction costs. At the same time, these vertical restraints can facilitate collusion, reduce intra- and inter-brand competition and foreclose markets.[38] The chapter showed that the balance of these effects is not an easy job and requires specific knowledge regarding antitrust and market analysis. These difficulties are also due to the fact that each vertical restraint (such as RPM, geo-blocking clauses, selective distribution system) requires a specific economic analysis.[39] For example, RPM and geo-blocking restrictions may combat free-riding, which is a procompetitive effect. RPM and geo-blocking clauses may also facilitate collusion and forecloses markets, which are anticompetitive effects. However, RPM may also combat double marginalization problems, while territorial protection may increase those problems.

Besides, it has been stated that balancing pro- and anticompetitive effects of vertical agreements also has limitations. First, incomplete information held by the parties harms the antitrust analysis. Second, the interrelations between producers and distributors over a specific time period and the resulting outcomes are not always the same (not even fully predictable). Actually, the effects of these interrelations are sometimes contradictory. Moreover, the economic assessment of vertical agreements is largely dependent on the study of the features of specific markets (such as market concentrations, rivalry, entry conditions, buying power) that add complexity to the analysis as a whole. The inter-temporal impacts of vertical agreements deny important information about the potential outcomes of certain practices, leading to a scenario of legal and economic uncertainty.

Therefore, information costs tend to be lower in societies that have a long-standing tradition in competition law (with the authority and firms more trained to assess vertical agreements) and where the culture of competition and access to

38. For more discussion, *see* sections 2.2 and 2.3 of Chapter 2.
39. Tables 2.1, 2.2 and 2.3 illustrate these diverse effects.

information is more present. On the contrary, information costs are higher in countries that have less experience in solving high complex cases, that have limited access to information regarding antitrust assessments, or just have an 'anaemic competition culture'.[40] Daniel Sokol, for instance, affirms that in a case where the competition authority is young (or with limited experience in assessing complex cases), human capital might be under-developed:

> With few professors and practitioners devoted to the area, it is difficult for agencies to recruit staff specifically trained in competition law and economics. The well-staffed agency, full of competition specialists is less likely to create errors of misguided prosecution or errors of non-prosecution of anti-competitive practices.[41]

Actually, several factors can contribute to create (or increase) the competition culture in a given jurisdiction, such as rethinking the university curriculum, increasing the role of competition advocacy and the role of the media, and if necessary, reforming institutions.[42] For instance, antitrust human capacity is primarily developed at the university level. This means that law schools and economic schools have an essential role in providing more teaching in this area to respond to the increasing demand for education in competition policies. Universities should adapt their courses to bring a general understanding of economic analysis of Competition Law (in a separate course or in the scope of other disciplines, such as in Contract Law), so that more people could be trained to solve highly complex cases, such as vertical restraints, but not limited to them.[43] Because the study of law and economics, mainly applicable to antitrust, provides a critical toolset for understanding the rationale of law based on the apprehension of how incentives shape human behaviour, the spread of this discipline may have a profound impact on society's behaviour, including business practices related to contract and commercial law.

As an example, Sokol discusses the lack of exposure to both Law and Economics courses and courses on Competition Law in Latin America.[44] In his research from 2009, he shows that from twenty-seven selected countries, thirteen of them have no course oriented to these disciplines. If there is no specific training in this regard, how would businessmen, lawyers or public authorities have knowledge on the legality of vertical agreements and their antitrust effects on markets? Even knowing that, since 2009, a lot has changed in Latin American countries in terms of antitrust knowledge and new antitrust practices, the gap between the need of antitrust knowledge and the sources of

40. Expression used by Pena, in J. Pena, 'Promoting Competition Policies from Private Sector in Latin America', *in* E. Fox & D. Sokol (eds), *Competition Law and Policy in Latin America*, Oxford, Hart Publishing, 2009, p. 469.
41. D. Sokol, 'The Development of Human Capital in Latin American Competition Policy', *in* E. Fox & D. Sokol (eds), *Competition Law and Policy in Latin America*, Oxford, Hart Publishing, 2009, p. 13.
42. P. A. Queiroz, *Direito Antitruste: Os fundamentos da promoção da concorrência*, São Paulo, Editora Singular, 2018, p. 302.
43. Most of the cases of abuse of dominant position, and other cases of horizontal agreements (different from hardcore cartels) also require an effect-based analysis and therefore tend to require very complex assessments.
44. Sokol, 2009, *supra* note 41, pp. 22-23.

information training is still very big. The author also stresses that the transfer of knowledge is a difficult process, since the transplant of experience from a more to a less experienced country is highly dependent of the capability of the latter to adapt foreign ideas and knowledge to their own reality.[45]

According to the empirical research carried out in Brazil on the status of the formal studies in Competition Law, less than 5% of the law schools offer disciplines related to Competition Law or Economic Law, with less than 2% offered as mandatory disciplines.[46] The research also shows that antitrust is still an underestimated discipline in the country. Pedro Aurélio de Queiroz indicates that some factors explain these low figures. The author states that the guidelines prepared by the Ministry of Education in Brazil and the National Education Council (in Portuguese, 'Conselho Nacional de Educação'ou 'CNE') regarding rules on higher education (CNE Resolution No. 9/2004) do not mention any disciplines related to Competition Law or Economic Law as a pedagogic area.[47] It should also be considered that, in Brazil, the National Bar Exam does not include Competition or Economic Law among the topics of examination. The absence of an antitrust discipline in this National Exam is certainly a factor that affects how the law schools in the country handle the topic.[48] This happens because the quality of the law schools in the country is mostly measured by the percentage of students that are approved in this National Exam, prepared by the Brazilian Bar Association (in Portuguese, 'Ordem dos Advogados do Brasil'). The reality in the country is that the traditional disciplines adopted by both the Ministry of Education and the Bar Association turn out to impose barriers to the inclusion of new subjects and more interdisciplinary topics. As the importance of antitrust disciplines seems to have been underestimated in the country, it is natural to expect that judges, public prosecutors, and lawyers also have less access to this specific education.

As a matter of fact, nowadays, CADE has 385 employees, of which 137 are non-administrative staff working on competition enforcement, including 40% lawyers, 25% economists, and the last 28% graduates in other areas.[49] With regard to CADE Commissioners, they used to traditionally be lawyers or economists because the law sets out in its Article 6 that such decision-making positions should be filled by lawyers or economists. However, recent appointments have not necessarily respected this procedural requirement. The current President, Alexandre Barreto de Souza, as an example, has studied management and public administration.[50]

The reality encountered in Brazil regarding education in Competition Law discipline is also reflected in several EU Member States. Indeed, taking into account the recent development of antitrust education in Portugal, Luís Morais explains that the

45. Sokol, 2009, *supra* note 41, p. 15.
46. L. Carvalho, 'O ensino da defesa e da promoção da concorrência nos cursos de graduação em Direito no Brasil', *Revista de Direito Empresarial* (July) 2008, pp. 167-235.
47. Queiroz, 2018, *supra* note 42, p. 302.
48. This point is reiforced by Forgioni in P. A. Forgioni, 'O que esperar do antitruste brasileiro no século XXI?', *Revista Jurídica Luso-Brasileira*, Vol. 1, No. 1, 2015, pp. 1737-1738.
49. CADE, *Annual Report 2018*, p. 41.
50. Alexandre Barreto de Souza has a mandate from 22/06/2017 until 21/06/2021. His background can be traced at: http://www.cade.gov.br/acesso-a-informacao/institucional/acesso-a-informacao/institucional/presidencia (15/4/2019).

law schools in the country started to slowly incorporate Competition Law disciplines in their curriculum after the '1999 Bologna Process',[51] which was an agreement among EU Member States about the higher education quality standards to make it more compatible and comparable.[52] However, according to Morais, it was the decentralization of the EU competition law that ultimately encouraged law faculties to create Competition Law disciplines in the country.[53] In the case of Portugal, just like many other EU Member States, the institutional change enhanced by Regulation 1/2003 promoted changes in the national curriculum of law studies. The Portuguese example demonstrates that, without an anticipatory process of institutional reform, it is very difficult to develop antitrust knowledge or the culture of competition in a given country. The following sections discuss in more detail the institutional factors that affect the path of antitrust enforcement.

Also regarding the spread of antitrust culture in the European context, Kovacic highlights the role of specific educational programmes that helped the implementation of antitrust law and policies in transition economies.[54] He argues that it was common to see public agents involved in market reforms after they have been studying or working in Western universities or who have been widely engaged in training programmes aimed at addressing the fundamental economic and legal underpinnings of competition policy. At this respect, Kovacic concludes that:

> Over time, the pool of indigenous experts may expand as university programs in business, economics, law, and public administration reformulate their curricula to teach courses relevant to developing a market economy. Transition economy agencies often find that professionals who have become expert in antitrust economics or law become extremely attractive to private sector employers.[55]

What stands out in the above paragraph is the role of qualifications among law enforcers and legal advisors also for some European Member States that for several years did not even have a market economy as reference.

The information costs analysis is associated not only to the spread of antitrust studies but also to the evolution of antitrust jurisprudence and the attempts of a competition authority in providing information to society. Regarding the Brazilian framework, over the years, CADE, especially after Resolution No. 17/2016, has not put much effort, either via their decision-making process or via soft-law instruments, into defining objective parameters for the economic assessment of vertical agreements.[56]

---

51. *See* more information about the Bologna Process at: http://europa.eu/rapid/press-release_MEMO-07-184_en.htm (22/5/2019).
52. L. D. S. Morais, *Direito da Concorrência: Perspectivas do seu ensino*, São Paulo, Editora Almedina, 2009, pp. 155-169.
53. Morais, 2009, *supra* note 52, pp. 172-182.
54. Kovacic, 2001, *supra* note 1, p. 306.
55. Kovacic, 2001, *supra* note 1, p. 306.
56. It is worth indicate that, in the past years, CADE has published some Guidelines that focuses exclusively on cartel and merger policies, such as the 'Guidelines on Competition Compliance Programs', 'Guidelines on CADE's Antitrust Leniency Program', 'Guidelines Cease and Desist Agreement for cartel cases' and 'Guidelines for the Analysis of Previous Consummation of Merger Transactions'. The content of these guidelines can be found at: http://en.cade.gov.br/topics/publications/guidelines (27/7/2019).

Moreover, CADE has relied heavily on settlements. The downside of settlement agreements is also the slow development of antitrust jurisprudence in Brazil towards the assessment of vertical agreements, since there is no effect-based assessment and/or decision published by CADE and the legal cases are not reviewed by national courts.[57]

The scenario is somehow diverse in Europe. The European Commission over the years has worked on providing NCAs and businesses with information on how to prepare an assessment of vertical practices, lowering the level of information costs in EU jurisdictions. It should be stressed that two main pillars have contributed to the access of information with the EU. These pillars are: (i) the consolidated antitrust jurisprudence, together with the updates of VBER and guidelines of application of Article 101 TFEU; and (ii) the ECN. Indeed, these pillars facilitated the transaction from an *ex ante* control of agreements to an *ex post* policy and, simultaneously, had a positive effect on the evolution of the information costs.[58]

The decisions and notices established by the Commission, in addition to the role of the Court of Justice in sometimes upholding or annulling decisions, were fundamental to the better understanding of the competition rules (including the complex assessment of Article 101 TFEU) and the goals of the Community. After almost forty years of enforcement of Resolution 17/1962, the rules on vertical agreements became more predictable to undertakings. In other words, several decades of notification system contributed to a good knowledge and acquaintance on how to assess the potential anticompetitive effects of vertical agreements taking into consideration the particularities of the Community, the entire legal system and its policy priorities. Indeed, the VBER and its guidelines became fundamental tools to business people to self-assess their contractual relations, and to national authorities when investigating anticompetitive practices.

Actually, as highlighted in Chapter 4, several NCAs, in the past years, have also launched their own guidelines, notices and studies to support the assessment of vertical agreements. For instance, in 2014, the AFCA produced an official opinion regarding RPM entitled 'Standpoint on Resale Price Maintenance' that also aims to guide society in relation to the possible scenarios where these price restrictions can negatively affect competition. In 2016, with the same purpose, the British CMA issued the study 'Vertical Restraints: New Evidence from a Business Survey'. Also, in 2016, the ACM in the Netherlands, published the document 'ACM's Strategy and Enforcement Priorities with Regard to Vertical Agreements'. Although the Dutch authority has not actively enforced many cases of vertical agreements in the past years, the ACM recognizes the need for a deep and careful look at these practices. In 2017, the German authority (*Bundeskartellamt*) launched a note on RPM in the food sector entitled 'Guidance Note on the Prohibition of Vertical Price-Fixing in the Brick-and-Mortar Food Retail Sector'. This guideline was published after the *Bundeskartellamt* imposed fines

57. For more information regarding the Brazilian legal framework, *see* Chapter 3.
58. For more information, *see* section 4.4 of Chapter 4.

amounting to EUR 260.5 million on twenty-seven companies for having engaged in price-fixing agreements between retailers and manufacturers in the food sector.[59]

Regarding the ECN, this network was created as a forum for regular contacts, consultation and discussion regarding the enforcement of Articles 101 and 102 TFEU. This network was created to help national authorities to enhance cooperation in a context that privileged the coherence, consistency and uniform application of the competition rules, given the diverse experiences among the NCAs in applying competition law. Considering the complexity of assessing antitrust cases, the ECN showed up as an important pillar to the national authorities. The idea of having the support of the Commission and of more experienced competition authorities, mainly for the new Member States with no tradition whatsoever in implementing competition rules, certainly also reduces the information costs discussed so far.

Taking into account the comparison of the experiences in Brazil and the EU, some questions emerge: How to overcome this informational deficit related to antitrust assessment and the lack of competition culture among business people and law enforcers? Can these costs be simply overcome by additional education in Competition Law and Economics? These are surely issues that need to be addressed by a number of jurisdictions that still lack enough competition culture.

5.5 INCENTIVE COSTS

The so-called incentive costs and information costs are usually interconnected, since the boundaries among are them not completely clear. Nevertheless, in this chapter, the incentive costs will be treated as the costs that influence the incentives of companies to engage in welfare-enhancing agreements or to stop participating in welfare-reducing agreements. Again, there are several methodologies that can classify these costs in the most different forms. Based on a law and economics theoretical approach, it is considered that the incentives of companies to engage in anticompetitive agreements are determined essentially by the following factors: (1) the level of fines imposed by antitrust agencies and courts, (2) the antitrust errors in assessing vertical agreements, (3) the role of private enforcement, and (4) the general trust in institutions. The following subsections will analyse in detail these factors.

5.5.1 Fines

The law and economics theory of crime and punishment asserts that offenders eventually stop committing crimes (or reduce the number of crimes), as a result of the

59. More information about the case can be found in the 2016 and 2017 Annual Reports of the German Competition Authority, the *Bundeskartellamt*.

increasing severity of the enforcement.[60] The level of enforcement is therefore measured by means of the size of fines and the probability of detection. Even though the original literature is on criminal law, the rationale can also be usefully applicable in the context of antitrust policies. Therefore, we consider that firms will engage in fewer restrictive agreements according to a greater probability of having antitrust authorities prosecuting their company and of higher levels of fines applicable to these practices. William Landes shows that effective antitrust fines must be equal to the damage caused to other market players by the offender, given a certain probability of apprehension.[61] However, as we know from previous discussions, the harm in the case of vertical agreements can be very difficult (when not impossible) to compute, since together with the anticompetitive outcomes there are always economic efficiencies to be balanced in this calculation.

The optimal amount of fines applicable to restrictive vertical agreements will vary depending on whether the country has an *ex ante* notification system of agreements or if it favours an *ex post* control of these practices. Under an *ex ante* notification system of agreements, the amount of fines imposed by the antitrust authority - in both cases of no-filing and/or existence of anticompetitive clauses - can actually determine whether companies will indeed comply or not with the law (meaning, whether they will notify the agreements or take the risk of being discovered). For now, let us assume that a certain country is changing its policy from a notification system to an *ex post* enforcement regime. In a context where the *ex post* enforcement stays unchanged, the ending of the notification system may lead to an increase in anticompetitive practices if the sanctions are low, or to a decrease in anticompetitive practices if the sanctions are high. In other words, if *ex post* enforcement efforts remain constant, an increase in fines would result in a decrease in the proportion of restrictive agreements, while an increase in fines would result in a 'reduction of moral inhibition against engaging in anti-competitive behaviour'.[62] As a consequence, the number of anticompetitive vertical agreements would increase. Some studies have demonstrated that the move to an *ex post* control of restrictive agreements is not optimal if the fines remain unchanged.[63]

Actually, a change in the policy of vertical agreements from an *ex ante* to *ex post* monitoring, as happened in Brazil and in the EU, affects firms' decision-making with regard to the choice of agreements they will opt to sign. According to Neven, 'as the system of ex-ante monitoring is removed, the system of ex-post monitoring should be re-calibrated and strengthened' by, for instance, a better screening of investigated

60. *See*, for instance, Becker, 1968, *supra* note 10; G. Stigler, 'The Optimal Enforcement of Law', *Journal of Political Economy*, Vol. 78, No. 3, 1970, pp. 526-536; G. Becker & G. Stigler, 'Law Enforcement, Malfeasance and Compensation of Enforcers', *Journal of Legal Studies*, Vol. 3, No. 1, 1974, pp. 1-18.
61. W. M. Landes, 'Optimal Sanctions for Antitrust Violations', *University of Chicago Law Review*, Vol. 50, No. 2, 1983, pp. 652-678.
62. K. Elzinga & W. Breit, *The Antitrust Penalties: A Study in Law and Economics*, New Haven, Yale University Press, 1976, p. 129.
63. *See*, for instance, G. Federico & P. Manzini, 'A Law and Economics Approach to the New European Antitrust Enforcing Rules', *Erasmus Law and Economics Review*, Vol. 1, No. 2, 2004, pp. 143-164. *See also*, Hahn, 2000, *supra* note 3.

cases, increasing the probability of enforcement of restrictive agreements, and re-evaluating of the amount of fines.[64] Business people are usually discouraged by the risk of sanctions they would incur if they implement more anticompetitive clauses to their vertical agreement. However, if fines are minimal, they would prefer to take the risk and sign unlawful agreements.[65]

If we look carefully at the European experience, the strengthening of *ex post* enforcement in the case of termination of *ex ante* notification of agreements was indeed one concern brought by the Commission in its policy evaluation document, the White Paper on Modernization of the EU Treaty (hereinafter 'White Paper').[66] In the first years of application of Regulation 1/2003, there were no changes in respect to the magnitude of fines for undertakings that engage in anticompetitive agreements. However, in 2006, new guidelines with specific methodologies to set fines for antitrust infringements were adopted by the European Commission.[67] These guidelines increased the deterrent effect of fines by determining, for instance: (i) that fines may be based on up to 30% of the company's annual sales to which the infringement relates, multiplied by the duration, in years, of the infringement; (ii) that an 'entry fee' may be applicable regardless of the length of the infringement; (iii) that fines for undertakings that continue to repeat the infringement may increase up to 100%.

These changes mean that, in respect to the application of fines at the EU level, the movement from an *ex ante* to an *ex post* monitoring of agreements was indeed accompanied by an increase in fines and the rules related to it in order to deter antitrust violations. At the national levels, however, the maximum allowed fine (of national laws) and the parameters for calculating the fine can differ significantly. Considering the same type of company and infringement, the differences in fines among Member States can be up to 25 times between the highest and the smallest fine.[68] It means that the level of deterrence among these countries also differs. In Europe, only a few NCAs have their own guidelines with specific methods to set fines, for instance, France and the UK.[69]

In Brazil, the policy evaluation documents that anticipated Resolution No. 17/2016 did not show any concern about strengthening *ex post* enforcement with the end of the notification system of vertical agreements. According to Article 37 of Brazilian Competition Law, fines for antitrust violation range from 0.1% to 20% of the

64. Neven, 2002, *supra* note 4, p. 351.
65. Neven, 2002, *supra* note 4, p. 361.
66. European Commission, *White Paper on Modernisation of the Rules Implementing Articles 85 and 86 of the EC Treaty*, 1999.
67. European Commission, *Guidelines on the Method of Setting Fines Imposed Pursuant to Article 23(2)(a) of Regulation No 1/2003*, 2006.
68. European Commission, *Impact Assessment Accompanying the Document Proposal for a Directive of the European Parliament and of the Council to Empower the Competition Authorities of the Member States to Be More Effective Enforcers and to Ensure the Proper Functioning of the Internal Market*, 2017, p. 20.
69. *See*, Autorité de la cuncurrence (France), *Notice of 16 May 2011 on the Method Relating to the Setting of Financial Penalties*, 2011; Competition and Markets Authority (UK), *CMA's guidance as to the appropriate amount of penalty*, 2018. It is worth noting that Germany, for instance, has a guideline with methods to set fines specific to cartel infringements. *See also*, Bundeskartellamt, *Guidelines for the setting of fines in Cartel Administrative Proceedings*, 2013.

company's gross revenues in the year prior to the beginning of the investigations, in the field of the business activity in which the violation occurred. The method for setting fines within this range, though, is not always clear, since the terms 'gross revenues', or 'the year prior to the beginning of the investigation' and 'field of the business' can be rather subjective. Even though the Brazilian Competition Law anticipates in Article 45 some parameters for the calculation of fines, including the 'seriousness of the violation' and the 'advantage obtained by the violator',[70] there are no clear guidelines oriented to develop objective methods to set fines. As a consequence, the interpretation of combined Articles 37 and 45 of the antitrust law has caused divergence in the national jurisprudence.

Gabriel Moreira Pinto conducted some empirical research about the different methodologies to decide fines in the Brazilian case law. He found out that, from 2004 to 2010, in most infringement decisions, CADE failed in clearly defining its method to calculate fines and in explaining the weight of the parameters established by Article 45.[71] More recently, João Paulo de Resende also carried out an analysis showing that, in a period of six months, CADE applied more than eighteen different methodologies to the calculation of fines in cartel cases.[72] The author explains, for instance, that CADE has considered diverse meanings to the term 'gross revenue', such as the 'profit of the company' in the *Milk Cartel* case,[73] the 'expected margin' in the *ForEx Cartel* case,[74] the 'value of bid-contract' in the '*CarWash*' investigation,[75] among other examples. The same inaccuracy has also been observed in the use of other economic and legal parameters.

In the cases of vertical restraints, CADE has not stipulated any fine higher than 2% of the company's gross revenues. From the cases explored in Chapter 3, CADE imposed fines in the *SKF* case of RPM of 1% of the company's gross revenues in 2013,[76] and 2% in the *Iguatemi* shopping mall cases.[77] In none of the cases was there an explicit explanation regarding the parameters taken by the authority. After the end of the notification system of vertical agreements in 2016, the level of sanctions remained unchanged in the country.

70. Article 45, Law No. 11.259/2011: 'Art. 45. In the application of the penalties set forth in this Law, the following shall be taken into consideration: I - the seriousness of the violation; II - the good faith of the transgressor; III - the advantage obtained or envisaged by the violator; IV - whether the violation was consummated or not; - 17/34 - V - the degree of injury or threatened injury to free competition, the national economy, consumers, or third parties; VI - the negative economic effects produced in the market; VII - the economic status of the transgressor; and VIII - any recurrence.'
71. G. Moreira Pinto, 'A dosimetria das multas impostas em resposta às infrações contra a ordem econômica', *Prêmio SEAE 2010 sobre Defesa da Concorrência*, 2010.
72. J. P. Resende, 'Ainda falta um guia de dosimetria de pena', *in* C. Campilongo & R. Pfeiffer (eds), *Evolução do antitruste no Brasil*, São Paulo, Editora Singular, 2018, p. 1077.
73. Case No. 08012.010744/2008-71.
74. Case No. 08700.004633/2015-04.
75. Case No. 08700.003226/2017-33.
76. *SKF v. Procon-SP*, Case No. 08012.001271/2001-447.
77. *Ambev 2*, Case No. 08012.001626/2008-71; *CADE v. Condomínio do Shopping Center Iguatemi/SP*, Case No. 08012.006636/97-43.

Furthermore, unlike the EU, any anticompetitive conduct (including vertical restrictions) in Brazil is also considered a crime, subjected to imprisonment of up to five years, under the Economic Criminal Law (Law No. 8.137/1990) and the Public Procurement Law (Law No. 8.666/1993). However, no business people have ever gone to prison as a consequence of anticompetitive misconduct. The very few cases of criminal prosecution in Brazil are cartel cases that are directly linked to corruption scandals.[78] The 'CarWash' operation is an example of that. Considered the biggest corruption scandal in history, the operation involved huge money-laundering schemes and fraud in public bids, which are in the scope of the antitrust authority.[79]

The last point that should be highlighted with respect to antitrust sanctions is that simply raising the amount of fines as a way of strengthening the *ex post* enforcement is not an optimal solution, since other variables play an important role in antitrust enforcement. Therefore, the next subsections will take a closer look into other institutional factors that affect the detection level: antitrust errors, private enforcement and institutional set-up.

5.5.2 Antitrust Errors

In general terms, experience in antitrust policymaking can be characterized as a situation in which agency and/or courts have analysed a large number of cases regarding a specific topic over the years and have learned from the outcomes of failures and successes in judgments and evaluations. The repetition of cases in both administrative and judicial levels over time not only creates an important source of knowledge for law enforcers but also permits the undertakings to have higher legal certainty on what is expected from them. If, for instance, a competition agency is new (or became recently effective) and just a few, if any, complex cases were assessed by the authority, the authority itself is more prone to errors. Besides, the companies will not have legal certainty on what type of business practices are illegal or not, and under which conditions. Subsection 5.3.2 emphasized the lack of experience as a source of information costs, since both law enforcers and undertakings, in these situations, have less access to information that comes from antitrust precedents. This subsection will stress experience as a factor that directly influences antitrust errors from both antitrust authorities and courts, and therefore affects the incentives of companies to engage in restrictive agreements.

Insights from the Social Learning Theory help explain how the lack of experience and/or consolidated jurisprudence creates enforcement costs.[80] This theory explains that all learning phenomena result from both direct experiences and observation of other people's behaviour. Albert Bandura argues that new patterns of behaviour can be acquired by observing the behaviour of others, without having to build up these

78. C. A. J. Schimidt, 'Crime e Castigo: Cartel no Brasil, algumas reflexões', *in* C. Campilongo & R. Pfeiffer (eds), *Evolução do antitruste no Brasil*, São Paulo, Editora Singular, 2018, p. 1186.
79. J. Watts, 'Operation Car Wash: Is This the Biggest Corruption Scandal in History?', *The Guardian*, 1 June 2017.
80. *See*, for instance, A. Bandura, *Social Learning Theory*, Englewood Cliffs, Prentice-Hall, 1977.

patterns gradually by tedious trial and error.[81] Moreover, the author also explains that people are repeatedly confronted with decisions that can lead to successful or unsuccessful outcomes. Because of that, over the time, successful responses to certain types of behaviour are then encouraged while inefficient ones are discarded over time.

Regarding the antitrust policies, this learning process means that if a certain jurisdiction has experience regarding assessing complex cases of vertical agreements, at both administrative and the judicial level, firms observe what has been done in the past and therefore they can take extra precautions to avoid anticompetitive practices. Therefore, firms can learn from past experience or even from observing other firms' and the competition authority's actions. At the same time, the competition authority is also involved in a learning process that is vulnerable to errors that can affect the evolution of the dynamics of competition in the markets. As explained in Chapter 2, antitrust assessments of vertical agreements can be complex because they involve a challenging balance of pro- and anticompetitive outcomes, and this complexity may generate errors that can be harmful to competition. As described by Alan Devlin and Michael Jacobs:

> More than any other area of civil law, antitrust is error prone. Its basic analytical methodology is hopelessly imprecise. The economic terms at the heart of many of its important doctrinal questions – terms such as 'cost,' 'market,' 'monopoly power,' and 'entry barrier' – are either vague, contestable, or both. In many cases, the answer to the question of interest – whether certain conduct is harmful to consumers – can depend upon first identifying and then comparing current or past harms and benefits with those likely, but not certain, to arise in the future. This comparison involves measuring the relative size of a known set of facts, on the one hand, and an uncertain but theoretically predictable future outcome, on the other.[82]

Indeed, as the paragraph above suggests, the errors that reflect the quality of decisions of antitrust authorities and courts can be classified as Type I and II errors. In statistics terms, on the one hand, a Type I error is described as the wrong rejection of a true null hypothesis.[83] It is also regarded as a 'false positive'. Regarding antitrust cases, a Type I error is a misjudgment in which law enforcers condemn a firm's behaviour which was not anticompetitive. Such errors may raise the desirable level of competitive intensity, increasing the degree of uncertainty or lowering the decision-making threshold for enforcement. Type I errors reflect an over-enforcement or over-regulation.[84] Type I errors pressure companies to take precautionary actions when they face the threat of being wrongly accused of anticompetitive behaviour. Consequently, businesses are less likely to participate in procompetitive business transactions, such as vertical agreements that bring economic efficiencies to markets. A Type I error can decrease total welfare in markets since they limit the availability of products and services to consumers.

---

81. Bandura, 1977, *supra* note 80, p. 5.
82. A. Devlin & M. Jacobs, 'Antitrust Error', *William & Mary Law Review*, Vol. 52, No. 1, 2010, pp. 86-87.
83. P. A. Morettin & W. O. Bussab, *Estatística Básica*, 5th ed., São Paulo, Editora Saraiva, 2003.
84. Devlin & Jacobs, 2010, *supra* note 82, pp. 86-87.

A Type II error, on the other hand, is described as the wrong rejection of a false null hypothesis.[85] It is also regarded as a 'false negative'. Considering competition law cases, a Type II error is a misjudgment in which law enforcers fail to condemn a conduct that is anticompetitive, meaning that such errors take place when anticompetitive practices or conducts are not punished. Type II errors reflect under-enforcement or under-regulation. Because of the scenario of under-enforcement caused by Type II error, firms may engage in more anticompetitive business practices, such as vertical restraints that foreclose markets. Type II errors can hence also decrease total welfare in markets since they, indirectly, also restrict the amount and variety of products and services that are available to consumers. Indeed, in any case, errors of Type I and II can create social costs and enormous disincentives to companies, in addition to provoking adverse effects on the welfare of consumers and distortions of the level of economic activity.[86] According to Michael Block and J. Gregory Sidak, antitrust errors introduce costs to society that cannot be easily eliminated by law enforcers, not even through compensation or imposition of high penalties.[87]

Let us take as example an *Agreement A*, a welfare-enhancing vertical agreement between a beverage producer and a wholesale distributor that creates efficiencies in the form of cost savings that are transferred to consumers as lower prices; and an *Agreement B*, a welfare-reducing distribution agreement with a retail price-fixing clause, in which the fixed-price was higher than competitive standards. A Type I error would mean that the antitrust agency blocks the welfare enhancing *Agreement A* or prosecutes the beverage companies treating them as if they were colluding instead of cooperating. In contrast, an error of Type II shapes the scenario in which the antitrust agency approves without restriction a welfare-reducing agreement as *Agreement B* or in the case of inertia of the agency in prosecuting the beverage companies involved in restrictive practices. It is worth noting the reaction of courts, antitrust agencies, and academics with regard to the antitrust error which has a bias towards 'false negatives', meaning that they tend to more easily admit the misjudgment related to an anticompetitive conduct, rather than to a procompetitive one.[88] This happens because the procompetitive behaviour that is erroneously condemned turns out to result in a permanent loss for the market. In our example, the efficiencies of *Agreement A* would never be passed on to the consumers, which would in theory cause less harm than the negative effects of a wrongly permitted anticompetitive conduct.[89]

The relevant issue at stake is that changes from an *ex ante* policy to an *ex post* monitoring of vertical agreements alter the probability of Type I and Type II errors, affecting the features of the agreements that are signed by firms. More frequent errors

85. Morettin & Bussab, 2003, *supra* note 83.
86. M. Block & J. Sidak, 'The Cost of Antitrust Deterrence: Why Not Hang a Price Fixer Now and Then?', *The Georgetown Law Journal*, Vol. 68, No. 5, 1980, pp. 1131-1138.
87. Block & Sidak, 1980, *supra* note 86.
88. A reference paper in this respect is F. Easterbrook, 'The Limits of Antitrust', *Texas Law Review*, Vol. 63, No. 1, 1984, pp. 1-40.
89. For more details regarding this discussion, *see*: Devlin & Jacobs, 2010, *supra* note 82; F. McChesney, 'Talking "Bout My Antitrust Generation: Competition for and in the Field of Competition Law"', *Emory Law Journal*, Vol. 52, 2003, pp. 1401-1412.

by antitrust agencies or courts in a certain jurisdiction, make businessmen less motivated to engage in welfare-enhancing contracts. According to Wils, 'errors or the risk of errors in the imposition of sanctions could lead to lawful and economically desirable conduct being deterred'.[90]

The end of a notification system of vertical agreements changes the sort of business practices that undertakings implement. If the antitrust agency or a court in a given country does not have experience in handling complex assessments of vertical agreements, the probability of Type II errors increases, and firms may be encouraged to engage in anticompetitive practices. However, if antitrust agencies and/or courts are overlooking vertical agreements, even the efficiency-enhancing ones, and the probability of Type I errors is high, this scenario could discourage better competitive practices. In this case, the number of Type I and Type II errors increases, while the available information for parties is less complete, and the law enforcer is less familiar with the actual application of substantial rules based on economic concepts.

In effect, a notification system of vertical agreements may reduce the above-mentioned error costs related to restrictive business practices, mainly if the quality of the assessment made by legal representatives at the moment of the notification is high. Therefore, the deterrent effect can be greater under a notification system of agreements, especially in the case when business people cannot be sure of the outcomes of the antitrust investigations or cannot predict the probability of being condemned.[91] In this context, antitrust error costs can be calibrated or adjusted considering the probability of detection or fines, or, more generally, depending on the intensity of the *ex post* enforcement. A reduction of error costs can thus be associated with a better screening of the cases to be investigated by the antitrust authority.[92]

In practice, law enforcers cannot avoid some of the antitrust error costs of enforcement, simply because there are uncertainties, the access to information is not perfect, the learning process is affected by institutional features and because generally judges are not particularly good at handling complex economic arguments.[93]

Looking at both European and Brazilian experiences, some lessons can be highlighted in relation to the learning process. In Europe, forty years of experience with the notification system of agreements gave European Commission a better knowledge and experience to assess the impact of agreements on economic welfare. When the notification regime was installed in 1962, the Commission or the Member States had no experience in assessing agreements, and the likelihood of committing errors was high, therefore the notification system of vertical agreements was an adequate policy. However, the accumulated experience over the years (particularly by the Commission) in handling complex economic analyses of vertical agreements, somehow justified the change towards an *ex post* control monitoring regime in 2003. As explained in Chapter 4, Regulation 1/2003 also decentralized antitrust enforcement in Europe, which means that, since then, NCAs as well as national courts are also subjected to the error costs.

90. Wils, 2003, *supra* note 19, p. 9.
91. Hahn, 2000, *supra* note 3, p. 72.
92. *See* analysis of Neven, 2002, *supra* note 4.
93. Easterbrook, 1984, *supra* note 88, p. 39.

As demonstrated so far in this book, the level of enforcement and the experience among Member States can considerably differ, due to, among others, different historical and institutional realities. In this scenario, the probability of antitrust errors also varies.

In Brazil, the existing antitrust jurisprudence is very limited. Also, the outcome of some important vertical cases indicated diverse perspectives on substantive topics among the CADE's Commissioners. With regard to RPM, until 2013, CADE had condemned no company for this antitrust practice. Most of the cases were dismissed because of the lack of market power of economic agents, lack of evidence, and/or lack of monitoring mechanisms and punishment for the dealer that did not follow the fixed resale prices. The jurisprudence until 2013 supported companies to carry out these business practices without apparent risks.[94] Since 2013, some divergent opinions among CADE's Commissioners started to be formulated in respect of the competitive outcomes of this practice. Moreover, RPM turned out to be considered as an anticompetitive practice in the judgment of the *SKF* case.[95] According to the company, no distributor was ever penalized for not following SKF's fixed markups, being free to set its own prices. The company also argued that the fixed markup was a request from the distributors themselves as a way of avoiding the free-riding problem as part of the 'price war' in the downstream market. CADE, however, defined that the vertical price-fixing established by the auto parts manufacturer SKF was considered illegal since defendants were not able to prove efficiencies. Besides, the case was considered illegal despite the fact that the distributors did not follow the fixed resale prices.

Since the *SKF* decision, companies are facing more legal uncertainty in respect of certain types of vertical contracts.[96] Firms must now be able to prove that the positive effects generated by vertical price-fixing will be passed on to consumers, altering the dynamics of the *ex post* enforcement of vertical restraints. If the burden of proof regarding the absence of adverse effects on competition relies on the company, it is very likely that it will be condemned by the authority, even though it can bring efficiencies to the markets.[97] This change of interpretation about the legal rules concerning RPM in Brazil may probably be subject to more error costs, once contracts can be considered illegal despite enhancing efficiencies in specific markets.

With regard to the practice of geo-blocking, CADE's jurisprudence is rather limited and outdated (from the early 2000s).[98] The most relevant cases are the ones involving exclusive territory clauses imposed by the Shopping Mall *Iguatemi*, in the city of São Paulo.[99] In this case, Iguatemi prohibited shop owners of luxury brands from opening other stores in malls that directly competed with Iguatemi and/or defining that the same shop owners could not have other shops within a certain radius of its mall

94. F. Amorim, *Fixação de preços de revenda no Sistema Brasileiro de Defesa da Concorrência: análise do direito sancionador antitruste à luz do princípio da segurança jurídica*, Master thesis filed at University of São Paulo, São Paulo, 2017.
95. *SKF v. Procon-SP*, Case No. 08012.001271/01-447.
96. For more information, *see* section 3.4.1 of Chapter 3.
97. Amorim, 2017, *supra* note 94, pp. 95-96.
98. For more information, *see* section 3.4.2 of Chapter 3.
99. *See*, *Participações Morro Vermelho Ltda. v. Condomínio Shopping Center Iguatemi e Shopping Centers Reunidos do Brasil Ltda*, Case No. 08012.009991/98-82 and *CADE v. Condomínio do Shopping Center Iguatemi/SP*, Case No. 08012.006636/97-43.

('radius clause'). Even though the authority recognized some economic efficiency of the clauses, such as the protection against free-riders, the result was the condemnation of the shopping mall, since the measures taken by the clauses were generating foreclosure and they were overall disproportionate. The effect-based analysis conducted by CADE over the year has been subjected to errors due to the adoption of a more qualitative approach and subjective reasoning, instead of a structured and objective economic assessment which includes the use of quantitative methods.

Additionally, as exposed in Chapter 3, in the past years, CADE has greatly depended on settlements. Settlements can actually generate diverse effects when it comes to error costs. On the one hand, settlements may decrease error costs, since firms sign the agreement with the authority and terminate the anticompetitive practice. The authority, in this case, reduces the administrative costs of carrying out the whole investigation, and the termination of the practice increases economic welfare. On the other hand, settlements may increase error costs, since companies might decide to sign the settlements and terminate the procompetitive agreements just in order not to bear the costs of litigation. Accordingly, the excessive use of settlements might also increase error costs.

In short, the lack of guidelines on the assessment of vertical agreements, the lack of judicial review added to the lack of experience in assessing complex cases increase the risks of misinterpretation of both the law enforcers and the business community, intensifying the risk of Types I and II errors in Brazil when it comes to the analysis of vertical restraints.

It should be noted that the recent globalization of antitrust laws and enforcement practices can help less experienced jurisdictions to avoid committing errors. Considering the international landscape, national competition agencies design their policies based on similar grounds, for instance, the promotion of market efficiency. This does not mean that antitrust rules must be the same in all jurisdictions, or even that the enforcement of competition law in different countries is free of tensions.[100] In this respect, Ezrachi explains that:

> Competition law is not immune to these dynamic society-driven processes. [...] it is inherently susceptive to a wide range of national variants. Although guided by economic analysis, one may identify distinct social, economic and political foundations which foster diversity. Different levels of economic development, market realities, government and enforcement structure all dictate differentiation in the composition of national competition provisions and their implementation.[101]

Indeed, in the attempt to apply international jurisprudence, the domestic economic reality and the goals of competition enforcement are only some of the many forces which often introduce tensions and inconsistencies. In the case of the EU, the market integration goal had a great role to play in defining the outcome of vertical restraints cases. However, the problems associated with market integration are not observed in many other jurisdictions such as Brazil. Therefore, by applying

100. A. Ezrachi, 'Sponge', *Journal of Antitrust Enforcement*, Vol. 5, No. 1, April 2017, pp. 49-75.
101. Ezrachi, April 2017, *supra* note 100, pp. 49-75.

international decisions (designed and based on their specific goals) to national realities, many less experienced countries in competition policies are subjected to even greater error costs of enforcement.

A last point to be noted in respect of errors in the decision-making process is the complexity of digital economies. The competition implications of vertical restraints in digital markets are inherently more complex because of multiple interactions, network externalities and vertical relationships between the marketplace platforms and consumers. Chapter 2 argued that this scenario potentially implies a more elaborated antitrust analysis with multiple foreclosure effects, and therefore, higher changes of antitrust error. The European Commission has been working on solving and clarifying the applicable rules when it comes to vertical agreements in online markets, but many questions remain unanswered.

For instance, new cases of selective distribution and platform bans contradict old jurisprudence in the topic, increasing the legal uncertainty of business people that intend to celebrate such contracts. The *Coty* case is an example of that situation. Towards the end of 2017, the ECJ decided that no antitrust violation had been verified in the selective distribution case against the luxury cosmetics company *Coty*, which banned authorized distributors from selling *Coty's* products in online platforms such as *Amazon* or *eBay*.[102] This outcome was different from the well-known jurisprudence in the topic, the *Pierre Fabri* precedent from the early 2010s, in which, the ECJ ruled that a prohibition on internet sales in the framework of selective distribution systems represents an infringement of competition by Article 101(1) TFEU.[103]

In Brazil, the few vertical cases involving digital markets ended up with settlement decisions, which, again, did not make a positive contribution to the development of the jurisprudence in the country.

5.5.3 The Role of the Judiciary and Private Enforcement

Vertical agreements can be detrimental to the overall economy, since they can drive competitors out of the market, and consumers can end up paying high prices for a product or service. These losses can therefore be compensated under the rules of tort law. If a country does not have an *ex ante* notification system of vertical agreements and public enforcement is not able to achieve effective enforcement, private actions can play an important role in national enforcement practices.

If a country has a notification system of agreements, the 'green flag' of the authority in respect of signing the agreement also protects the companies against future litigation. However, if the companies do not have confirmation from the antitrust authorities with respect to the legality of the agreements, they are not only subjected to possible prosecution by the authority itself but are also not covered against private litigations. This uncertainty in respect of private actions generates costs to parties. In countries where private actions are very common, companies may have less incentive

102. *Coty Germany GmbH v. Parfümerie Akzente GmbH*, Case No. C-230/16, decision Luxembourg Court of Justice of the European Union on 6 December 2017.
103. *Pierre Fabre v. L'Autorité de la concurrence*, Case No. 439/09.

to engage in anticompetitive agreements, and the opposite is also true. If private actions are not a reality in a given jurisdiction, companies may engage in more restrictive agreements, since the probability of being sued is low. In some jurisdictions, private antitrust actions are more welcome than others. For instance, in the US, an average 90% of the antitrust cases come from private litigation,[104] but this is not a reality in many jurisdictions for several reasons.

It is worth highlighting that the structure of the judiciary system directly impacts the incentive to initiate private actions. Furthermore, a system of private *ex post* control of anticompetitive agreements requires supporting rules that enable an adequate assessment by the judiciary, and these flanking rules are not always existent in common law jurisdictions as they are in most European countries or even in Brazil.[105] In the scope of private enforcement, both in the EU and in Brazil, civil law procedures require that the plaintiffs present, in the case files, the relevant information to support their case. However, they often have difficulties in gathering the complex information and evidence to prove the anticompetitive infringement. This is different from the public enforcement systems. In the administrative model followed by both jurisdictions, the competition authority has greater investigative powers and has the right to collect evidence with or without the firm's consent (for instance, in the form of dawn raids).[106]

In a country with under-developed or dysfunctional courts, it does not make too much sense to give incentives to private rights as a way of enforcing the anticompetitive vertical agreements. Expanding on this idea, Donncadh Woods et al. also point to some other obstacles regarding antitrust private actions.[107] The first obstacles highlighted by the author are that parties might not always have adequate incentives to start a claim before the courts, mainly because judiciary costs can be very high. Second, proving the infringement of welfare-reducing vertical agreements can also be challenging for claimants. Third, the calculation of the real loss related to the existence of a restrictive agreement in the marketplace is very costly and difficult to assess, as there is not enough expertise to identify the losses. Fourth, and most important of all, companies (e.g., distributors) might decide not to enter into a private action in order to keep good commercial relations (e.g., with their suppliers). Finally, some agencies and courts are known for moving slowly, both because of the significant number of pending cases and also because of several legal tools that allow parties to the case to unduly delay the process.

Looking at what has happened in the EU, the Directive 2014/104/EU entered into force after ten years of having the *ex post* control of agreements, removing procedural

104. *See* Wils, 2003, *supra* note 19.
105. Moschel, 2000, *supra* note 34, p. 498.
106. Pirrung, 2004, *supra* note 31, p. 97. It should be noted that the investigative power of antitrust agencies is often focused in cartel cases, but less common in the vertical cases.
107. D. Woods, A. Sinclair & D. Ashton, 'Private Enforcement of Community Competition Law: Modernization and the Road Ahead', *Competition Policy Newsletter*, Vol. 2, Summer, 2004, p. 33.

obstacles to private actions under EU law.[108] The Directive is applicable to every individual or collective antitrust damage action, which include cases of compensation for damages originated by restrictive agreements. Thus, important changes were brought by the Directive, such as: (i) parties now have easier access to required evidence; (ii) the final infringement decision of an NCA also constitutes full evidence before the national courts; (iii) victims have at least five years to bring damages claims before courts, after the moment the victim finds out about the damages caused by an antitrust infringement; (iv) victims are also entitled to full compensation for the harm, including the right to the receipt of interest regarding the period of time since the harm occurred until the payment of full compensation. Despite the limitations of this Directive, the changes brought by it, to a certain extent, lowered the level of uncertainty of private actions and helped to increase the credibility of the judicial system.

The outcomes of the European experience fostered further discussions in Brazil regarding the clarification of rules of private antitrust claims.[109] CADE's recent Resolution No. 21 from 12 September 2018 aimed at clarifying the documents produced by the administrative proceedings, such as leniency documents, that can be used in courts when starting a private action. There has also emerged an initiative from the Senate, Project Law No. 283/2016, aiming at facilitating and encouraging private actions with regard to anticompetitive conduct. One of the main prepositions of this Project Law is to increase the time period regarding the right to start an action from three to five years after CADE's decision. CADE has been directly involved in this legislative process that is still to be approved by the Chamber of Deputies.

Despite the relevance of these legislative attempts, there are two important considerations with regard to the Brazilian case. First, these rules are mostly applicable to cartel cases, and there is a very low perception from society that it can also be applicable to other anticompetitive practices such as restrictive vertical agreements. Second, the efficient use of private enforcement for vertical agreements requires the use of the economic analysis of law by judges and members of the judiciary that Brazil has not necessarily developed so far.

The discussion regarding the role of judiciary power in antitrust cases is, of course, not limited to private actions but also to the judicial review of CADE's administrative decisions. In Brazil, CADE's decisions are subject to judicial review. Until the mid-2000s, CADE's decisions were not so effective, since most of them were suspended by the judiciary. From 1994, when the old Brazilian Competition Law entered into force, until 2005, only 18% of CADE's infringement decisions were essentially confirmed by courts.[110] In 2002-2004, for instance, less than 4% of the fines imposed by the Brazilian authority were actually paid by parties. This scenario started

108. Directive 2014/104/EU of the European Parliament and of the Council of 26 November 2014 on certain rules governing actions for damages under national law for infringements of the competition law provisions of the Member States and of the European Union Text with EEA relevance.
109. The European Directive 2014/104/EU was indeed quoted several times by CADE in the technical note that followed the Public Consultation No. 5/2016.
110. CADE, *Defesa da Concorrência no Brasil: 50 anos*, 2013, p. 132.

to slowly change after 2008, when the agency's success rate in court disputes started to increase.[111] In a study conducted by the Brazilian Society of Public Law (in Portuguese '*Sociedade Brasileira de Direito Público*' or just *SBDP*) in 2011, it was pointed out that almost 50% of CADE's decisions on administrative proceedings regarding anticompetitive conduct were confirmed by national courts.[112] Other data presented by CADE in 2013 indicate that about 80% of CADE's decisions are now upheld by the judiciary.[113]

5.5.4 The General Trust in Institutions

The general trust in institutions appears to be relevant when discussing antitrust enforcement costs. In this respect, developing economies such as Brazil are particularly vulnerable. Also in the EU, there are some less developed countries that face similar institutional challenges, such as Bulgaria, Croatia, Czech Republic, Estonia, Greece, Latvia, Lithuania, Romania, and Slovakia.[114] The public and private enforcement of competition law in less developed countries should be characterized in the context of insufficient economic development, incipient competition regimes, lack of competition culture, economic fragility, and most importantly for the current discussion, the institutional weakness.[115]

The costs raised by the distrust of institutions are particularly important in the context of *ex post* control of vertical agreements, but not limited to it. Under an *ex post* monitoring regime, undertakings may have more incentives to engage in anticompetitive practices, because of the low probability of detection. The likelihood of being caught is also strongly related to the administrative and judicial structure of the given jurisdiction, as well as all the other bodies that are related to it.

From the institutional perspective, it would first be useful to mention the general conceptualization of institutions brought by Douglas North:

> Institutions are the rules of the game of a society, or, more formally, are the humanly devised constraints that structure human interactions. They are composed of formal rules (statute law, common law, regulation), informal constraints (conventions, norms of behaviour and self-imposed codes of conduct), and the enforcement characteristics of both. Organizations are the players: group of individuals bound by a common purpose to achieve objectives. They include political bodies (political parties, the senate, the regulatory agency); economic bodies (firms, trade unions, family farms, cooperatives); social bodies (churches,

111. In 2008, there were 343 new cases for judicial review; in 2009, 150 new cases; in 2010, 62 new cases; in 2011, 58. CADE, 2013, *supra* note 110, p. 131.
112. Sociedade Brasileira de Direito Público (SBDP), *Revisão Judicial das Decisões do Conselho Administrativo de Defesa Econômica (CADE): Pesquisa empírica e aplicada sobre os casos julgados pelos Tribunais Regionais Federais (TRFs), Superior Tribunal de Justiça (STJ) e Supremo Tribunal Federal (STF)*, Belo Horizonte, Editora Fórum, 2010.
113. CADE, 2013, *supra* note 110, p. 136.
114. For more information about the development of EU regions, *see* European Union (2017), *Eurostat Regional Yearbook*, available at: https://ec.europa.eu/eurostat/documents/3217494/8222062/KS-HA-17-001-EN-N.pdf (26/5/2019).
115. Pena, *supra* note 40, p. 480.

clubs, athletic associations); and educational bodies (schools, colleges, vocational training centres).[116]

In general terms, North and other scholars associated to the 'New Institutional Economics' have examined how institutional quality affects public policy.[117] As an example of institutional quality, one can highlight: (i) voice and accountability (citizen participation in the selection of governments); (ii) political stability; (iii) government effectiveness (capability to produce and implement good policies); (iv) regulatory quality (incidence of market-friendly policies); (v) rule of law; and (vi) control of corruption.[118] In the context of antitrust law, countries with mature institutions, greater capabilities and resources have greater prospects of using efficiently ambitious competition policies.[119]

In a comparative historical analysis of institutions, one of the main ideas is that the choices made at the time of formation of the institutions and the resulting political decisions have a constraining effect on their future development due to the inertial tendency of institutions that block or hinder subsequent changes.[120] The concept of 'path dependence' is precisely offered as the analytical tool to understand the importance of temporal sequences and the development of social events and processes over time. According to the path dependence theory, once a specific trajectory has been adopted, it would take a great deal of effort or even an external shock to change the direction and course of institutions at later times.[121] This means that the current structure and functioning of any institution can be understood only partially if the analysis is not integrated in a historical perspective. Despite the attempts of some competition agencies, there will always be some difficulties to guarantee a competitive environment. The challenges of cultural components are most of the times difficult to overcome, because they are historically and politically rooted.

Institutional stability is one of the factors to be considered when promoting competition policy, and this comprises both *ex ante* preventive educational measures, and *ex post* enforcement control. The antitrust authority is therefore responsible for promoting appropriate institutional arrangements for its purposes defined by law.[122]

For this book, I consider that a competition law itself is not sufficient to guarantee optimal levels of enforcement, since the institutional environment can jeopardize the efforts of the authorities. In Europe, for instance, the Commission, in cooperation with the ECN, has difficulties in transplanting the competition culture and institutional

116. D. North, 'The New Institutional Economics and Third World Development', *in* J. Harris, J. Hunter & C. Lewis (eds), *Economics and Third World Development*, Oxon, Routledge, 1995, p. 23.
117. Regarding the work of North, *see*, for instance, D. North, *Institutions, Institutional Change and Economic Performance*, Cambridge, Cambridge University Press, 1990; D. North, 'Economic Performance Through Time', *American Economic Review*, Vol. 84, No. 3, 1994, pp. 359-368.
118. List prepared by World Bank in the following working paper: D. Kaufmann, A. Kraay & P. Zoido-Lobaton, 'Governance Matters', *World Bank Policy Research Working Paper*, No. 2196, 1999.
119. Kovacic, 2001, *supra* note 1.
120. *See*, North, 1990, *supra* note 117.
121. *See*, North, 1990, *supra* note 117.
122. Amorim, 2017, *supra* note 94.

set-up to guarantee optimal competition policy across the different EU Member States. The Report entitled 'Ten Years of Regulation 1/2003' concluded that NCAs have to be empowered to co-enforce competition rules in Europe, in order to make a positive contribution to the strengthening of EU antitrust enforcement.[123] Yet, the same report suggested that several NCAs still have room for improvement, among others, by finding adequate enforcement tools to deter anticompetitive violations. These concerns were again raised by the impact assessments documents of Directive 1/2019 that aims 'to empower the competition authorities of the Member States to be more effective enforcers and to ensure the proper functioning of the internal market'.[124]

In Brazil, CADE also faces challenges when it comes to building effective enforcement mechanisms that at the same time deter anticompetitive effects and encourage a competition culture among businesspeople. Looking back at the Brazilian experience, antitrust law was born as a way to protect the 'popular economy', and after the 1988 Constitution and Law No. 8.884/1994, took the position of creating a competitive market. Actually, the old Competition Law from 1994 was created in the context of privatization of state-owned companies. In Brazil, a top-down model of competition policy was configured.[125] In a top-down model, there is the transposition of norms (in this case, of competition law), without a correlative sociopolitical movement, which ends up having a small effect on society. The legal reforms of countries that have a top-down approach may be insufficient to create a competition culture. These countries may need more serious institutional reforms against abuses of economic power, which also involves movements against private interests that interfere in a more efficient law- and decision-making.[126]

All these institutional issues are directly linked to the main discussion of this chapter on the optimal design of competition policies applicable to vertical agreements. When choosing between an *ex ante* notification system of agreements, an *ex post* control system or something in between, the regulator (mostly antitrust agencies) should avoid overweighting the directive administrative costs of having to analyse notifications, but also look at several other factors related to the development of antitrust knowledge and institutional set-up analysed in this chapter. These factors are usually underestimated by policymakers although they play a big role in the definition of incentives to parties on whether to engage or not in anticompetitive practices.

---

123. European Commission, *Ten Years of Antitrust Enforcement under Regulation 1/2003: Achievements and Future Perspectives*, 2014.
124. *See*, for instance, European Commission, *Impact Assessment Accompanying the Document Proposal for a Directive of the European Parliament and of the Council to Empower the Competition Authorities of the Member States to Be More Effective Enforcers and to Ensure the Proper Functioning of the Internal Market*, 2017.
125. Queiroz, 2018, *supra* note 42, p. 312.
126. It is worth noting that Brazil, since 2014 has been passing to the biggest political crises of the country due to a series of corruption scandals. Among the politicians involved in these scandals are two former Presidents, Lula da Silva (who is currently in prison), and Dilma Rousseff that was impeached and removed from its office in 2016.

5.6 ADMINISTRATIVE COSTS

Administrative costs can be defined as direct costs borne by the law enforcers and firms to comply with the applicable regulation. Administrative costs are usually the ones that are easier to consider when it comes to estimating enforcement costs. For this purpose, I will divide the administrative costs into two different components, the fixed administrative costs and the variable administrative costs. From microeconomic theory, fixed costs are the ones that do not depend on the amount of quantity produced, and variable costs are the ones that change with the variation of output.[127] However, since we are not talking about production costs, but enforcement costs, I will consider fixed administrative costs the ones that basically do not vary with the passage of time, degree of experience of public agents and of antitrust experts, or the level of maturity of the institutional set up. The variable administrative costs, on its turn, are the ones that vary with the degree of experience that public agents and antitrust experts acquire over time, and with the level of maturity of the institutional set-up. The following paragraphs will explain these two components in detail.

The fixed administrative costs are simply the cost of maintaining the antitrust agencies, prosecutors and courts, from the infrastructure to the human resources. The cost of staff is often the biggest cost of an antitrust agency. When thinking about the costs borne by private parties, they are usually related to the cost of lawyers and experts, and fees of antitrust agencies.

In the context of the enforcement of vertical agreements, a notification system can be costly both to the undertakings and to the antitrust authorities. The undertakings, under a notification system of agreements, bear the costs of the notification fees and the costs of hiring lawyers. The firms also might bear the costs of renegotiations, for instance, if the authority gives a signal of a potential anticompetitive concern, and, in extreme cases, the costs of redrafting the whole contract and vertical clauses. Under a notification system of vertical agreements there are also the costs linked to the disclosure of information between the parties of the agreement that can be quite high in cases where the authority decides to reject the operation. The antitrust authorities themselves, under an *ex ante* notification system, have to consider the costs of their staff to proceed with the analysis of filling forms, and most importantly, they bear the risk of analysing a huge number of contracts, including the ones that present no antitrust risk whatsoever to the markets.

Under the *ex post* regime of agreements, the costs for antitrust authorities drop drastically, since they will only randomly assess the most severe agreements. However, for the parties, it is not always clear which legal framework reduces the administrative costs. This is the case because, even under the *ex post* control regime, parties still have to hire lawyers to help the self-assessment of their contracts, although they will not be 100% sure that their agreement is lawful. Apart from these legal costs, under the *ex post* regime, firms are vulnerable to the risks of future litigation that can be much bigger than a simple notification fee. Antitrust litigations can take years to be solved if taking

127. For the analysis of different measures of costs, *see* G. Mankiw & M. P. Taylor, *Microeconomics*, 4th ed., Hampshire, Cengage Learning, 2017, pp. 116-122.

into account both administrative decisions and judicial reviews and therefore the costs to parties are very unpredictable.

Administrative costs tend to be overstated in the lawmaking process, not only because they are easier to compute but also because of the budget constraints of antitrust authorities. Antitrust regulators usually have a certain budget for hiring a limited number of staff and most of the time they choose to allocate the money in the assessment of more severe or of a politically more interesting case.

The European Commission White Paper explicitly brought up the issue of the administrative burden of the notification of agreements, since the resources expended in those cases could be allocated to more severe cases such as cartel prosecutions. However, this administrative burden of the notification system, argued by the Commission, was criticized by some scholars who showed that it was overweighed. As presented in Chapter 4, Riley argued that the notification of vertical agreements was already an 'irrelevant procedure with marginal impact on the enforcement of EU competition law' by the time Regulation 1/2003 entered into force and, therefore, there were almost no costs to the Commission to abandon this policy.[128] Indeed, even though in the late 1960s the Commission was handling more than 30,000 notifications a year, this amount was substantially reduced by the introduction of comfort letters, block exemptions (mainly the 1999 Block Exemption Regulation), and notices. For instance, only seventy-one agreements were notified in 2003, before the new regulation entered into force.[129] It means that with the adoption of complementary rules to the notification system, the administrative burden of the authority also goes down.

However, even though administrative costs may have been overstated by the Commission in the White Paper, the lack of resources of some EU Member States is a reality that has been calling the attention of the European authority in the past years. The policy evaluation document that anticipated Directive 1/2019 shows that several EU Member States have insufficient resources and a significantly lower level of enforcement decisions.[130] The document compared countries with similar GDP, showing that national authorities with limited resources also face excessively lower levels of antitrust decisions compared to the NCAs with a higher level of resources in the same time period.[131]

Similar analysis could be formulated concerning the Brazilian experience. From January 2015 to November 2016, a period when Brazil faced clear rules of notification of both vertical and horizontal agreements,[132] only thirty-five associative agreements

128. A. Riley, 'EC Antitrust Modernization: The Commission Does Very Nicely – Thank You! Part One: Regulation 1 and the Notification Burden', *European Competition Law Review*, Vol. 11, 2003a, p. 604.
129. According to the *XXXIII Report on Competition Policy 2003*, 216 agreements were notified in 1998, followed by 162 in 1999, 101 in 2000, 94 in 2001 and 101 in 2002.
130. European Commission, 2017, *supra* note 124.
131. European Commission, 2017, *supra* note 124, p. 28. The European Commission does not reveal in this policy evaluation document to which Member State each data belongs, but it shows that NCAs which have more limited resources (e.g., Countries 1 and 2) present less enforcement decisions (14 and 13 decisions respectively) compared to the NCAs with a higher level of resources (e.g., Countries 3 and 4: 28 and 48 decisions respectively) in the same time period.
132. Period when CADE Resolution No. 10/2014 was into force.

among horizontals and verticals were assessed by the authority, corresponding to less than 5% of cases analysed by the authority in the same period. One could say that the notification system of vertical agreements in Brazil did not necessarily overload CADE's staff. However, budget constraint is currently a problem faced by the authority, since the hiring of two-hundred additional staff foreseen by the Competition Law No. 12.529/2011 has not materialized due to wider government budget cuts. According to an OECD report, the Brazilian antitrust authority is known as one of 'the most understaffed competition enforcement regimes in the world'.[133]

Antitrust authorities tend to overstate the administrative burden of a notification system of vertical agreements because they are simply not interested in such cases. Authorities are usually interested in enforcing more high-profile cases that would increase their reputation, such as international price-fixing cartels, and, consequently, this private interest pulls the lawmaking in the direction of choosing a less costly policy option for vertical agreements. The downside of having private interests behind the regulatory process is that optimal welfare outcomes cannot always be achieved.

Finally, the variable administrative costs of enforcement can change depending on the degree of experience of antitrust authorities and their institutional maturity. As a result, it is wrong to assume that all the authorities bear similar costs when it comes to assessing vertical agreements, under *ex ante* or *ex post* control of such commercial practices. Indeed, the greater the experience of a particular antitrust agency, the better qualified its staff is, and less time and resources are spent in the assessment of each vertical agreements' case. Consequently, the costs for the authority (or for the legal representatives of firms) are lower. This component of the administrative costs is very relevant for the next step of this analysis that refers to the building of the Antitrust Cost Curve related to the enforcement of vertical agreements.

5.7 THE ANTITRUST COST CURVE

5.7.1 Building the Cost Curve

This chapter started by highlighting the work of Hahn,[134] Neven,[135] Barros,[136] and Loss et al.,[137] who all somehow identified the importance of experience and institutional set-up to define an optimal policy for restrictive agreements. Briefly speaking, according to these authors, notification policies of agreements are preferred by the less experienced law enforcers when assessing anticompetitive conduct and when their perception of undertakings with regard to the probability of getting caught is low. This existing literature, as described before, has some limitations, since it is shaped in the EU context of modernization of competition rules, and did not focus on the different

133. OECD, *Peer Reviews of Competition Law and Policy: Brazil*, 2019, p. 10.
134. Hahn, 2000, *supra* note 3.
135. Neven, 2002, *supra* note 4.
136. Barros, 2003, *supra* note 6.
137. Loss at al., 2008, *supra* note 7.

policies required for vertical agreements and for other restrictive practices. Moreover, the theoretical literature has not been further developed in recent years.

Below, the discussion is reintroduced by the formulation of illustrative curves in the context of a qualitative and normative analysis. This attempt will consider that the total cost of enforcement of vertical agreements are equal to *C*, which embodies the sum of *C1* (information cost), *C2* (incentive cost) and *C3* (administrative cost).

For this qualitative analysis, it is considered first that enforcement costs are associated to the evolution of incentive and information costs that are a function of α, which measures the antitrust experience acquired over time with regard to the economic assessment of complex vertical agreement cases (Figure 5.1). Experience, in this case, is not measured by 'time', but rather, assessment of cases. It is worth noting that using 'time' as a variable of the cost curves has several limitations. Historical and sociopolitical reasons can affect the course of time it takes for a certain jurisdiction to achieve a good experience. As highlighted along this book, the influence of different groups of agents (e.g., industry and their lobby groups, politicians, lawyers) in the law- and decision-making process can delay the due development of the legal rules, directly affecting the relevance of the time dimension.

Second, enforcement cost is related to the evolution of incentive and information costs that are also a function of β, which measures the quality and maturity of the institutional set-up (Figure 5.2). The institutional set-up is related to all institutional features/elements that affect the institutional maturity and quality mentioned in section 5.4.4, mainly the capabilities of law enforcers to guarantee optimal levels of enforcement. The choice of these measures is related to the level of antitrust experience and the quality and maturity of the institutional set-up is in accordance with the cost analysis conducted in the previous sections. Indeed, these two variables turned out to be at the centre of our discussions related to both information and incentive costs and, therefore, they are adequate for our purpose.

Third, for this analysis, it is possible to interpret that the administrative costs can also be a function of α and β, and therefore they are not constant in time. As explained in section 5.6.2, the more experienced is the law enforcer, the quicker (and therefore the less costly) will be the decision-making process.

When it comes to information and incentive costs, Table 5.1 indicates which costs are directly influenced by α and β. The symbol ' + + ' indicates the situation where the costs are highly influenced by variables α and β, the symbol ' + ' indicates the situation where the costs are slightly influenced by variables α and β, and the symbol '-' refers to a situation where the costs are not influenced by any of the variables.

Table 5.1 Enforcement Costs: Degree of Influence of Antitrust Experience and the Institutional Set-Up

Enforcement Costs	α	β
	Information costs	
Costs of gathering information	+ +	+
Costs of assessing the competitive effects	+ +	+
	Incentive costs	
Fines	-	+ +
Antitrust error	+ +	+ +
Structure of judiciary	+	+ +
Distrust in institutions	+	+ +

Note: α refers to antitrust experience and β refers to institutional set-up.
Source: Compiled by the author.

Table 5.1 shows that information costs - composed by the costs of gathering market information and the costs of assessing the economic effects of vertical agreements (both efficiencies and anticompetitive effects) - are highly influenced by the antitrust degree of experience. This is the case because the more mature and experienced is the competition agency, the greater are the chances of having knowledgeable staff to conduct the assessments of vertical agreements. Information costs are also slightly influenced by the level of the institutional set-up variable, since, for instance, the gathering of market information might also depend on how stable and trustworthy the competition authority is in the eyes of business people.

Considering the incentive costs in Table 5.1, they are all highly influenced by the level of institutional set-up. For example, the incentive costs of not having an optimal fine scheme (and/or optimal methods of applying fines) are highly dependent on the level of maturity of the authority. The comparative analysis showed that some European countries with long-standing tradition in Competition Law, such as the UK, France and Germany have specific guidelines when it comes to this topic. Having clear rules concerning this topic decreases the enforcement costs. Antitrust error costs are also highly influenced by the degree of experience of the law enforcers. The more experienced and more mature is the authority, the smaller are the errors in the decision-making process.

Relying on both law and economics and the social learning theories, Figures 5.1 - 5.3 are proposed.

Figure 5.1 Evolution of Information and Incentive Costs in Assessing Vertical Agreements: The Influence of Antitrust Experience

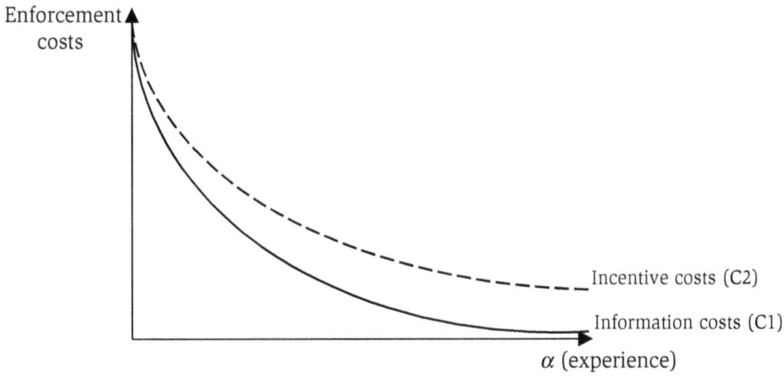

Source: Compiled by the author.

In Figure 5.1, the cost curves (*C1* and *C2*) are non-linear downward sloping curves. The first property that should be highlighted is related to the negative slope of the curves. In both incentive and information costs curves there is a negative relation between the variables, i.e., the bigger the experience of law enforcers in conducting full economic assessment in vertical cases, the smaller are the enforcement costs related to it. The second important property is their convex shape, meaning that the slope of the curves decreases at a decreasing rate. In practical terms, if an antitrust authority has no experience whatsoever in assessing complex vertical agreement cases ($\alpha = 0$), the perceived value of the first assessment (to both business people and law enforcers) will be bigger than the perceived value of the second assessment, and so on. By the time the authorities have assessed multiple cases, the value of a marginal decision over the topic becomes minimal. It is worth noting that the elasticity of the different moments of the curve changes because it depends on how sensitive the impact on costs of a given jurisdiction's learning from the new cases.

There is some other information that can be extracted from Figure 5.1. Even though the incentive costs (*C2*) and information cost (*C1*) curves have a similar shape, *C2* is usually higher than *C1*, and this can be explained by the fact that incentive costs are highly dependent on the same institutional factors that influence the curve of information costs, such as effective antitrust prosecution, fast and specialized judiciary, elements that are slightly captured by α (Table 5.1). Lastly, although the perceived value of the antitrust experience might increase over time, the levels of incentive and information costs will never be zero, since the ongoing changing conditions related to market performance, emergence of new markets (e.g., digital markets), and new types of contractual clauses may enhance the consideration of low but positive enforcement costs. In other words, there will always be uncertain factors that may affect this variable.

A similar analysis can be drawn taking into account the enforcement cost curves where total costs are a function of the quality of the institutional set-ups.

Figure 5.2 Evolution of Information and Incentive Costs in Assessing Vertical Agreements: The Influence of the Quality and Maturity of the Institutional Set-Up

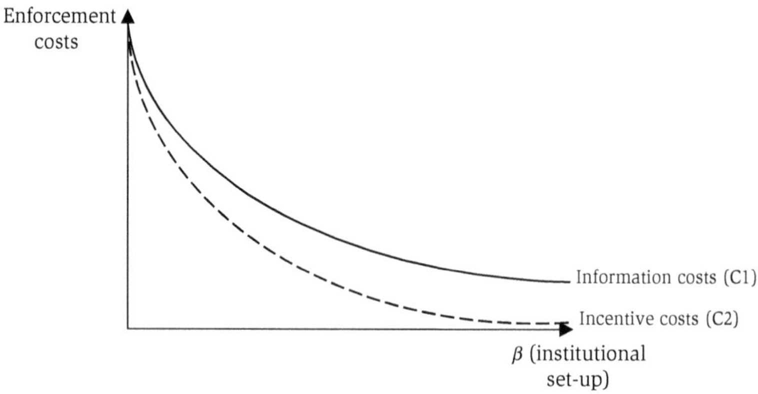

Source: Compiled by the author.

The same as in Figure 5.1, the *C1* and *C2* curves in Figure 5.2 are non-linear downward sloping curves. In more detail, there is a negative relation between incentive and information costs, and the institutional set-up variable. In other words, the greater the levels of institutional maturity and quality, the smaller the enforcement costs associated with the institutional set-up. The information and incentive costs curves are convex. If a jurisdiction has no antitrust law, no rules for vertical agreements, no specialized court, no accountability, and so on (i.e., to say, if $\beta = 0$), the perceived value for society of the first institutional change – for instance, the creation of an antitrust agency and competition law – will be bigger than the perceived value of the following institutional changes, that may create secondary rules, guidelines, rules for private enforcements, and so on. In this case, *C1* is higher than *C2*, since institutional factors by themselves do not capture all the costs associated with information and knowledge. Lastly, despite the maturity and trustworthy nature of the institutions, the enforcement costs for both curves will never be zero, since there will always be uncertain factors that may affect this variable, such as private interests of groups of agents that are constantly putting pressure on the law decision-making process.

In sequence, Figure 5.3 presents the enforcement costs of vertical agreements in a simplified cost curve *I*, equal to *C1* + *C2*, that is a function of Φ, a variable that captures both antitrust experience and the maturity and quality of the institutional set-up. In Figure 5.3, the administrative cost curve is represented by curve *C3*. The *C3* curve is downward sloping, since it is influenced by both information and incentive costs. However, it is flatter than the curve *I*, since the administrative costs also have a fixed component that does not depend on that function Φ, and therefore keeps the curve *C3* less steep.

Figure 5.3 Evolution of Antitrust Enforcement Costs in Assessing Vertical Agreements

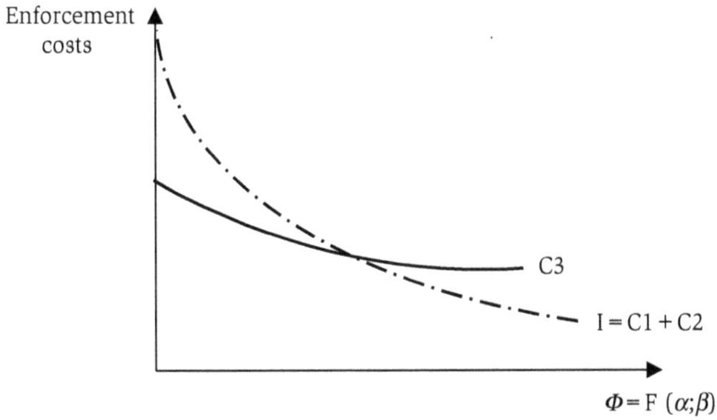

Source: Compiled by the author.

As we will demonstrate in the next subsection, the proposed curves, together with the comparative law and economic analysis, give us the basis for a normative analysis.

5.7.2 The Three-Stage Policy Framework Applicable to Vertical Agreements

This book has highlighted some antitrust policy options applied to vertical agreements, such as: *ex ante* notification of agreements, mixed policies (such as block-exemption regimes), and *ex post* control of restrictive agreements by public and private enforcement. It also emphasized that information and incentive costs are lower under the notification system than under block exemption regimes or *ex post* monitoring, since parties, in the moment of the notification, are obliged to share with the authority the content of each agreement and information about the market. However, administrative costs are higher in a notification system, since not only do the companies have to bear the procedure costs and cost of lawyers to do the notification but also the antitrust agency has to guarantee enough staff to assess these notifications. This comparison of enforcement costs and policy option is illustrated in Table 5.2

Table 5.2 Enforcement Costs under Ex Ante and Ex Post Control Systems

Enforcement Costs	Ex Ante *Notification*	Ex Post *Control*
Information costs	+	+ +
Incentive costs	+	+ +
Administrative costs	+ +	+

Source: Compiled by the author.

Taking into consideration the policy framework and the enforcement cost curves of assessing vertical agreements, it is possible to identify preferable policies for each phase of the cost curves. It is worth noting that, for this analysis, the approach that underlies the choice of antitrust enforcement policy is oriented towards welfare maximization by seeking to *minimize enforcement costs.*

Generally speaking, to minimize the costs of enforcement in a given jurisdiction, a notification system of vertical agreements will be an optimal policy when information and incentive costs are higher than the administrative costs of the *ex ante* system of notification. However, the favouring of an *ex post* monitoring system of restrictive agreements will be preferred in the moment when information and incentive costs are lower than the administrative costs of the notification. Lastly, mixed policies for vertical agreements will be preferred policies in the moment when the cost curve *I* becomes less inelastic, but the level of enforcement costs (information and incentive) are still higher than the administrative cost curve. *See* Figure 5.4.

Figure 5.4 The Three-Stage Policy Framework Applicable to Vertical Agreements

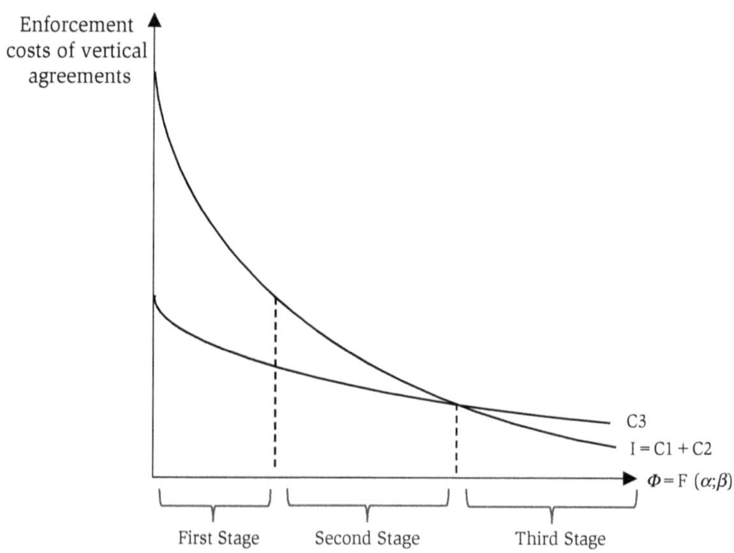

Source: Compiled by the author.

According to the proposed framework, during the First Stage of curve *I*, public enforcement and a pure *ex ante* notification of vertical agreements should be the most adequate policies to be encouraged. This is the case because the notification system of agreements has an important educational function and should be respected by the agencies. Moreover, the notification system should be presented as an ambitious competition policy in order to foster full advocacy and law enforcement. In this stage of implementation of an antitrust law, it is more efficient and overall less costly to adopt the obligation towards notification.

As soon as some institutional basis is set up, and the law enforcers have some level of experience in assessing complex vertical agreement cases, the Second Stage can be characterized and, therefore, mixed policy options should be introduced in the jurisdiction. As example of mixed policies one can identify: block exemptions regimes (as the ones introduced by the EU) in which the antitrust authority defines which types of agreements are presumed to be legal, and under which circumstances; and/or blacklisted regimes, in which the authority defines the types of vertical agreements that are presumed to be illegal. The other example of a mixed policy would be the implementation of a simplified consultation procedure, so that companies could obtain additional clarification from the authorities regarding their commercial practices. All the above examples of mixed policies guarantee some degree of legal certainty to companies, and at the same time reduce the enforcement costs associated to it, including error costs of future litigations.

It is worth noting that, within the scope of the proposed curve (Figure 5.4), the point of the curve that separates the First and the Second Stage is a blurry one, i.e., it can be more to the right or to the left of the curve depending on each case. This occurs because each jurisdiction reacts differently over the time in terms of capturing antitrust experience and improving the quality of its institutional set-up. In Figure 5.4, the different reactions can also be expressed by different slopes of the *I* curve. For instance, one can consider a country A where a sole RPM assessment is enough to create clear rules on how the country balances the pro- and anticompetitive effects of vertical agreements. In this case, since the slope of the *I* curve is bigger (the *I* curve is more inelastic), the period related to Stage 1 is a very short one. In other countries, however, the repetition of the assessment of several cases may be necessary to acquire greater knowledge on the topic. In these cases, the *I* curve tends to be flatter and the period in which Stage 1 is optimal becomes longer. In short, the point of the curve that shows the passage from Stage 1 to Stage 2 moves to the right.

When a jurisdiction achieves the Third (and last) Stage, individuals and law enforcers are most probably better informed about the types of business practices that restrict competition. Moreover, law enforcers are more efficient in enforcing the law since institutions are also more trustworthy. In this last stage, the adoption of a sole *ex post* monitoring system of vertical agreements and of preferences to private litigation must be encouraged.

There are some extra considerations to be made in regard to the illustrative curves. First, objective parameters of time that define for how long each jurisdiction should keep the same policies in each stage are very hard to formulate. Again, each jurisdiction has different institutional backgrounds and cultural values that directly influence the pace of policy implementation oriented to vertical agreements. Second, and most importantly, from law and economics theory, various combinations of policies and sanctions can establish similar levels of enforcement.[138] This means that the change from the first to the second stage should be carried out together with the publication of guidelines that directly inform business people and law enforcers about the types of vertical agreements that are considered restrictive in a given jurisdiction. Moreover, the change from the second to the third stage (or even from the first to the third stage in the cases of countries that do not consider mixed policies) should be carried out with the strengthening of *ex post* control mechanisms. This change means the redefinition of fines, the increase of investigative powers, and the clarification of rules about private actions, but is not limited to them.

5.7.3 Limitation of the Framework: Political Economy Distortions

It must be acknowledged that the proposed three stage policy framework has limitations, since it does not represent every possible situation of changes in law regarding vertical agreements. This section presents one of these alternative scenarios.

As discussed in Chapter 2, regulation can be motivated and explained by public interest arguments, meaning that the law and policy decision makers operate to ensure the promotion of economic efficiency. However, in certain contexts, the law- and decision-making processes may not be guided by what is optimal for society, or they may not achieve the public interest goals. These scenarios certainly do not promote economic efficiency.

Regarding the lack of the predominance of public interest, public choice theorists highlight the powerful influence of special-interest groups over the whole law- and decision-making process. In the antitrust field, not different from economic regulation in general, the agencies, the judges, the antitrust bureaucrats[139] and their legal representatives are relevant stakeholders involved in the process of making either a new law or changes to existing laws. Private interests of the different groups of agents can directly affect the lawmaking process and the adequate assessment of the changes in antitrust regulation regarding rules for restrictive vertical agreements. Private interests may affect the balance among the total enforcement costs' components and anticipate or even delay the evolution from Stage 1 to Stage 2 and Stage 3 in the curve.

The evolution between the three stages may not be linear. For instance, in the assessment of the law, some authorities might exaggerate the role of administrative costs when deciding on whether to impose an *ex ante* notification system of agreements or an *ex post* monitoring one. This may happen since the enforcement of vertical agreements creates substantial costs to the competition authority and does not proportionally increase its reputation as a law enforcer. By overestimating the value of administrative costs, the authority might decide to implement a unique *ex post*

138. *See*, for instance, P. Polisky & S. Shavell, 'The Optimal Tradeoff Between the Probability and Magnitude of Fines', *American Economic Review*, Vol. 69, No. 5, 1979, pp. 880-891.
139. Expression used by Tollison in R. Tollison, 'Public Choice and Antitrust', *Cato Journal*, Vol. 4, Winter, 1985, p. 905.

enforcement scheme in an earlier stage of implementation of antitrust law. If this occurs earlier than in the so-called 'Stage 3', the efficiency of law enforcement will not be maximized.

The public choice perspective, that is to say, the thesis that government authorities, businesses, and legal representatives attempt to influence the law- or decision-making process in order to pursue benefits for themselves, may lead one to conclude that both the Brazilian and the European legal changes favoured, in a premature way, the adoption of an *ex post* control of vertical agreements. The reasons for the inefficient outcome may be related to the influence of private interests in the regulatory process. Regarding the Brazilian experience, Chapter 3 found that the self-interest of both CADE and competition lawyers may explain the enactment of Resolution No. 17/2016. Neither did CADE include in its policy assessment document any reference to the goals of competition law in the country nor did it give clear reasoning explaining the choice of this specific regulation. Hence, one may hypothesize that the exclusion of vertical agreements from the Brazilian notification system was influenced by the private interests of relevant agents.

The same holds true in the EU case. Chapter 4 presented some literature that explains the context in which the 2004 Reform of EU Competition Law happened, as well as the potential winners and losers of the premature change in policy. The analysis of the European experience opens up a debate about the Commission's main argument regarding the huge administrative costs of adopting the notifications of agreements. In reality, according to Riley, the notification was already an 'irrelevant procedure with marginal impact on the enforcement of EU competition law' and the reductions in administrative costs associated to changes in its policy to the Commission were actually minimal.[140] Law firms providing antitrust advocacy to the undertakings also profited from the decentralized *ex post* control of Regulation 1/2003.[141] This happened because, following the 2004 Reform, companies should privately self-assess their agreements (to minimize antitrust risks and to know better how to deal with competitors) and *ex post* litigations were also encouraged.[142]

In sum, the relevance of private interests cannot be neglected in any normative analysis involving competition law, especially in the cases of less developed EU countries and in the cases of developing countries such as Brazil, or even in the cases of countries with lower experience in applying competition law. It is worth noting that developing countries that do not clearly present the goals of their competition laws are more subjected to the influence of private interests in their regulatory process.

5.8 POLICY RECOMMENDATION FOR THE EU AND BRAZIL

This chapter proposes a normative analysis of policies oriented to vertical agreements. The main question was formulated at the beginning of the chapter: *Does a policy change*

140. Riley, 2003a, *supra* note 128, p. 604.
141. A. Wigger, 'Revising the European Competition Reform: The Toll of Private Self-Enforcement', *Working Papers Political Science of Vrije Universiteit Amsterdam*, No. 07, 2004.
142. Wigger, 2004, *supra* note 141, at 14-15.

from an ex ante *notification system to an* ex post *monitoring of vertical agreements always enhance the efficiency of the enforcement of competition law?* The answer to this question is negative and the comparative law and economics analysis of the EU and Brazil experiences support this important conclusion.

From what has been previously discussed, antitrust regulators should consider three main costs to be minimized in their lawmaking process: information costs, incentive costs and administrative costs. Information and incentive costs are mostly related to the antitrust experience of law enforcers with regard to the assessment of complex vertical agreement cases, and to the maturity and quality of the institutional set-up in each jurisdiction that can be shaped by several factors including institutional quality and the capability of law enforcers to guarantee optimal levels of enforcement. Meanwhile, the administrative costs are the monetary costs faced by the law enforcers and firms to comply with the applicable regulation. Regarding the public authorities, the administrative costs are the costs of maintaining the antitrust agencies, prosecutors and courts, from the physical infrastructure to the human resources. In order to guarantee an optimal level of antitrust enforcement, all three costs should be considered by antitrust authorities in its lawmaking process. However, this has not always been the case.

Based on law and economics enforcement theories and drawing on the comparative analysis of the experiences of the EU and Brazil, this chapter formulated illustrative enforcement cost curves to develop a qualitative and normative analysis. A three-stage policy framework applicable to vertical agreements was proposed, in which, depending on its antitrust experience and institutional set-up, the jurisdiction should choose among a notification of agreements by public authorities (Stage 1), a mixed policy option such as block exemption regimes (Stage 2) or an *ex post* control by both public and private agents (Stage 3). The normative analysis also suggests that various combinations of policies and sanctions can establish similar levels of enforcement. For instance, the change from Stage 1 to Stage 2, or from Stage 1 (or 2) to Stage 3, may also be accompanied by complementary policies, such as the publication of guidelines, the increase in fines, the clarification of procedural rules for private actions, and the creation of specialized courts, among others.

The chapter concludes that both the Brazilian and the European experiences favoured, in a premature way, the adoption of *ex post* control of vertical agreements. Because of that, complementary policies should be implemented in both jurisdictions in order to enhance optimal levels of enforcement of restrictive vertical agreements, and therefore, to move towards optimal levels of social welfare.

In the EU, by the time Regulation 1/2003 entered into force ending the notification system of vertical agreements, several Member States did not even have a competition agency, which means that their α and β values were close to zero.[143] According to the proposed policy framework, a notification system of vertical agreements is preferred when a country has no experience in applying competition law and

143. It is worth noting that when a competition law is inexistent in a certain country, meaning, when α (experience) and β (institutional set-up) are close to zero, this does not mean that there is no welfare loss in this jurisdiction.

also when the institutional set-up is limited. One can argue that the ECN would help filling the experience gap by transplanting the experience of the European Commission and the maturity of NCAs (such as Germany and France). However, this argument has several limitations since the top-down approach proposed by the European Commission has not easily permitted the full spread of competition culture across different Member States.[144] These points lead us to the conclusion that the implementation of *ex post* control was precipitated in particular European countries.

There are, of course, lessons to be learned from the EU experience to other jurisdictions, as well as points of improvement to be taken into consideration by European authorities. In respect to the lessons to be learned, there are several positive aspects of the EU 2004 Reform that are aligned to the proposed normative analysis. One lesson is that the adoption of an *ex post* control of vertical agreements has happened in stages for most of the Member States (mainly the founder Member States). Other lessons are related to the fact that the European authority, that under the *ex post* regime, published guidelines to the self-assessment of vertical agreements and also took several measures to enhance antitrust enforcement, such as increasing enforcement powers of the Commission and Member States, increasing fines, implementing new rules for private actions, that indeed decrease the information and incentive costs to a level that is equal to or less than the potential administrative costs of bearing a notification system.

Regarding the points of improvement of the overall enforcement of anticompetitive vertical agreements in Europe, this book highlights important measures to be taken both at the EU level, mostly by the European Commission, and at the Member States level, i.e., by NCAs. At the EU level, the Commission should first conclude the revision of the VBER to be entered into force in 2022 in an effective way. The Commission must add to the revised regulation further legal requirements and clarifications concerning new forms of contractual relations and abuses that are arising in the context of digital markets and the new roles of e-commerce platforms. For instance, the Commission could indicate what is the legal framework that covers the cases of MFN clause provisions, and how to assess the potential effects of wide and narrow MFN clauses. Also, more clarification regarding platform bans is required. The new legal provisions should guarantee better information to the self-assessment of vertical agreements, and most importantly guarantee a higher level of consistency in the application of the legal rules across Member States.

A second important point to be made when it comes to policies at EU level is that the Commission should add efforts to efficiently monitor the implementation of the Directive 2019/1/EU, which has as its objective the empowerment of competition authorities by better designing their institutional set-up. This implies that the Commission bears now the responsibility not only to enact the legal rules but also to guarantee that there are enough enforcement mechanisms to apply those rules across the Member States. In order to achieve the goals of this policy, it is necessary to ensure full awareness of the different levels of enforcement across Member States. Lastly, about

144. This fact supports one of the reasoning that underlies Directive 2019/1/EU.

the ECN, the optimal exchange of experiences among EU Member States could be accomplished via the creation of an official ECN vertical agreement working group. Naturally, the expected cooperation within this particular group guarantees better consistency in the application of EU competition policies relevant to vertical agreements.

At the national level, there are three main points that should be highlighted. The first one, also within the scope of the Directive 2019/1/EU, is that the authorities should efficiently allocate their resources to build an adequate institutional set-up, at both the administrative and judicial level. This implies having minimal investigatory tools (including technological instruments) and higher decision-making powers, which also depend on hiring highly qualified staff to carry out the complex assessments required by Article 101 TFEU. In this regard, the second point should be highlighted, which is the need for more training of national law enforcers in the economic analysis of antitrust cases across all Member States. Moreover, these educational programmes should be further developed at both the administrative and judicial level.[145] The last point to be noted is the need for better organization and cataloguing of internal data and case files of NCAs, in order to help identifying potential antitrust actions that require better enforcement focus. It has been shown in this book that, nowadays, there is still almost no public and categorized information on the enforcement of vertical agreements among the different Member States. And this is also the case because their annual reports fail to give a full picture of the on-going investigations. It is worth recalling that the focus of this book is looking at the big picture of potential drawbacks of EU enforcement systems, and not at the particular needs of each national authority.

On the Brazilian perspective, the country could have also profited from a longer period of notification system of vertical agreements. First, the country did not acquire enough experience in assessing complex vertical agreement cases. Apart from that, the country lacks efficient educational programmes in competition law, it has also judicial bodies that are not open to interdisciplinary approaches, and the law- and decision-making processes are characterized by high levels of corruption and political influences. However, since the Brazilian law applicable to vertical agreements has changed twice in the past five years, being the last change made in 2016 to favour *ex post* control of these practices, it will probably not be revised in the near future. Therefore, other complementary policies should be carefully considered in the country in order to improve enforcement levels and minimize enforcement costs.

Given the analysis about the main threats for an effective antitrust enforcement concerning vertical agreements developed in this chapter, here are some suggested policy proposals that can directly reduce information, incentive, and administrative costs in Brazil.

145. It is important to acknowledge that the European Commission has invested in some projects related to the training of national judges in EU Competition Law. However, these projects need should be extended, and they should make sure that law enforcers indeed attend these courses. For more information about these training programmes, *see*: https://ec.europa.eu/competition/court/training (20/8/2019).

Assessment of the first threat: Lack of consolidated antitrust jurisprudence with regard to vertical agreements and the excessive use of settlements in Brazil.

Competition policy in Brazil would benefit from specific guidelines on vertical agreements, indicating how business people and the antitrust authority could improve the economic assessment of these commercial practices. Soft-law instruments, such as guidelines, have been widely used by antitrust agencies around the world, including other regulatory bodies, since they improve the institutional environment throughout activities that enhance social learning. Guidelines help companies and their legal advisors to interpret the rules, especially in the case of complex matters involving interdisciplinary knowledge. The creation of guidelines about vertical agreements would even help CADE's Commissioners to better explore the available information in each case and make more uniform decisions on vertical cases, ensuring greater legal certainty. Considering the scope of the content, the guidelines should describe the concept of the main vertical agreements (e.g., RPM, geo-blocking, selective distribution) as well as the economic criteria to analyse their potential effects in the markets. In this attempt, the Brazilian guidelines could adapt the *Guidelines on Vertical Restraints*, prepared by the European Commission, by taking into consideration the goals of competition policy in the country. Finally, with the growth of vertical contracts in the context of e-commerce, it would be very important that the guidelines also include explanations about how to perform an optimal economic assessment of contracts in the context of digital economies.

It is worth noting that the Brazilian competition policy applicable to vertical agreements could also be improved by the use of legal exemptions in specific markets. Antitrust literature in Brazil explain that there is room to interpret about the viability of legal exemptions in the country, since the current legislation does not explicitly foresee/or prohibit such practice.[146]

Assessment of the second threat: CADE's institutional design and lack of specialized staff

Nowadays, CADE's internal units and departments are primarily specialized in mergers and cartel cases, leaving the vertical cases handled by merger units. This practice puts into question the priorities of CADE's investigations. CADE should add to its institutional priorities the enforcement of other forms of anticompetitive conducts than cartels, which also have deleterious effects on markets. As a policy recommendation, the assessment of vertical restraints cases should be held in specialized units, with a team of lawyers and economists who are highly skilled in making the economic analysis of the dual-side effects of vertical agreements. The opening of a specialized unit (or specialized enforcement teams), and the hiring and/or relocating, for example, of highly educated staff, would increase the quality and efficiency of CADE's investigations. This specialization would also enhance the consistency of the administrative

146. *See* discussion in C. Salomão Filho, *Direito Concorrencial: as estruturas*, 3rd ed., São Paulo, Editora Malheiros, 2007; P. A. Forgioni, *Direito Concorrencial e Restrições Verticais*, São Paulo, Revista dos Tribunais, 2007, p. 128.

decisions. As CADE's resources tend to be very limited, the specialized unit could also handle other unilateral conduct apart from vertical cases, which usually also require very complex economic assessments. Regarding the European best practices, for instance, the European Commission clearly distinguishes the units that deal with mergers, from the ones that deal with cartels, complex antitrust cases, policy evaluation and state-aid cases. In the case of the European Commission, these units are even further divided according to the sectors of the economy. However, it is considered that, in Brazil, the simple creation of a specialized unit for vertical agreements would already be a great progress in the improvement of the institutional design of antitrust policies.

Assessment of the third threat: Lack of clarity regarding antitrust sanctions and the methodology to set fines.

When CADE opted to change the policy of vertical agreements to an *ex post* enforcement system, the sanctions for antitrust violation remained unchanged. In order to ensure that an *ex post* enforcement system of agreements gives the right incentives to companies, i.e., incentives to sign procompetitive vertical agreements instead of restrictive ones, the increase in antitrust fines is a policy decision to be considered by the Brazilian authority. Today, in the Brazilian reality, companies have incentives to actually design restrictive contract clauses, since CADE's *ex post* enforcement has been rare, the fines are minimal and rarely enforceable by the courts. Indeed, CADE should not only consider increasing the level of fines for cases of vertical restraints but also create clear methodologies for setting the fines and enforcing them. Looking at the European experience, it is worth recalling that several countries in Europe with more antitrust experience, such as Germany, the UK and France, have nowadays specific guidelines that clarify the methods used in setting antitrust sanctions and fines. This can certainly be used as an inspiration for improving the antitrust tools and practices in Brazil.

Assessment of the fourth threat: Non-existence of specialized antitrust courts, and unclear rules for proposing private actions.

This item involves the role of the Brazilian judicial system in enforcing antitrust policy, both regarding the judicial review of CADE's administrative decisions and the assessment of antitrust damage claims. The Brazilian judiciary is not fully prepared to perform a merit analysis in antitrust matters, and it ends up focusing most of its decisions on formal errors of the administrative processes, rather than on the full analysis of the case. Therefore, it is recommended that the creation of specialized courts be considered, with judges that are trained to conduct an economic analysis of the legal cases, which would also bring more efficiency to the due processes. It is important to point out that there is no legal impediment to create specialized courts for antitrust matters in the country, since Brazil has a history of creating specialized courts in diverse topics, such as military crimes, corruption, financial crimes, environmental cases. In a comparative law and economics perspective, the experience of the EU shows that the good performance of antitrust authorities is also better perceived due to the existence of specialized courts. In accordance with this recommendation, the Brazilian judges should have additional training of the economic analysis of law in antitrust cases (including courses of basic law and economics concepts and methods, microeconomics, antitrust economics, among others), since the improvement of the institutional environment should be articulated with building new educational perspectives.

Assessment of the fifth threat: Lack of transparency, influence of private interests in the lawmaking process and risk of regulatory capture.

Although CADE accomplished public consultations prior to the publication of its legal Resolutions, several other practices need to be developed and implemented to improve the transparency of the lawmaking process. In this sense, CADE must adopt the best practices regarding transparency and impact assessment of its regulations, which includes, among others: (i) the introduction of a roadmap (summary of the topic) and feedback periods that anticipate the public consultations; (ii) the extension of deadlines for public consultations, (iii) the spread of the use of social media and communication strategies in Brazil to encourage the participation of potential stakeholders in the lawmaking process; (iv) the publication of a detailed technical note with justifications for the proposed changes in lawmaking, including, for instance, a cost benefit analysis methodology of the new rule. Regarding the lessons from Europe, the reviewing process of the rules applied to vertical agreements was followed by an extensive impact assessment analysis. The impact assessment for the new VBER (to enter into force in 2022) started already in November 2018, with the roadmap and first feedbacks of different stakeholders and countries.

Another relevant recommendation for the Brazilian antitrust policy would be the introduction of a more transparent system for the appointment and nomination of CADE's Commissioners and President, for instance, by allowing the interested candidates to directly apply for a transparent selection process of these positions based on qualification and skills. This topic is of particular importance in the historical moment that Brazil is passing through, since the country has been in the spotlight because of issues of corruption and political influence in most of its Ministries, Secretariats and Agencies.

Assessment of the sixth threat: Lack of social knowledge on antitrust matters.

This last recommendation is a rather general, but still a very important one. Although CADE has the legal responsibility to explore the knowledge on competition law within universities, research groups, companies, associations, consultancies, law firms (with or without competition expertise), and among other stakeholders, the outcomes have been limited. An example of an initiative to be taken by the authority is the promotion of institutional actions across the various States in Brazil, such as the organization of forums, programmes, and other events to favour the spread of awareness of antitrust conduct.

Moreover, CADE's compliance guidelines do not focus on the precautions to be taken by business people to avoid restrictive vertical agreements. The existing compli ance guidelines are rather focused on the prevention of sharing information among firms in the context of cartel and pre-merger scenarios. Therefore, an amendment to the current compliance guideline, adding concerns oriented to vertical agreements, could be an alternative policy to tackle the issue. Also, within the scope of new educational strategies and practices, one last point that deserves attention is the need to reformulate the curriculum of economics and law schools to ensure that students have the option to study antitrust-related disciplines throughout the entire national territory (as separate or together with other related disciplines).

Finally, it is noteworthy that the previous recommendations should be considered in a holistic public policy perspective to guarantee the optimal enforcement of an antitrust policy. In other words, there should be an integrated effort to improve the institutional design, the learning strategies and the policy tools.

CHAPTER 6

Conclusions

This book has reviewed the enforcement of the Brazilian and the EU antitrust policies oriented to vertical agreements from an institutional perspective. It has considered both the evolution of the legal framework and the application of the existing policies in practice. The book highlighted the main challenges of the current approaches taken by the competition authorities in these jurisdictions and formulated specific proposals for improvements. Because Brazilian competition rules were originally inspired by the European legal framework, it also resumes discussions regarding comparative law and the efficiency of transplanting laws and good practices. The following sections will recall the main questions and answers that were raised by this comparative study.

It is worth noting that when it comes to the analysis of vertical agreements, we highlighted that the effects of these practices are limited and less problematic when compared to the effects of horizontal agreements. Hence, the policy options of the former type of restrictions should be carefully assessed. The complexity of vertical agreements also requires the conceptualization by the competition authorities of what is harmful to society, in order to guarantee that restrictions to competition do not take place. And whether a country will choose a lighter or stricter approach towards vertical agreements will depend on what are the goals of competition policy, i.e., what policymakers believe their competition policy should aim at protecting.

6.1 SUMMARY OF THE FINDINGS

Chapter 2 of this book proposed the following group of economic-oriented questions: *Under which conditions should vertical agreements be considered efficiency enhancing? How can vertical agreements lead to anticompetitive outcomes?*

It was argued that vertical agreements have different effects on the marketplace. On the one hand, these commercial practices can bring economic efficiencies to markets, increasing the total welfare. On the other hand, they can generate negative outcomes, be harmful to consumers and producers, reducing the total welfare of the specific market. Chapter 2 explored three main efficiency arguments: the double markup problem, the preventing of free-riding in both upstream and downstream markets, and the reduction of transaction costs of the firms that are in a vertical structure. In addition, the chapter indicated three main anticompetitive effects: the increase of collusive practices, the reduction of intra- and inter-brand competition, and the foreclosure of markets.

The complex nature of vertical agreements makes it difficult for law- and decision makers to assess the welfare outcomes of such practices. This book showed that a vertical restraint can constitute a solution to a market failure, and at the same time encourage anticompetitive behaviour. Moreover, different forms of vertical restraints have diverse outcomes in the markets, and therefore require case-by-case assessments. For example, RPM and geo-blocking restrictions may combat free-riding, which is a procompetitive effect. RPM and geo-blocking clauses may also facilitate collusion and forecloses markets, which are anticompetitive effects. However, RPM may combat double marginalization problems, while territorial protection may increase those problems.

Chapter 2 also showed that what is called 'regulatory dilemma' may be reinforced in the context of digital economies, e-commerce transactions, and marketplace platforms. New forms of vertical restraints are being observed in online markets, which raise concerns on their potential anticompetitive effects. This is because the assessment of the competition implications of vertical restraints in digital markets seems inherently more complex on behalf of multiple interactions, network externalities and vertical relationships between the marketplace platforms and consumers. This scenario potentially implies a more careful antitrust analysis with multiple foreclosure effects.

In sequence, Chapters 3 and 4 aim at answering the following legal-oriented questions: *What are the possible legal treatments for vertical agreements? What are the promises and drawbacks of the legal treatment chosen by Brazil and by the EU? To what extent has the evolution of the Brazilian and European regulation been conditioned by the interests of private relevant actors?*

Brazil and the EU passed through a similar change in antitrust policy applicable to vertical agreements: from an *ex ante* notification system of agreements to an *ex post* control of restrictive practices, although with some crucial differences. In the EU, the change from an *ex ante* to an *ex post* control happened after forty years of a notification system of agreements, and it was accompanied by other complementary policies, such as the enactment of the Block Exemption Regulation and Guidelines for helping firms self-assess the potential anticompetitive effects of their contracts. In Brazil, the Resolution No. 17/2016 removed the vertical relationship threshold for notification, leaving the enforcement of anticompetitive vertical agreements in Brazil solely dependent on *ex post* control. In contrast with Europe, the Brazilian authority did not publish any guidelines to better inform business people nor did it take any specific measures to strengthen the *ex post* control.

With regard to the Brazilian context, it is undeniable that competition policies in Brazil have evolved considerably in the past decades. Brazil is one example of an emerging economy that has put efforts in implementing a competition policy, and, as a result, it 'has consolidated its position among the main antitrust jurisdictions around the world'.[1] However, when it comes to Brazil's experience in regulating vertical agreements, Chapter 3 argued that the established legal framework that excluded vertical agreements from the notification system and favoured the *ex post* control, presents limitations. The study has demonstrated that these limitations can represent threats for the optimal enforcement of competition law. Among the identified threats, it is highlighted: (i) the lack of consolidated antitrust jurisprudence with regard to vertical agreements and excessive use of settlements in Brazil; (ii) CADE's institutional design and lack of specialized staff; (iii) the lack of clarity regarding antitrust sanctions and the methodology to set fines; (iv) the non-existence of specialized antitrust courts, and unclear rules for proposing private actions; (v) the lack of transparency and the influence of private interests in the lawmaking process; and (vi) the lack of social knowledge on antitrust matters.

These items are related, in general terms, to the unstable learning process of the enforcer and business community with regard to the assessment of vertical restraints. This situation leads to great legal uncertainty and to the prevalence of private-interest motives in the lawmaking process. Both problems lead to sub-optimal regulations and lower levels of antitrust enforcement.

In more detail, when analysing case law under CADE's *ex post* enforcement, the antitrust jurisprudence is not consolidated enough to guarantee legal certainty to parties when assessing their vertical agreements. For instance, Chapter 3 highlighted that for RPM cases, there is no clear rule or clear jurisprudence regarding the topic. Besides, in these cases, CADE's Tribunal is also not completely sure on whether to define such practice as a per se illegality.

In the scope of Chapter 3, it also showed that one of the goals of competition policies in Brazil is to protect competition and prevent markets from being harmed by agents with a high degree of economic power, by preserving an environment where companies have effective incentives to compete, innovate and attend to consumers' demands. The use of the presumption of illegality in RPM cases does not necessarily respect these goals, because RPM can bring economic efficiencies to markets. These economic efficiencies can help creating a level playing field among competitors that are intrinsically expressed in the constitutional principles, and therefore they should not be ignored by the Brazilian authority in the analysis of any vertical cases, even when it involves price restrictions.

Moreover, CADE relies heavily on settlements. The downsides of settlement agreements are the reduction of legal certainty in the marketplace and the slow development of the jurisprudence in Brazil towards the economic assessment of vertical agreements. With settlements, there is no effect-based assessment and/or decision published by CADE and legal cases are not reviewed by the national courts.

Even considering all the achievements of the authority in the last decade, mostly in terms of merger control and cartel policies, CADE still faces challenges in defining objective parameters for assessing vertical agreements (including the definition of

1. OECD, *Peer Review of Competition Law and Policy: Brazil*, 2019, p. 15.

whether some practices are per se illegal or not) and also does not have enough staff to do such work. This means that the Brazilian authority has favoured *ex post* enforcement with a lack of staff to do so.

Another important topic of Chapter 3 was the identification of the self-interest of relevant actors as a possible explanation for the enactment of Resolution No. 17/2016. As the policy assessment documents of Resolution No. 17/2016 did not make any reference to the goals of the country, nor gave a clear reasoning to the choice of this specific regulation, one could hypothesize that the exclusion of vertical agreements from the notification system has been based on the private interests of relevant agents. Moreover, Schuartz's theory of 'deconstitutionalization' of the Brazilian competition rules is somehow confirmed. This is because the application of the rule of reason in vertical cases seems to be neglected and the lawmaking process and the implementation of competition law have not been observing the constitutional principles of the country.

In other words, the choice for the exclusion of vertical agreements from the notification system was not properly justified in the lawmaking process. First, the goals and constitutional principles of the country were not considered by the authority. Second, the aptitude of business people in self-assessing their contracts and the capability of the antitrust authority to deter restrictive anticompetitive agreements were not completely reflected.

With regard to the European context, Chapter 4 shows that historically, Regulation 1/2003 replaced the centralized *ex ante* notification system of vertical agreements to a decentralized *ex post* control of these business practices. It presented some alternative literature that suggests that behind the 'decentralization', the Commission did not lose its central role in the enforcement of competition law in Europe, since it kept (and even expanded) most of its investigatory and lawmaking powers. Despite the political economy discussions and the suggested alternative readings, this book shows that there are still very important lessons to be drawn from the European experience and the 2004 Reform.

These lessons are mainly related to the instruments that are used by the NCAs to guarantee the enforcement of vertical restraints, in the *ex post* control scenario. Within the sections there are three of these instruments that can be called 'pillars': (i) the existence of a consolidated antitrust jurisprudence, of a VBER and of specific guidelines; (ii) the creation of a network among authorities that permitted some coordination, sharing of experiences and better competence allocation among the Member States and the Commission; and (iii) the intensification of *ex post* control instruments.

Chapter 4 also highlighted that over the years, even with the presence of the three enforcement pillars, there are still open questions to be considered when thinking about optimal enforcement of vertical restraints in the EU context. Two challenges were identified. The first challenge refers to the controversies about the application of regulations and soft law instruments to cases involving the digital economy. The two chosen case analyses (selective distribution and price parity arrangements) illustrate that countries such as Germany, France, and the UK are facing important controversies and are presenting different interpretations of Article 101 TFEU and of the content of the VBER. The new realities of a more globalized, technology-driven and digitalized competitive environment may suggest the need for a clearer framework for assessing and balancing anti- and procompetitive effects of such restrictive practices. The second challenge is related to the different levels of enforcement of Article 101 TFEU among the Members States. This chapter argued that not all the national authorities developed adequate enforcement procedures over time. The analysis suggests that the institutional disparities remain a point of concern to be overcome by the Commission in the coming years.

From what has been discussed, one can note that the challenges faced by several EU countries - even with the support of the Commission - are also faced by several developing countries around the world. The difficulties of establishing a proper competition authority, with sufficient resources to enforce all antitrust topics (including the complex cases of vertical restraints), with specialized courts, among other items, are not a problem encountered only in the European reality. For this reason, the understanding of the EU experience and its challenges are valuable for this comparative study.

Finally, Chapter 5 discussed the answers to the law and economics group of sub-questions that enhances the normative analysis: *Does a change in antitrust policies from* ex ante *to* ex post *control of vertical agreements always enhance the efficiency of the enforcement of competition law? What are the direct and indirect enforcement costs in a notification system of vertical agreements and in an* ex post *monitoring system? Which elements affect those different costs?*

From the analysis, we concluded that not always the change from an *ex ante* to an *ex post* control of vertical agreements is capable of enhancing the efficiency of law enforcement. The comparative law and economics analysis of the EU and Brazil experiences support this important conclusion. Actually, the choice of an optimal antitrust enforcement policy applicable to vertical agreement should seek to *minimize enforcement costs*. And the assessment of these enforcement costs by policymakers shall consider three dimensions of costs: information costs, incentive costs and administrative costs.

Information and incentive costs are mostly related to the lack of antitrust experience of law enforcers with regard to the assessment of complex vertical agreement cases, and to the lack of maturity and quality of the institutional set-up in each jurisdiction that can be shaped by several factors. Information costs will often be high in jurisdictions where there is limited case law regarding vertical agreements, no specific guidelines regarding the topic, and non-specialized or highly qualified staff. Incentive costs, in its turn, are influenced by several institutional factors. They can be defined as the costs that influence the incentives of companies to engage in welfare-enhancing agreements or to stop participating in welfare-reducing agreements. Incentive costs are often high in jurisdictions where there is generally a low level of antitrust deterrence, no clear rules regarding setting fines, a high incidence of antitrust errors in the decision-making process, apart from a non-active judiciary and general distrust in institutions. Meanwhile, the administrative costs are the direct costs faced by the law enforcers and firms to comply with the applicable regulation. Chapter 5 also showed that administrative costs tend to be overstated in the lawmaking process, not only because they are easier to compute, but also because of the budget constraints of antitrust authorities.

Based on the costs analysis, on the EU and Brazilian experiences, and on law and economics enforcement theories, Chapter 5 formulated illustrative enforcement cost curves to answer to the main question suggested to the readers, *How should an antitrust policy be designed to efficiently deter anticompetitive vertical agreements and encourage procompetitive ones?*

The antitrust policy should observe the three-stage policy framework applicable to vertical agreements in order to guarantee that the three enforcement costs are minimized.

Figure 6.1 The Three-Stage Policy Framework Applicable to Vertical Agreements

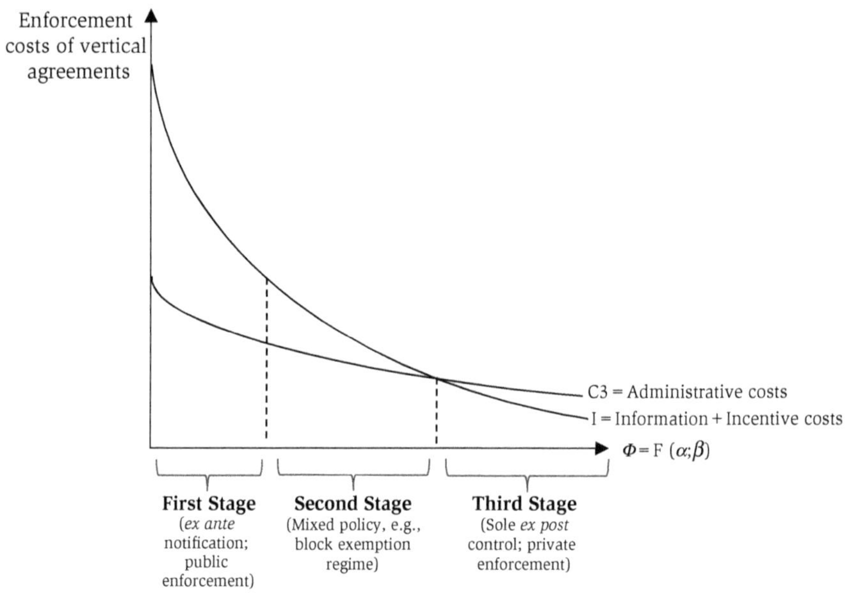

Note: Φ, a variable that captures both antitrust experience (α), and the maturity and quality of the institutional set-up (β)

Source: Compiled by the author.

According to the novel framework, there is no unique design of antitrust policy that is capable of deterring anticompetitive vertical agreements and encourage pro-competitive ones in every jurisdiction. In reality, the country should opt among a notification of agreements by public authorities (Stage 1), a mixed policy option such as block exemption regimes (Stage 2) or an *ex post* control by both public and private agents (Stage 3), depending on its antitrust experience and institutional set-up. The normative analysis also suggests that various combinations of policies and sanctions can establish similar levels of enforcement. For instance, the change from Stage 1 to

Stage 2, or from Stage 1 (or 2) to Stage 3, may also be accompanied by complementary policies, such as the publication of guidelines, the increase in fines, the clarification of procedural rules for private actions and, the creation of specialized courts, among others.

One limitation of the proposed three-stage policy framework is that private interests of different groups of agents, including the antitrust regulators, can directly affect the analysis. This may happen because private interests affect the balance among the total enforcement costs' components. For instance, in the assessment of the law, some authorities might exaggerate the role of administrative costs when deciding on whether to impose an *ex ante* notification system of agreements or an *ex post* monitoring one. This may happen since the enforcement of vertical agreements creates substantial costs to the competition authority and does not proportionally increase its reputation as a law enforcer.

Looking at the proposed stages of implementation of policies oriented to vertical agreements, the book concludes that both the Brazilian experience and the European one (in respect of the new Member States) were premature in favouring the *ex post* control of vertical agreements. Because of that, complementary policies should be implemented in these jurisdictions in order to guarantee optimal levels of enforcement of restrictive vertical agreements, therefore, optimal levels of welfare.

6.2 POLICY RECOMMENDATION

Along the chapters of this book, it has been discussed that, in Brazil, law enforcement still has some challenges in ensuring that anticompetitive vertical agreements are effectively enforced in the country. Therefore, I proposed six policy recommendation to the country.

First, competition policy in Brazil would benefit from specific guidelines on vertical agreements, indicating how business people and the antitrust authority could improve the economic assessment of these commercial practices. Guidelines help companies and their legal advisors to interpret the rules, especially in the case of complex matters involving interdisciplinary knowledge. The creation of guidelines about vertical agreements would even help CADE's Commissioners to better explore the available information in each case and make more uniform decisions on vertical cases, ensuring greater legal certainty. Considering the scope of the content, the guidelines should describe the concept of the main vertical agreements (e.g., RPM, geo-blocking, selective distribution) as well as the economic analysis criteria to analyse their potential competitive effects and potential economic efficiencies. The guidelines should also not exclude clarifications concerning new forms of vertical contractual relations and abuses that are arising in the context of digital markets and e-commerce platforms.

When it comes to strengthening *ex post* enforcement in the country, CADE, in the second place, should add to its institutional priorities the enforcement of other forms of anticompetitive conduct rather than cartels, which also have deleterious effects on markets. As a policy recommendation, the assessment of vertical restraints cases should be held in specialized units, with a team of lawyers and economists who are highly skilled in making the economic analysis of the dual-sided effects of vertical agreements. The opening of a specialized unit (or specialized enforcement teams), and the hiring and/or relocating, for example, of highly educated staff, would increase the quality and efficiency of CADE's investigations. Third, CADE should also increase the pattern of antitrust fines for cases related to vertical restraints and create clear methodologies for setting the fines and enforcing them. Unfortunately, the current Brazilian *ex post* enforcement of vertical restraints (rare administrative and judicial enforcement, minimal fines) may generate the wrong incentives for companies that tend to be more willing to design restrictive contract clauses.

Sequentially, as a fourth item of recommendation, I suggested the creation of specialized courts, with judges that are trained to conduct an economic analysis of the legal cases, which would also bring more efficiency to the due processes. In fifth place, in order to develop and implement improvements in the transparency of the lawmaking process, CADE must adopt best practices regarding transparency and impact assessment of its regulations. I highlight hereby some of these best practices (i) the introduction of a roadmap (summary of the topic) and feedback periods that anticipate the public consultations; (ii) the extension of deadlines for public consultations; (iii) the spread of the use of social media and communication strategies in Brazil to encourage the participation of potential stakeholders in the lawmaking process; (iv) the publication of a detailed technical report. Apart from these items, there should also be the introduction of a more transparent system for the appointment and nomination of CADE's Commissioners and President, for instance, by allowing interested candidates to directly apply for a transparent selection process of these positions based on qualifications and skills.

Finally, CADE should promote institutional actions across the various States in Brazil, such as the organization of forums, programmes, and other events to favour the spread of awareness of antitrust conduct. This recommendation aims at exploring the knowledge on competition law within universities, research groups, companies, associations, consultancies, law firms (with or without competition expertise), and among other stakeholders.

When it comes to the policy recommendations to the EU, these are aimed at the EU level (European Commission) and at the national level (NCAs). At the EU level, the Commission should first conclude the revision of the VBER to be entered into force in 2022 in an effective way. The Commission must add to the revised Regulation further legal requirements and clarifications concerning new forms of contractual relations and abuses that are arising in the context of digital markets and the new roles of e-commerce platforms. For instance, the Commission could assure more clarification regarding platform bans, and also indicate what is the legal framework that covers the cases of MFN clause provisions, and how to assess the potential effects of wide and narrow MFN clauses. Even though the economic literature regarding the effects of MFNs is still very limited, which makes it difficult to authorities relying on a specific criterion for the assessment of these clauses, the new legal provisions should guarantee better information to the self-assessment of vertical agreements, and most importantly guarantee a higher level of consistency in the application of the legal rules across Member States.

A second important point to be made when it comes to policies at EU level is that the Commission should add efforts to efficiently monitor the implementation of the Directive 2019/1/EU, which has as its objective the empowerment of competition authorities by better designing their institutional set-up. This implies that the Commission bears now not only the responsibility to enact the legal rules but also to guarantee that there are enough enforcement mechanisms to apply those rules across the Member States. In order to achieve the goals of this policy, it is necessary to be fully aware of the different levels of enforcement across Member States. Lastly, about the ECN, the optimal exchange of experiences among EU Member States could be accomplished via the creation of an official ECN vertical agreement working group. Naturally, the expected cooperation within this particular group guarantees better consistency in the application of EU competition policies relevant to vertical agreements.

At the national level, there are three main points that I would like to highlight. The first one, also within the scope of the Directive 2019/1/EU, is that the authorities should efficiently allocate their resources to build an adequate institutional set-up, at both the administrative and judicial level. This implies having minimal investigatory tools (including technological instruments) and higher decision-making powers, which also depend on hiring highly qualified staff to carry out the complex assessments required by Article 101 TFEU. In this regard, I would like to highlight the second point which is the need for more training of law enforcement officers in the economic analysis of antitrust cases. Moreover, these educational programmes in each Member State should be developed at both the administrative and judicial level. The last point to be noted is the need for better organization and cataloguing of internal data and case files of NCAs, in order to help identifying potential antitrust actions that require better enforcement focus. I have shown that, nowadays, there are still almost no public and categorized information on the enforcement of vertical agreements among the different Member States. And this is also the case because their annual reports fail to give a full picture of the on-going investigations. It is worth recalling that the focus of this book is looking at the big picture of potential drawbacks of EU enforcement systems and not at the particular needs of each national authority.

It is worth noting that the description of many of the above-discussed threats to an effective enforcement in Brazil can also be understood as threats to the competition authorities of the EU Member States, mainly to those with less experience in implementing and enforcing competition laws (such as the ones from the new Member States). Therefore, some of the public policies recognized as suggestions for enhancing the Brazilian policy framework also serve as recommendations, to some extent, to certain European competition authorities.

Clearly, Brazil is the focus of this book. This does not imply, however, that the findings are not useful for other countries' competition policies. At the worldwide level, there are still significant barriers to the enforcement of competition law in many countries, and a lack of focus on the enforcement of more complex conduct such as of vertical restraints. I would like to stress that countries with more recent competition policies, like China, India, Mexico, and Russia, are facing even greater threats to law enforcement across their territories.[2] The territorial dimension of these countries, just like in Brazil, makes it hard for national authorities with limited budgets to control exclusionary practices, primarily those implemented in the most remote regions of the countries. Indeed, the main findings of this book imply a general warning of policy failures raised by transplanting of competition rules.

Ultimately, I would like to draw attention to the outcomes of the coronavirus pandemic for antitrust policies. After the coronavirus outbreak in early 2020 and the acceleration of e-commerce, it is expected that companies in all sectors will engage in new or more intense vertical alliances, as an important strategy of cost reduction and market expansion. Indeed, several competition authorities have already announced points of enforcement for the coming years and companies, more than ever, must carefully assess how the local antitrust regulation affects their business strategies. This scenario reinforces the tensions and complexities that already existed and brings new elements for future research.

6.3 FUTURE RESEARCH

The topic of regulation of vertical agreements is a complex one. While this book aims to offer a more comprehensive theoretical and institutional framework for determining the optimal policies of vertical agreements through a comparative study between Brazil and the EU, there are relevant questions that build on this book.

Regarding the European law and economics research, further analysis of antitrust enforcement actions of specific Member States could be encouraged. Mainly because of language barriers, and a lack of access to relevant data and case files in English, this research did not focus on the specificities of the case law of national authorities. However, I understand that a more extensive analysis of national jurisprudence will add inputs to the normative framework proposed so far. The same suggestion applies for other developing countries with recent implementation of competition policies, such as India, Mexico, Russia and China. The assessment of their case law and legal framework would certainly enrich and give new perspectives to this study.

Other research questions can be derived from this book. It is well-known that the harmonization of legal rules imposed by European Commission with Regulation 1/2003 has provoked different impacts on the enforcement of competition rules across the Member States. In this sense, further research could discuss the 'price' of this harmonization process or its welfare consequences within all European Member States, either with or without long-standing tradition in applying competition rules.

Finally, considering the discussion about competition in digital markets, further research is needed to capture the economic effects of new forms of vertical agreements.

2. *See*, for instance, recent contributions *in* N. Philipsen, S. E. Weishaar & G. Xu, *Market Integration: The EU Experience and Implications for Regulatory Reform in China*, Heidelberg, Springer, 2016; F. Jenny & Y. Katsoulacos, *Competition Law Enforcement in the BRICS and in Developing Countries: Legal and Economic Aspects*, Basel, Springer, 2016; P. Burnier da Silveira, *Competition Law and Policy in Latin America: Recent Developments*, Alphen aan den Rijn, Kluwer International, 2017.

Hub-and-spoke conspiracies, price-algorithms restrictions, and vertical restraints on e-commerce platforms are only a few of the anticompetitive practices that are currently a challenge to policymakers. Therefore, more normative analysis on how technological innovations affect legal rules applicable to antitrust law would certainly be a refinement of this book.

References

Abreu, F. & Honda, J., 'Associative Agreements under the Brazilian Antitrust Law', *in* C. Zarzur, L. Katona & M. Villela (eds), *Overview of Competition Law in Brazil*, São Paulo, Editora Singular, 2015.

Amorim, F., *Fixação de preços de revenda no Sistema Brasileiro de Defesa da Concorrência: análise do direito sancionador antitruste à luz do princípio da segurança jurídica*, Master thesis filed at University of São Paulo, São Paulo, 2017.

Angelozzi, G., *História do Direito no Brasil*, Rio de Janeiro, Freitas Bastos Editora, 2009.

Atiyah, P., *The Rise and Fall of Freedom of Contract*, Oxford, Oxford University Press, 1979.

Azevedo, P. F., 'Contratos de Exclusividade em Shopping Centers', *in* E. Pereira, E. Lagroteria & J. P. Lea (eds), *Concorrência e Regulação: Estudos e Pareceres Econômicos*, 1st ed., São Paulo, Editora Singular, 2004, pp. 163-186.

Azevedo, P. F., 'Restrições verticais e Defesa da Concorrência: A experiência Brasileira', *Textos para Discussão FGV-EESP*, No. 264, 2010.

Bagnoli, V., *Direito Econômico e Concorrencial*, 7th ed., São Paulo, Revista dos Tribunais, 2017.

Barcellos, R., *O Contrato de Shopping Center e os Contratos Atípicos Interempresariais*, São Paulo, Editora Atlas, 2009.

Bandura, A., *Social Learning Theory*, Englewood Cliffs, Prentice-Hall, 1977.

Barros, P., 'Looking Behind the Curtain: Effects from Modernization of European Union Competition Policy', *European Economic Review*, Vol. 47, No. 4, 2003, pp. 613-624.

Becker, G., 'Crime and Punishment: An Economic Approach', *Journal of Political Economy*, Vol. 76, No. 2, 1968, pp. 169-217.

Becker, G. & Stigler, G., 'Law Enforcement, Malfeasance and Compensation of Enforcers', *Journal of Legal Studies*, Vol. 3, No. 1, 1974, pp. 1-18.

Becker, G., 'A Theory of Competition among Pressure Groups for Political Influence', *Quarterly Journal of Economics*, Vol. 98, No. 3, 1983, pp. 371-400.

Bishop, S. & Walker, M., *Economics of E.C. Competition Law: Concepts, Application and Measurement*, 3rd ed., London, Sweet and Maxwell, 2010.

Block, M. & Sidak, J., 'The Cost of Antitrust Deterrence: Why Not Hang a Price Fixer Now and Then?', *The Georgetown Law Journal,* Vol. 68, No. 5, 1980, pp. 1131-1138.

Boik, A, & Corts, K., 'The Effects of Platform Most-Favored-Nation Clauses on Competition and Entry', *The Journal of Law and Economics*, Vol. 59, No. 1, 2016, pp. 105-134.

Bork, R., 'The Rule of Reason and the Per Se Concept: Price-Fixing and Market Division', *Yale Law Review,* Vol. 75, No. 5, 1965, pp. 775-847.

Bork, R., *The Antitrust Paradox: A Policy at War with Itself,* New York, Basic Books, 1978.

Brook, O. & Cseres, K., 'Member States' Interest in the Enforcement of EU Competition Law: A Case Study of Article 101 TFEU', *in* M. Varju (ed.), *Between Compliance and Particularism: Member State Interests and European Union Law,* Cham, Springer Publishing, 2019.

Brown, J. R. & Goolsbee, A., 'Does the Internet Make Markets More Competitive? Evidence from the Life Insurance Industry', *Journal of Political Economy,* Vol. 110, No. 3, 2002, pp. 481-507.

Brynjolfsson, E., Hu, Y. & Smith, M., 'Consumer Surplus in the Digital Economy: Estimating the Value of Increased Product Variety at Online Booksellers', *Management Science,* Vol. 49, No. 11, 2003, pp. 1580-1596.

Budzinski, O., 'Towards an International Governance of Transborder Mergers? Competition Networks and Institutions Between Centralism and Decentralism', *NYU Journal of Internation Law and Politics,* Vol. 36, No. 1, 2003, pp. 1-52.

Buccirossi, P., 'Vertical Restraints on E-commerce and Selective Distribution', *Journal of Competition Law and Economics,* Vol. 11, No. 3, 2015, pp. 747-773.

Budzinski, O. & Christiansen, A., 'Competence Allocation in the EU Competition Policy System as an Interest-Driven Process', *Journal of Public Policy,* Vol. 25, No. 3, 2005, pp. 313-337.

Budzinski, O., 'An Economic Perspective on the Jurisdictional Reform of the European Merger Control System', *European Competition Journal,* Vol. 2, No. 1, 2006, pp. 119-140.

Budzinski, O., *The Governance of Global Competition: Competence Allocation in International Competition Policy,* Cheltenham, Edward Elgar Publishing, 2008.

Burnier da Silveira, P., *Competition Law and Policy in Latin America: Recent Developments,* Alphen aan den Rijn, Kluwer International, 2017.

Buxbaum, H., 'Private Enforcement of Competition Law in the United States: Of Optimal Deterrence and Social Costs', *in* J. Basedow (ed.), *Private Enforcement of EC Competition Law,* International Competition Law Series, Zuidpoolsingel, Wolters Kluwer, 2007.

CADE, *Defesa da Concorrência no Brasil: 50 anos,* 2013.

CADE, *Annual Report 2018.*

Campilongo, C. & Pfeiffer, R., *Evolução do antitruste no Brasil,* São Paulo, Editora Singular, 2018.

Cardenal, M. B. S., 'Vertical Restraints on E-Commerce in the Context of the Single Digital Market Initiative of the European Commission', *Stanford-Vienna European Union Law Working Paper,* No. 23, 2017.

Carvalho, L., 'O ensino da defesa e da promoção da concorrência nos cursos de graduação em Direito no Brasil', *Revista de Direito Empresarial,* July 2008, pp. 167-235.

Cauffman, C. & Philipsen, N. J., 'Who Does What in Competition Law: Harmonizing the Rules on for Damages for Infringements of the EU Competition Rules', *in* B. Akkermans, J. Hage, N. Kornet & J Smits (eds), *Who Does What in European Private Law?,* Ius Commune Europaeum No. 137, Cambridge-Antwerp-Portland, Intersentia, pp. 245-287.

Cengiz, F., 'Multi-Level Governance in Competition Policy: The European Competition Network', *European Law Review,* Vol. 35, No. 5, 2010, pp. 660-677.

CEPS, *Assessing the costs and benefits of regulation: Study for the European Commission,* 2013.

Chiritoiu, B. M., 'Convergence Within the European Competition Network: Legislative Harmonization and Enforcement Priorities', *in* A. Almăşan & P. Whelan (eds), *The Consistent Application of EU Competition Law: Substantive and Procedural Challenges,* Cham, Springer International Publisher, 2017.

Coase, R., 'The Nature of the Firm', *Economica,* Vol. 4, November, 1937, pp. 386-405.

Colino, S., *Vertical Agreements and Competition Law: A Comparative Study of the EU and US Regimes,* Portland, Hart Publishing, 2010.

Collins, H., *The Law of Contract,* 2nd ed., London, Butterworths, 1993.

Colomo, P. I., *The Shaping of EU Competition Law,* Cambridge, Cambridge University Press, 2018.

Comanor, W. & Kirkwood, J., 'Resale Price Maintenance and Antitrust Policy', *Contemporary Economic Policy,* Vol. 3, 1985, pp. 9-16.

Comanor, W., 'Vertical Price-Fixing, Vertical Market Restrictions, and the New Antitrust Policy', *Harvard Law Review,* Vol. 98, No. 5, 1985, pp. 983-1002.

Cristofaro, P., 'A categorização dos ilícitos concorrenciais e o direito concorrencial brasileiro', *in* C. Campilongo & R. Pfeiffer (eds), *Evolução do antitruste no Brasil,* São Paulo, Editora Singular, 2018.

Cross, F., 'The Role of Lawyers in Positive Theories of Doctrinal Evolution', *Emory Law Journal,* Vol. 45, 1996, pp. 523-527.

Cseres, K., 'Multi-Jurisdictional Competition Law Enforcement: The Interface Between European Competition Law and the Competition Laws of the New Member States', *European Competition Journal,* Vol. 3, No. 2, 2007, pp. 465-502.

Cseres, K., 'Comparing Laws in the Enforcement of EU and National Competition Laws', *European Journal of Legal Studies,* Vol. 3, No. 1, 2010, pp. 7-44.

Cseres, K., 'The Impact of Regulation 1/2003 in the New Member States', *Competition Law Review,* Vol. 6, No. 2, 2010b, pp. 145-182.

de la Mano, M. & Jones, A., 'Vertical Agreements under EU Competition Law: Proposals for Pushing Article 101 Analysis, and the Modernization Process, to a Logical Conclusion', *King's College London Law School Research Paper,* No. 23, 2017.

Devlin, A. & Jacobs, M., 'Antitrust Error', *William & Mary Law Review,* Vol. 52, No. 1, 2010, pp. 75-132.

Dobson, P., 'Vertical Restraints Policy Reform in the European Union and United Kingdom', *Loughborough University Business School Research Series*, No. 2, 2005.

Duke, A., 'Public Enforcement', *in* J. Duns, A. Duke, & B. Sweeney (eds), *Comparative Competition Law,* Cheltenham, Edward Elgar Publishing, 2015.

Duns, J., Duke, A., & Sweeney, B., (eds), *Comparative Competition Law,* Cheltenham, Edward Elgar Publishing, 2015.

Easterbrook, F., 'The Limits of Antitrust', *Texas Law Review,* Vol. 63, No. 1, 1984, pp. 1-40.

Ebb, L., 'The *Grundig-Consten* Case Revisited: Judicial Harmonization of National Law and Treaty Law in the Common Market', *University of Pennsylvania Law Review,* Vol. 115, No. 6, 1967, pp 855-889.

Elzinga, K. & Breit, W., *The Antitrust Penalties: A Study in Law and Economics*, New Haven, Yale University Press, 1976.

European Commission, *Green Paper on Vertical Restraints in EC Competition Policy*, 1997.

European Commission, *White Paper on Modernisation of the Rules Implementing Articles 85 and 86 of the EC Treaty*, 1999.

European Commission, *Commission Notice on cooperation within the Network of Competition Authorities*, 2004.

European Commission, *Guidelines on the method of setting fines imposed pursuant to Article 23(2)(a) of Regulation No 1/2003,* 2006.

European Commission, *Guidelines on Vertical Restraints,* 2010.

European Competition Network, *Results of the questionnaire on the reform of Member States (MS) national competition laws after EC Regulation No. 1/2003,* 2013.

European Commission, *Ten Years of Antitrust Enforcement under Regulation 1/2003*, 2014.

European Commission, *A Digital Single Market Strategy for Europe,* 2015.

European Commission, *Final report on the E-commerce Sector Inquiry*, 2017.

European Commission, *Impact Assessment Accompanying the document Proposal for a Directive of the European Parliament and of the Council to empower the competition authorities of the Member States to be more effective enforcers and to ensure the proper functioning of the internal market*, 2017.

European Commission, 'EU competition rules and marketplace bans: Where do we stand after the Coty judgment?', *Occasional discussion papers by the Competition Directorate–General of the European Commission*, 2018.

European Commission, *Consultation Strategy for the evaluation of the Vertical Block Exemption Regulation*, 2019.

Ezrachi, A. & Stucke, M., *Virtual Competition: The Promise and Perils of the Algorithm-Driven Economy*, Cambridge, Harvard University Press, 2016.

Ezrachi, A., 'Sponge', *Journal of Antitrust Enforcement*, Vol. 5, No. 1, April 2017, pp. 49-75.

Federico, G. & Manzini, P., 'A Law and Economics Approach to the New European Antitrust Enforcing Rules', *Erasmus Law and Economics Review,* Vol. 1, No. 2, 2004, pp. 143-164.

Ferro, M. S., 'Institutional Design of National Competition Authorities: EU Requirements', *Competition Law Review*, Vol. 13, No. 2, 2018, pp. 109-137.

Fingleton, J., 'The Distribution and Attribution of Cases among the Members of the Network: The Perspective of the Commission/NCAs', *in* C. Ehlermann & I. Atanasuy (eds), *Constructing the EU Network of Competition Authorities,* Oxford, Hart Publishing, 2005.

Forrester, I., 'Modernization: An Extension of the Powers of the Commission?', *in* D. Geradin (ed.), *Modernization and Enlargement: Two Major Challenges for EC Competition Law,* Antwerp, Intersentia, 2004.

Forgioni, P. A., *Contratos de distribuição*, São Paulo, Editora Revista dos Tribunais, 2005.

Forgioni, P. A., *Direito Concorrencial e Restrições Verticais*, São Paulo, Revista dos Tribunais, 2007.

Forgioni, P. A., 'O que esperar do antitruste brasileiro no século XXI?, *Revista Jurídica Luso-Brasileira*, Vol. 1, No. 1, 2015, pp. 1713-1742.

Forgioni, P. A., *Os fundamentos do antitruste,* 9th ed., São Paulo, Editora Revista dos Tribunais, 2016.

Forgioni, P. A., *Contratos Empresariais: Teoria Geral e Aplicação*, 4ª ed., São Paulo, Revista dos Tribunais, 2019.

Frazão, A., *Direito da Concorrência: pressupostos e perspectivas*. São Paulo, Editora Saraiva, 2017.

Georgieva, Z., 'Competition Soft Law in French and German Courts: A Challenge for Online Sales Bans Only?', *Maastricht Journal of European and Comparative Law,* Vol. 24, No. 2, 2017, pp. 175-193.

Geradin, D. & Pereira Neto, C. M., *Restrições verticais adotadas por empresas dominantes: uma análise do Direito Concorrencial no Brasil e na União Europeia,* Edição Bilingue, São Paulo, Editora Revista dos Tribunais, 2013.

Geradin, D., Layne-Farrar, A., & Petit, N., *EU Competition Law and Economics,* Oxford, Oxford University Press, 2012.

Gerard, D., 'The Effects-Based Approach under Article 101 TFEU and Its Paradoxes: Modernization at War Itself?', J. Bourgeois & D. Waelbroeck (eds), *Ten Years of Effects-Based Approach in EU Competition Law Enforcement*, Brussels, Bruylant, 2012.

Gerber, D., 'Modernizing Competition Law: A Developmental Perspective', *European Competition Law Review,* Vol. 4, 2001, pp. 122-130.

Grau, E. R., *A Ordem Econômica na Constituição de 1988*, 15th ed., São Paulo, Malheiros Editores, 2012.

Grau, E. & Forgioni, P. A., 'Restrição à concorrência, autorização legal e seus limites, Lei 8.884, de 1994, e Lei 6.279/1979 ("Lei Ferrari")', *Revista do IBRAC,* Vol. 6, 1999, pp. 5-27.

Gomes, A. C. & Camargo e Gomes, M. E. A, 'Ouvidoria do CADE: contribuições para o equilíbrio entre autonomia e accountability', *in* C. Campilongo & R. Pfeiffer (eds), *Evolução do antitruste no Brasil*, São Paulo, Editora Singular, 2018.

Gonçalves, P. A., *Fixação e Sugestão de Preços de Revenda em Contrato de Distribuição*, 2nd ed., São Paulo, Editora Singular, 2016.

Gonzales, A. & Micco, A., 'Private Versus Public Antitrust Enforcement: Evidence from Chile', *Journal of Competition Law & Economics*, Vol. 10, No. 3, 2014, pp. 691-709.

Hahn, V., 'Antitrust Enforcement: Abuse Control or Notification?', *European Journal of Law and Economics*, Vol. 10, No. 1, 2000, pp. 69-91.

Hawk, B., 'System Failure: Vertical Restraints and EC Competition Law', *Common Market Law Review*, Vol. 32, No. 4, 1995, pp. 937-989.

Hortaçsu, A., Martínez-Jerez, F. & Douglas, J., 'The Geography of Trade in Online Transactions: Evidence from eBay and Mercadolibre', *American Economic Journal: Microeconomics*, Vol. 1, No. 1, 2009, pp. 53-74.

Hovenkamp, H., *Principles of Antitrust*, St. Paul, West Academic Publishing, 2017.

Jenny, F. & Katsoulacos, Y., *Competition Law Enforcement in the BRICS and in Developing Countries: Legal and Economic Aspects*, Basel, Springer, 2016.

Jones, A. & Sufrin, B., *EU Competition Law: Text, Cases and Materials*, 5th ed., Oxford, Oxford University Press, 2014.

Jullien, B. & Rey, P., 'Resale Price Maintenance and Collusion', *The RAND Journal of Economics*, Vol. 38, No. 4, 2007, pp. 983-1001.

Kaplow, L., 'Rules Versus Standards: An Economic Analysis', *Duke Law Journal*, Vol. 42, No. 3, 1992, pp. 557-629.

Kaufmann, D., Kraay, A. & Zoido-Lobaton, P., 'Governance Matters', *World Bank Policy Research Working Paper*, No. 2196, 1999.

Kerber, W. & Vezzoso, S., 'EU Competition Policy, Vertical Restraints, and Innovation: An Analysis from an Evolutionary Perspective', paper presented at *10th International Joseph A. Schumpeter Society Conference (ISS)*, Milan, 9-12 June 2004.

Kingston, S., 'A "New Division of Responsibilities" in the Proposed Regulation to Modernize the Rules Implementing Article 81 and 82 EC? A Warning Call', *European Competition Law Review*, Vol. 22, No. 8, 2001, pp. 340-348.

Klein, B., Crawford, R. & Alchian, A., 'Vertical Integration, Appropriable Rents, and the Competitive Contracting Process', *The Journal of Law & Economics*, Vol. 21, No. 2, 1978, pp. 297-326.

Klein, B., 'The Apple E-books Case: When Is a Vertical Contract a Hub in a Hub-and-Spoke Conspiracy?', *Journal of Competition Law & Economics*, Vol. 13, No. 3, 2017, pp. 423-474.

Kochan, D., 'The Commenting Power: Agency Accountability Through Public Participation Public Participation', *Oklahoma Law Review*, Vol. 70, No. 3, pp. 601-622.

Kovacic, W., 'Institutional Foundations for Economic Legal Reform in Transition Economies: The Case of Competition Policy and Antitrust Enforcement', *Chicago Kent Law Review*, Vol. 77, 2001, pp. 265-306.

Kovacic, W., 'Rating the Competition Agencies: What Constitutes Good Performance?', *George Mason Law Review*, Vol. 16, No. 4, 2009, pp. 903-926.

Kovacic, W., Hollman, H. & Grant, P., 'How Does Your Competition Agency Measure Up?', *European Competition Journal,* Vol. 7, No. 1, 2011, pp. 25-45.

Krattenmaker, T. & Salop, S., 'Anticompetitive Exclusion: Raising Rivals' Costs to Achieve Power over Price', *The Yale Law Journal,* Vol. 96, No. 2, 1986, pp. 209-293.

Landes, W. M., 'Optimal Sanctions for Antitrust Violations', *University of Chicago Law Review,* Vol. 50, No. 2, 1983, pp. 652-678.

Lao, M., 'Resale Price Mantenance: The Internet Phenomenon and "Free Rider" Issues', *Antitrust Bulletin,* Vol. 55, No. 2, 2010, pp. 473-512.

Lever, J., 'The German Monopolies Commission's Report of the Problems Consequent upon the Reform of the European Cartel Procedures', *European Competition Law Review,* Vol. 23, No. 7, 2002, pp. 321-325.

Lieber, E. & Syverson, C., 'Online Vs. Offline Competition', *in* M. Peitz & J. Waldfogel (eds), *The Oxford Handbook of the Digital Economy,* Oxford, Oxford University Press, 2012.

Logelain, P. *Competition Law: Self-Assessment of Contracts – Interaction of EU Competition Law with Contract Law and Tort Law,* Bruxelles, Larcier, 2011.

Long, W., Schramm, R. & Tollison, R., 'The Economic Determinants of Antitrust Activity', *in* F. Mc Chesney & W. F. Schughart II (eds), *The Causes and Consequences of Antitrust: The Public Choice Perspective,* Chicago, The University of Chicago Press, 1995.

Loss, F., Malavolti-Grimal, E., Verge, T. & Berges-Sennou, F., 'European Competition Policy Modernization: From Notifications to Legal Exception', *European Economic Review,* Vol. 52, No. 1, 2008, pp. 77-98.

Mankiw, G. & Taylor, M. P., *Microeconomics,* 4th ed., Hampshire, Cengage Learning, 2017.

Mankiw, G., *Principles of Microeconomics,* 8th ed., Boston, Cengage Learning, 2018.

Marvel, H. & McCafferty, S., 'Resale Price Maintenance and Quality Certification', *RAND Journal of Economics,* Vol. 15, No. 3, 1984, pp. 346-359.

Marvel, H., 'How Fair Is Fair Trade?', *Contemporary Economic Policy,* Vol. 3, 1985, pp. 23-35.

Mathewson, F. & Winter, R., 'The Law and Economics of Resale Price Maintenance', *Review of Industrial Organization,* Vol. 13, No. 1/2, 1998, pp. 57-84.

Mattos, C., 'Um pouco da História da Lei 12.529/11', *in* C. Campilongo & R. Pfeiffer (eds), *Evolução do antitruste no Brasil,* São Paulo, Editora Singular, 2018.

Mattos, P., 'Regulação econômica e social e participação pública no Brasil', *IX Congreso Internacional del CLAD sobre la Reforma del Estado y de la Administración Pública,* Madrid, Spain, 2004.

Mc Chesney, F. & Schughart II, W. F., *The Causes and Consequences of Antitrust: The Public Choice Perspective,* Chicago, The University of Chicago Press, 1995.

Mc Chesney, F., 'Talking "Bout My Antitrust Generation: Competition for and in the Field of Competition Law"', *Emory Law Journal,* Vol. 52, 2003, pp. 1401-1412.

Menard, C., 'On Clusters, Hybrids, and Other Strange Forms: The Case of the French Poultry Industry', *Journal of Institutional and Theoretical Economics,* Vol. 152, No. 1, 1996, pp. 154-183.

Menard, C., 'The Economics of Hybrid Organizations', *Journal of Institutional and Theoretical Economics*, Vol. 160, No. 3, 2004, pp. 345-376.

Morais, L. D. S., *Direito da Concorrência: Perspectivas do seu ensino*, São Paulo, Editora Almedina, 2009, pp. 155-169.

Moreira Pinto, G., 'A dosimetria das multas impostas em resposta às infrações contra a ordem econômica', *Prêmio SEAE 2010 sobre Defesa da Concorrência*, 2010.

Morettin, P. A. & Bussab, W. O., *Estatística Básica*, 5th ed., São Paulo, Editora Saraiva, 2003.

Moschel, W., 'Change of Policy in European Competition Law?', *Common Market Law Review*, Vol. 37, No. 3, 2000, pp. 495-499.

Motta, M., *Competition Policy: Theory and Practice*, Cambridge, Cambridge University Press, 2004.

Neven, D., Papandropoulos, P. & Seabright, P., *Trawling for Minnows: European Competition Policy and Agreements Between Firms*, London, Center for Economic and Policy Research (CEPR), 1998.

Neven, D., 'Removing the Notification of Agreements: Some Consequences of Ex-post Monitoring', *in* A. Bogdandy, P. Mavroidis & Y. Meny (eds), *European Integration and International Cooperation: Studies in International Economic Law in Honour of Claus-Dieter Ehlermann*, The Hague, Kluwer Law International, 2002.

Ng, W., *The Political Economy of Competition Law in China*, Cambridge, Cambridge University Press, 2018.

Nicolaides, P., 'Development of a System for Decentralised Enforcement of EC Competition Policy', *Intereconomics*, Vol. 37, No. 1, 2002, pp. 41-51.

Niels, G., Jenkins, H. & Kavanagh, J., *Economics for Competition Lawyers*, 2nd ed., Oxford, Oxford University Press, 2016, p. 247.

North, D., *Institutions, Institutional Change and Economic Performance*, Cambridge, Cambridge University Press, 1990.

North, D., 'Economic Performance Through Time', *American Economic Review*, Vol. 84, No. 3, 1994, pp. 359-368.

North, D., 'The New Institutional Economics and Third World Development', *in* J. Harris, J. Hunter & C. Lewis (eds), *Economics and Third World Development*, Oxon, Routledge, 1995.

OECD, *Vertical Restraints for online sales*, 2013.

OECD, *Relationship between Public and Private Antitrust Enforcement: Brazil*, 2015.

OECD, *The competition analysis of vertical restraints in multi-sided markets – Note by Cafarra and Kuhn*, 2017.

OECD, *Peer Review of Competition Law and Policy: Brazil*, 2019.

Ogus, A., 'The Economic Basis of Legal Culture: Networks and Monopolization', *Oxford Journal of Legal Studies*, Vol. 22, No. 3, 2002, pp. 419-443.

Ogus, A., *Regulation: Legal Form and Economic Theory*, Oxford, Hart Publisher, 2004.

Patel, K. K. & Schweitzer, H., (eds), *The Historical Foundations of EU Competition Law*, Oxford, Oxford University Press, 2013.

Peltzman, S., 'Toward a More General Theory of Regulation', *Journal of Law and Economics*, Vol. 19, No. 2, 1976, pp. 211-240.

Pena, J., 'Promoting Competition Policies from Private Sector in Latin America', *in* E. Fox & D. Sokol (eds), *Competition Law and Policy in Latin America*, Oxford, Hart Publishing, 2009.

Pérez, S. & Scheur, S., 'The Evolution of the Law on Article 85 and 86 EEC: Ordoliberalism and Its Keynesian Challenge', *in* K. K. Patel & H. Schweitzer (eds), *The Historical Foundations of EU Competition Law*, Oxford, Oxford University Press, 2013.

Pfeiffer, R. A. C., *Defesa da concorrência e bem-estar do consumidor*, PhD thesis filed at University of São Paulo, São Paulo, 2010.

Philipsen, N., Weishaar, S. E. & Xu, G., *Market Integration: The EU Experience and Implications for Regulatory Reform in China*, Heidelberg, Springer, 2016.

Pindyck, R. & Rubinfeld, D., *Microeconomics*, 7th ed., Essex, Pearson Hall, 2009.

Pirrung, M., 'EU Enlargement Towards Cartel Paradise? An Economic Analysis of the Reform of European Competition Law', *Erasmus Law and Economics Review*, Vol. 1, 2004, pp. 77-109.

Polisky, P. & Shavell, S., 'The Optimal Tradeoff Between the Probability and Magnitude of Fines', *American Economic Review*, Vol. 69, No. 5, 1979, pp. 880-891.

Porter, M. E., *Competitive Strategy: Techniques for Analyzing Industries and Competitors*, New York, Free Press, 1980.

Posner, R., 'Theories of Economic Regulation', *The Bell Journal of Economics and Management Science*, Vol. 5, No. 2, 1974, pp. 335-358.

Posner, R., 'The Social Costs of Monopoly and Regulation', *Journal of Political Economy*, Vol. 83, No. 4, 1975, pp. 807-827.

Posner, R., 'The Rule of Reason and the Economic Approach: Reflections on the Sylvania Decision', *University of Chicago Law Review*, Vol. 45, No. 1, 1977, pp. 1-20.

Posner, R., *Antitrust Law*, 2nd ed., Chicago, The University of Chicago Press, 2001.

Posner, R., 'Vertical Restraints and Antitrust Policy', *University of Chicago Law Review*, Vol. 72, 2005, pp. 229-241.

Possas, M. & Pondé, P. 'A análise de eficiência em práticas restritivas verticais: custos de transação e cláusulas de raio no ercado de shopping center', *in* C. Campilongo & R. Pfeiffer (eds), *Evolução do antitruste no Brasil*, São Paulo, Editora Singular, 2018, pp. 1012-1056.

Queiroz, P. A., *Direito Antitruste: Os fundamentos da promoção da concorrência*, São Paulo, Editora Singular, 2018.

Resende, J. P., 'Ainda falta um guia de dosimetria de pena', *in* C. Campilongo & R. Pfeiffer (eds), *Evolução do antitruste no Brasil*, São Paulo, Editora Singular, 2018.

Reuter,T., 'Private Antitrust Enforcement and the Role of Harmed Parties in Public Enforcement', *European Journal of Law and Economics*, Vol. 41, 2016, pp. 479-507.

Rey, P. & Stiglitz, J., 'The Role of Exclusive Territories in Producer's Competition', *The RAND Journal of Economics*, Vol. 26, 1995, pp. 431-451.

Rey, P. & Caballero-Sanz, F., 'The Policy Implication of the Economic Analysis of Vertical Restraints', *European Commission Economic Paper*, No. 119, 1996.

Riley, A., 'EC Antitrust Modernization: The Commission Does Very Nicely - Thank You! Part One: Regulation 1 and the Notification Burden', *European Competition Law Review*, Vol. 11, 2003a, pp. 604-615.

Riley, A., 'EC Antitrust Modernization: The Commission Does Very Nicely - Thank You! Part Two: Between the Idea and the Reality: Decentralization under Regulation', *European Competition Law Review*, Vol. 12, 2003b, pp. 657-672.

Rodriguez, A. & Menon, A., *The Limits of Competition Policy: The Shortcommings of Antitrust in Developing and Reforming Countries*, Biggleswade, Kluwer Law International, 2010.

Sahuguet, N., Steenbergen, J., Verge, T., & Walckiers, A., 'Vertical Restraints: Towards Guidance to Iron Out Perceived Enforcement Discrepancies Across Europe?', *Journal of European Competition Law & Practice*, Vol. 7, No. 4, 2016, pp. 274-279.

Salomão Filho, C., *Direito Concorrencial: as condutas*, 1a. ed., São Paulo, Editora Malheiros, 2007.

Salomão Filho, C., *Direito Concorrencial: as estruturas*, 3rd ed., São Paulo, Editora Malheiros, 2007.

Salomão Filho, C., 'Evolução ou Involução do direito antitruste?', *in* C. Campilongo & R. Pfeiffer (eds), *Evolução do antitruste no Brasil*, São Paulo, Editora Singular, 2018.

Sampaio Ferraz, M. M., 'Fixação de preço de revenda no e-commerce: uma análise à luz da jurisprudência nacional e internacional', *Revista do IBRAC*, Vol. 23, No. 2, 2017, pp. 448-464.

Santacruz, R., 'Exclusividade e competição no mercado de shopping centers', *in* C. Mattos (org.) (ed.), *A revolução do antitruste no Brasil 2*, São Paulo, Editora Singular, 2008.

Scherer, F. M., *Industrial Market Structure and Economic Performance*, 2nd ed., Chicago, Rand McNally, 1980.

Schimidt, C. A. J., 'Crime e Castigo: Cartel no Brasil, algumas reflexões', *in* C. Campilongo & R. Pfeiffer (eds), *Evolução do antitruste no Brasil*, São Paulo, Editora Singular, 2018.

Schreuders, W., 'Welcome in Brussels on the Rhine: A Positive Perspective on the EU', *in* M. Faure, W. Schreuders & L. Visscher (eds), *Don't Take it Seriously: Essays in Law and Economics in Honours of Roger Van den Bergh*, Cambridge, Intersentia, 2018.

Schuartz, L. F., 'A desconstitucionalização do direito de defesa da concorrência', *Revista do IBRAC*, Vol. 16, No. 1, 2009, pp. 325-351.

Schughart II, W. F., 'Public-Choice Theory and Antitrust Policy', *in* F. Mc Chesney & W. F. Schughart II (eds), *The Causes and Consequences of Antitrust: The Public Choice Perspective*, Chicago, The University of Chicago Press, 1995.

Schwartz, W., 'An Overview of the Economics of Antitrust Enforcement', *Georgetown Law Journal*, Vol. 68, 1980, pp. 1075-1102.

Shavell, S., 'The Optimal Structure of Law Enforcement', *Journal of Law & Economics*, Vol. 36, No. 1, 1993, pp. 255-287.

Simonsen, R., *História Econômica do Brasil*, São Paulo, Companhia Editora Nacional, 1957.

Smits, R., 'The European Competition Network: Selected Aspects', *Legal Issues of European Integration,* Vol. 32, No. 6, 2005, pp. 175-192.

Sociedade Brasileira de Direito Público (SBDP), *Revisão Judicial das Decisões do Conselho Administrativo de Defesa Econômica (CADE): Pesquisa empírica e aplicada sobre os casos julgados pelos Tribunais Regionais Federais (TRFs), Superior Tribunal de Justiça (STJ) e Supremo Tribunal Federal (STF),* Belo Horizonte, Editora Fórum, 2010.

Sokol, D., 'The Development of Human Capital in Latin American Competition Policy', *in* E. Fox & D. Sokol, *Competition Law and Policy in Latin America,* Oxford, Hart Publishing, 2009.

Souam, S., 'Optimal Antitrust Policy under Different Regimes of Fines', *International Journal of Industrial Organization,* Vol. 19, No. 1, 2001, pp. 1-26.

Souter, W., *Coherence in EU Competition Law,* Oxford, Oxford University Press, 2016.

Spengler, J., 'Vertical Integration and Antitrust Policy', *Journal of Political Economy,* Vol. 58, No. 4, 1950, pp. 347-352.

Stigler, G., 'The Optimal Enforcement of Law', *Journal of Political Economy,* Vol. 78, No. 3, 1970, pp. 526-536.

Stigler, G., 'The Theory of Economic Regulation', *The Bell Journal of Economics and Management Science,* Vol. 2, No. 1, 1971, pp. 3-21.

Stiglitz, J, 'Principal and Agent', *The New Palgrave: A Dictionary of Economics,* Vol. 3, 1987, pp. 966-971.

Sulivan, L. A., *Antitrust,* Minnesota, West Publishing, 1976.

Swaak, C. R., *European Community Law and the Automobile Industry,* Deventer, Wolters Kluwer, 1999.

Telser, L., 'Why Should Manufacturers Want Fair Trade', *The Journal of Law & Economics,* Vol. 3, October 1960, pp. 86-105.

Todorov, F., & Torres Filho, M., 'History of Competition Policy in Brazil: 1930-2010', *The Antitrust Bulletin,* Vol. 57, No. 2, 2012, pp. 207-257.

Tollison, R., 'Public Choice and Antitrust', *Cato Journal,* Vol. 4, Winter, 1985, pp. 905-916.

Van den Bergh, R., 'Towards Efficient Self-Regulation in Markets for Professional Services', *in* C. D. Ehlermann & A. Atanasiu (eds), *European Competition Law Annual,* Oxford, Hart Publishing, 2004.

Van den Bergh, R. & Camesasca, P., *European Competition Law and Economics: A Comparative Perspective,* 2nd ed., London, Sweet & Maxwell, 2006.

Van den Bergh, R., 'Should Consumer Protection Law Be Publicly Enforced? An Economic Perspective on EC Regulation 2006/2004 and Its Implementation in the Consumer Protection Laws of the Member States', *in* W. van Boom & M. Loos (eds), *Collective Enforcement of Consumer Law,* Groningen, Europa Law Publishing, 2007.

Van den Bergh, R., 'Vertical Restraints: The European Part of the Policy Failure', *The Antitrust Bulletin,* Vol. 61, No. 1, 2016, pp. 167-185.

Van den Bergh, R., *Comparative Competition Law and Economics,* Cheltenham, Edward Elgar, 2017.

Vaz, I., *Direito Econômico da Concorrência,* Rio de Janeiro, Editora Forense, 1993.

Venit, J. 'Brave New World: The Modernization and Decentralization of Enforcement under Article 81 and 82 of the EC Treaty', *Common Market Law Review,* Vol. 40, No. 3, 2003, pp. 545-580.

Verissimo, M. P., 'A "regra da razão" e o controle de condutas anticompetitivas pelo CADE', *in* C. Campilongo & R. Pfeiffer (eds), *Evolução do antitruste no Brasil*, São Paulo, Editora Singular, 2018.

Watts, J., 'Operation Car Wash: Is This the Biggest Corruption Scandal in History?', *The Guardian,* 1 June 2017.

Werden, G., 'Network Effects and Conditions of Entry: Lessons from the Microsoft Case', *Antitrust Law Journal,* Vol. 69, No. 1, 2011, pp. 87-111.

Wigger, A., 'Revising the European Competition Reform: The Toll of Private Self-Enforcement', *Working Papers Political Science of Vrije Universiteit Amsterdam,* No. 07, 2004.

Wijckmans, F & Tuytschaever, F., *Vertical Agreements in EU Competition Law,* 3rd ed., Oxford, Oxford University Press, 2018.

Wilks, S., 'Agency Escape: Descentralization or Dominance of the European Commission in the Modernization of Competition Law?', *Governance: An Institutional Journal of Policy, Administration and Institutions,* Vol. 18, No. 3, 2005, pp. 431-452.

Williamson, O., *Markets and Hierarchies: Analysis and Antitrust Implications*, New York, Free Press, 1975.

Williamson, O., 'Assessing Vertical Market Restrictions: Antitrust Ramifications of the Transaction Cost Approach', *University of Pennsylvania Law Review,* Vol. 127, No. 4, 1979, pp. 953-993.

Williamson, O., *The Economic Institutions of Capitalism,* New York, Free Press, 1985.

Williamson, O., 'Comparative Economic Organization: The Analysis of Discrete Structural Alternatives', *Administrative Science Quarterly,* Vol. 36, No. 2, 1991, pp. 269-296.

Williamson, O., *The Mechanisms of Governance,* New York, Oxford University Press, 1996.

Wils, W., 'Should Private Antitrust Enforcement Be Encouraged in Europe?', *World Competition*, Vol. 26, No. 3, 2003, pp. 472-488.

Wils, W., 'Ten Years of Regulation 1/2003: A Retrospective', *Journal of European Competition Law and Practice,* Vol. 4, No. 4, 2013, pp. 293-301.

Wils, W., 'Private Enforcement of EU Antitrust Law and Its Relationship with Public Enforcement: Past, Present and Future', *World Competition*, Vol. 40, No. 1, 2017, pp. 3-46.

Woods, D., Sinclair, A. & Ashton, D., 'Private Enforcement of Community Competition Law: Modernization and the Road Ahead', *Competition Policy Newsletter,* Vol. 2, (Summer) 2004, pp. 31-37.

Wright, J., 'Evidence-Based Antitrust Enforcement in the Technology Sector', *CPI Antitrust Chronicle,* Volume March, 2013.

Zarzur, C., Katona, L. & Villela, M., *Overview of Competition Law in Brazil,* São Paulo, Editora Singular, 2015.

Index

INTERNATIONAL COMPETITION LAW SERIES

1. Ignacio De Leon, *Latin American Competition Law and Policy: A Policy in Search of Identity*, 2001 (ISBN 90-411-1542-0).
2. Wim Dejonghe & Wouter Van de Voorde (eds), *M & A in Belgium*, 2001 (ISBN 90-411-1594-3).
3. Yang-Ching Chao, Gee San, Changfa Lo & Jiming Ho (eds), *International and Comparative Competition Law and Policies*, 2001 (ISBN 90-411-1643-5).
4. Martin Mendelsohn & Stephen Rose, *Guide to the EC Block Exemption for Vertical Agreements*, 2002 (ISBN 90-411-9813-X).
5. Clifford A. Jones & Mitsuo Matsushita (eds), *Competition Policy in the Global Trading System: Perspectives from the EU, Japan and the USA*, 2002 (ISBN 90-411-1758-X).
6. Christian Koenig, Andreas Bartosch, Jens-Daniel Braun & Marion Romes (eds), *EC Competition and Telecommunications Law*. Second Edition, 2009 (ISBN 978-90-411-2564-4).
7. Jürgen Basedow (ed.), *Limits and Control of Competition with a View to International Harmonization*, 2002 (ISBN 90-411-1967-1).
8. Maureen Brunt, Economic Essays on Australian and New Zealand Competition Law, 2003 (ISBN 90-411-1991-4).
9. Ky P. Ewing, Jr., *Competition Rules for the 21st Century: Principles from America's Experience*, Second Edition, 2006 (ISBN 90-411-2477-2).
10. Joseph Wilson, *Globalization and the Limits of National Merger Control Laws*, 2003 (ISBN 90-411-1996-5).
11. Peter Verloop & Valérie Landes (eds), *Merger Control in Europe: EU, Member States and Accession States*, Fourth Edition, 2003 (ISBN 90-411-2056-4).
12. Themistoklis K. Giannakopoulos, *Safeguarding Companies' Rights in Competition and Anti-dumping/Anti-subsidies Proceedings*, Second Edition, 2011 (ISBN 978-90-411-3404-2).
13. Marjorie Holmes & Lesley Davey (eds), *A Practical Guide to National Competition Rules across Europe*, Second Edition, 2007 (ISBN 978-90- 411-2607-8).
14. Sigrid Stroux, *US and EU Oligopoly Control*, 2004 (ISBN 90-411-2296-6).
15. Tzong-Leh Hwang and Chiyuan Chen (eds), *The Future Development of Competition Framework*, 2004 (ISBN 90-411-2305-9).

16. Phedon Nicolaides, Mihalis Kekelekis and Maria Kleis, *State Aid Policy in the European Community: Principles and Practice,* Second Edition, 2008 (ISBN 978-90-411-2754-9).
17. Doris Hildebrand, *Economic Analyses of Vertical Agreements: A Self- Assessment*, 2005 (ISBN 90-411-2328-8).
18. Frauke Henning-Bodewig, *Unfair Competition Law: European Union and Member States*, 2005 (ISBN 90-411-2329-6).
19. Duarte Brito & Margarida Catalão-Lopes, *Mergers and Acquisitions: The Industrial Organization Perspective,* 2006 (ISBN 90-411-2451-9).
20. Nikos Th. Nikolinakos, *EU Competition Law and Regulation in the Converging Telecommunications, Media and IT Sectors*, 2006 (ISBN 90-411- 2469-1).
21. Mihalis Kekelekis, *The EC Merger Control Regulation: Rights of Defence. A Critical Analysis of DG COMP Practice and Community Courts' Jurisprudence*, 2006 (ISBN 90-411-2553-1).
22. Mark R. Joelson, *An International Antitrust Primer: A Guide to the Operation of United States, European Union and Other Key Competition Laws in the Global Economy*, Third Edition, 2006 (ISBN 90-411-2468-3).
23. Themistoklis K. Giannakopoulos, *A Concise Guide to the EU Anti-dumping/ Anti-subsidies Procedures*, 2006 (ISBN 90-411-2464-0).
24. George Cumming, Brad Spitz & Ruth Janal, *Civil Procedure Used for Enforcement of EC Competition Law by the English, French and German Civil Courts*, 2007 (ISBN 978-90-411-2471-5).
25. Jürgen Basedow (ed.), *Private Enforcement of EC Competition Law,* 2007 (ISBN 978-90-411-2613-9).
26. Jung Wook Cho, *Innovation and Competition in the Digital Network Economy: A Legal and Economic Assessment on Multi-tying Practices and Network Effects*, 2007 (ISBN 978-90-411-2574-3).
27. Akira Inoue, *Japanese Antitrust Law Manual: Law, Cases and Interpretation of the Japanese Antimonopoly Act*, 2007 (ISBN 978-90-411-2627-6).
28. René Barents, *Directory of EC Case Law on Competition,* 2007 (ISBN 978-90-411-2656-6).
29. Paul F. Nemitz (ed.), *The Effective Application of EU State Aid Procedures: The Role of National Law and Practice*, 2007 (ISBN 978-90-411-2657-3).
30. Jurian Langer, *Tying and Bundling as a Leveraging Concern under EC Competition Law,* 2007 (ISBN 978-90-411-2575-0).
31. Abel M. Mateus & Teresa Moreira (eds), *Competition Law and Economics – Advances in Competition Policy and Antitrust Enforcement*, 2007 (ISBN 978-90-411-2632-0).
32. Alberto Santa Maria, *Competition and State Aid: An Analysis of the EC Practice*, 2007 (ISBN 978-90-411-2617-7).
33. Barry J. Rodger (ed.), *Article 234 and Competition Law: An Analysis,* 2007 (ISBN 978-90-411-2605-4).

34. Alla Pozdnakova, *Liner Shipping and EU Competition Law,* 2008 (ISBN 978-90-411-2717-4).
35. Milena Stoyanova, *Competition Problems in Liberalized Telecommunications: Regulatory Solutions to Promote Effective Competition*, 2008 (ISBN 978-90-411-2736-5).
36. *EC State Aid Law/Le Droit des Aides d'Etat dans la CE. Liber Amicorum Francisco Santaolalla Gadea*, 2008 (ISBN 978-90-411-2774-7).
37. René Barents, *Directory of EU Case Law on State Aids,* Third Edition, 2019 (ISBN 978-94-035-1101-6).
38. Ignacio De Leon, *An Institutional Assessment of Antitrust Policy: The Latin American Experience*, 2009 (ISBN 978-90-411-2478-4).
39. Doris Hildebrand, *The Role of Economic Analysis in EU Competition Law: The European School*, Fourth Edition, 2016 (ISBN 978-90-411-6245-8).
40. Eugène Buttigieg, *Competition Law: Safeguarding the Consumer Interest. A Comparative Analysis of US Antitrust Law and EC Competition Law*, 2009 (ISBN 978-90-411-3119-5).
41. Ioannis Lianos & Ioannis Kokkoris (eds), *The Reform of EC Competition Law: New Challenges,* 2010 (ISBN 978-90-411-2692-4).
42. George Cumming & Mirjam Freudenthal, *Civil Procedure in EU Competition Cases before the English and Dutch Courts*, 2010 (ISBN 978-90-411-3192-8).
43. A.E. Rodriguez & Ashok Menon, *The Limits of Competition Policy: The Shortcomings of Antitrust in Developing and Reforming Economies*, 2010 (ISBN 978-90-411-3177-5).
44. Mika Oinonen, *Does EU Merger Control Discriminate against Small Market Companies? Diagnosing the Argument with Conclusions*, 2010 (ISBN 978-90-411-3261-1).
45. Eirik Østerud, *Identifying Exclusionary Abuses by Dominant Undertakings under EU Competition Law: The Spectrum of Tests*, 2010 (ISBN 978-90-411-3271-0).
46. Marco Botta, *Merger Control Regimes in Emerging Economies: A Case Study on Brazil and Argentina*, 2011 (ISBN 978-90-411-3402-8).
47. Jürgen Basedow & Wolfgang Wurmnest (eds), *Structure and Effects in EU Competition Law: Studies on Exclusionary Conduct and State Aid*, 2011 (ISBN 978-90-411-3174-4).
48. George Cumming (ed.), *Merger Decisions and the Rules of Procedure of the European Community Courts*, 2012 (ISBN 978-90-411-3671-8).
49. Eduardo Molan Gaban & Juliana Oliveira Domingues (eds), *Antitrust Law in Brazil: Fighting Cartels,* 2012 (ISBN 978-90-411-3670-1).
50. Giandonato Caggiano, Gabriella Muscolo & Marina Tavassi (eds), *Competition Law and Intellectual Property: A European Perspective,* 2012 (ISBN 978-90-411-3447-9).
51. Ben Van Rompuy, *Economic Efficiency: The Sole Concern of Modern Antitrust Policy? Non-efficiency Considerations under Article 101 TFEU*, 2012 (ISBN 978-90-411-3870-5).

52. Liyang Hou, *Competition Law and Regulation of the EU Electronic Communications Sector: A Comparative Legal Approach*, 2012 (ISBN 978-90-411-4047-0).
53. Barry Rodger, *Landmark Cases in Competition Law: Around the World in Fourteen Stories*, 2012 (ISBN 978-90-411-3843-9).
54. Andreas Scordamaglia-Tousis, *EU Cartel Enforcement: Reconciling Effective Public Enforcement with Fundamental Rights*, 2013 (ISBN 978-90-411-4758-5).
55. Bernardo Cortese (ed.), *EU Competition Law: Between Public and Private Enforcement*, 2014 (ISBN 978-90-411-4677-9).
56. Barry Rodger (ed.), *Competition Law: Comparative Private Enforcement and Collective Redress across the EU*, 2014 (ISBN 978-90-411-4559-8).
57. Nada Ina Pauer, *The Single Economic Entity Doctrine and Corporate Group Responsibility in European Antitrust Law*, 2014 (ISBN 978-90-411-5262-6).
58. Urška Petrovčič, *Competition Law and Standard Essential Patents: A Transatlantic Perspective*, 2014 (ISBN 978-90-411-4960-2).
59. David Telyas, *The Interface between Competition Law, Patents and Technical Standards*, 2014 (ISBN 978-90-411-5418-7).
60. Katerina Maniadaki, *EU Competition Law, Regulation and the Internet: The Case of Net Neutrality*, 2014 (ISBN 978-90-411-4140-8).
61. Horacio Vedia Jerez, *Competition Law Enforcement and Compliance across the World: A Comparative Review*, 2015 (ISBN 978-90-411-5815-4).
62. Kadir Ba, *The Substantive Appraisal of Joint Ventures under the EU Merger Control Regime*, 2015 (ISBN 978-90-411-5816-1).
63. Alberto Santa Maria, *Competition and State Aid: An Analysis of the EU Practice*, Second Edition, 2015 (ISBN 978-90-411-5818-5).
64. Lúcio Tomé Feteira, *The Interplay between European and National Competition Law after Regulation 1/2003: "United (Should) We Stand?"*, 2016 (ISBN 978-90-411-5663-1).
65. Giovanni Pitruzzella & Gabriella Muscolo (eds), *Competition and Patent Law in the Pharmaceutical Sector: An International Perspective*, 2016 (ISBN 978-90-411-5927-4).
66. Małgorzata Cyndecka, *The Market Economy Investor Test in EU State Aid Law: Applicability and Application*, 2016 (ISBN 978-90-411-6102-4).
67. Damiano Canapa, *Trademarks and Brands in Merger Control: An Analysis of the European and Swiss Legal Orders*, 2016 (ISBN 978-90-411-6717-0).
68. Inge Graef, *EU Competition Law, Data Protection and Online Platforms: Data as Essential Facility*, 2016 (ISBN 978-90-411-8324-8).
69. Anders Jessen, *Exclusionary Abuse after the* Post Danmark I *Case: The Role of the Effects-Based Approach under Article 102 TFEU*, 2017 (ISBN 978-90-411-8996-7).
70. Baskaran Balasingham, *The EU Leniency Policy: Reconciling Effectiveness and Fairness*, 2017 (ISBN 978-90-411-8479-5).
71. Eugene Stuart & Iana Roginska-Green, *Sixty Years of EU State Aid Law and Policy: Analysis and Assessment*, 2018 (ISBN 978-90-411-8869-4).

72. Anna Renata Pisarkiewicz, *Margin Squeeze in the Electronic Communications Sector: Critical Analysis of the Decisional Practice and Case Law,* 2018 (ISBN 978-90-411-6246-5).
73. Ploykaew Porananond, *Competition Law in the ASEAN Countries: Regional Law and National Systems,* 2018 (ISBN 978-90-411-9102-1).
74. Corinne Ruechardt, *EU State Aid Control of Infrastructure Funding,* 2018 (ISBN 978-90-411-9099-4).
75. Amalia Athanasiadou, *Patent Settlements in the Pharmaceutical Industry under US Antitrust and EU Competition Law,* 2018 (ISBN 978-94-035-0113-0).
76. Miroslava Marinova, *Fidelity Rebates in Competition Law: Application of the 'As Efficient Competitor' Test,* 2018 (ISBN 978-94-035-0570-1).
77. Gabriella Muscolo & Marina Tavassi, *The Interplay Between Competition Law and Intellectual Property: An International Perspective,* 2019 (ISBN 978-90-411-8687-4).
78. Fevzi Toksoy, Bahadir Balki & Hanna Stakheyeva, *Merger Control in the EU and Turkey: A Comparative Guide,* 2019 (ISBN 978-94-035-0934-1).
79. Paulo Burnier da Silveira & William Evan Kovacic (eds), *Global Competition Enforcement: New Players, New Challenges*, 2019 (ISBN 978-94-035-0283-0).
80. Giovanna Massarotto, *Antitrust Settlements: How a Simple Agreement Can Drive the Economy*, 2019 (ISBN 978-94-035-1133-7).
81. Marc Veenbrink, *Criminal Law Principles and the Enforcement of EU and National Competition Law: A Silent Takeover?*, 2020 (ISBN 978-94-035-1434-5).
82. Ferdinand Wollenschläger, Wolfgang Wurmnest & Thomas M.J. Möllers (eds), *Private Enforcement of European Competition and State Aid Law: Current Challenges and the Way Forward,* 2020 (ISBN 978-94-035-0281-6).
83. Jorge Marcos Ramos, *Firm Dominance in EU Competition Law: The Competitive Process and the Origins of Market Power*, 2020 (ISBN 978-94-035-2030-8).
84. Ingrid Margrethe Halvorsen Barlund, *Leniency in EU Competition Law*, 2020 (ISBN 978-94-035-1722-3).
85. Jan Blockx, Mens Rea *in EU Antitrust Law: When Intentions Matter*, 2020 (ISBN 978-94-035-2353-8).
86. Maria Wasastjerna, *Competition, Data and Privacy in the Digital Economy: Towards a Privacy Dimension in Competition Policy?*, 2020 (ISBN 978-94-035-2220-3).
87. Maria Fernanda Caporale Madi, *Regulating Vertical Agreements: A Comparative Law and Economics Review of the EU and Brazil*, 2020 (ISBN 978-94-035-2650-8).

www.ingramcontent.com/pod-product-compliance
Ingram Content Group UK Ltd.
Pitfield, Milton Keynes, MK11 3LW, UK
UKHW020811290926
15470UKWH00003B/1089

9 789403 526508